Tell it like it is: How our schools fail Black children

Edited by Brian Richardson

middle class bias 35
sense of identity 47)

UNIVERSITY OF CHICHESTER LIBRARIES

AUTHOR:

D1343723

TITLE:

371.97 TEL

DATE: 2/06

SUBJECT: TES

UNIVERSITY OF OXFORD ...... LIBRARIES

AUTHOR:

TITLE

DATE

Tell it like it is:
How our schools fail Black children

Edited by Brian Richardson

Bookmarks Publications  Trentham Books

Tell it Like It Is: How our schools fail Black children
Edited by Brian Richardson
Published September 2005
Bookmarks Publications, c/o 1 Bloomsbury Street, London WC1B 3QE
Trentham Books, Westview House, 734 London Road, Stoke on Trent ST4 5NP
ISBN 1905192061
Printed by Bath Press
Design and production by Bookmarks Publications
Cover Picture: Jess Hurd www.reportdigital.co.uk

Contents

Editor's acknowledgements

It is a tribute to the dedication and commitment of so many people to progressive anti-racist education that what began as a series of conversations and emails at the end of 2004 has grown into this present volume. Of course none of this would have happened without Bernard Coard's original outstanding and challenging study and it was his 2004 update to the original which sparked a new interest in his work and has led to the publication of this collection. We must also salute those pioneers such as John La Rose, Eric and Jessica Huntley, Buzz Johnson and the community activists who first put the words of Coard and others into print and circulated them throughout Britain and the wider world.

A number of people have played a particularly vital role in bringing this project to fruition. Paul Mackney, the general secretary of the National Association of Teachers in Further and Higher Education (Natfhe), deserves particular praise for being the first person to respond to Coard's rallying cry of high quality education for all by circulating the 2004 essay, suggesting a reprint of the original pamphlet, and for convening the first series of meetings that led to this book.

Bookmarks Publications took up this idea and played a vital role in helping to make the book what it is – both a tribute to Bernard Coard's original work and a reflection of the contemporary debates about Black children in education today. A special mention should go to the Bookmarks production team. Hannah Dee provided me with invaluable editorial advice and assistance, while Mary Phillips and Peter Robinson worked above and beyond the call of duty and did a fantastic job in ensuring that the book was out in time for Black History month 2005. As well as his endorsement, Ken Livingstone, the Mayor of London, has provided financial support which helped to ensure that we have been able to publish the book and we hope at a price within the budget of the schools, colleges, communities and families we want to reach.

I must thank all the writers and interviewees for their passionate and thoughtful contributions, and Benjamin Zephaniah and Linton Kwesi Johnson for allowing us to include a selection of their work in this publication. Gillian Klein at Trentham Books offered her usual wise, encouraging and constructively critical editorial advice. Thank you also to my workmates and colleagues at the Southern and Eastern Region TUC, and in particular Mick Connolly, the regional secretary. Beccy Palmer, who organised the interview with the Tricycle Group in Brent, is one of those selfless, unsung and inspirational characters who really does help to make a difference.

I would like to dedicate this book to my colleagues in the Communities Empowerment Network and to the teachers in Manchester, Leeds and London that I have worked with, many of whom are close personal friends, who go into schools and colleges every day and try to make a difference to all young people's lives. Finally I owe a particular debt of gratitude to Eve R Light. I could not have completed my work on this project without the love, encouragement and support she unfailingly provides, and her suggestions, advice and input.

A note on terminology

Bernard Coard's original pamphlet which forms a central core of this publication focused specifically upon the 'West Indian Child'. This present book is subtitled 'How Our Schools Fail Black Children'. Although much of the analysis in this volume relates to African-Caribbean children – and boys in particular – we use the term Black to mean those people of African, Asian, Caribbean and South East Asian descent and other groups who are discriminated against on the grounds of their race, culture, colour, nationality or religious practice. We recognise that this definition may be problematic for some individuals and groups and we respect the right of each individual, including the contributors to this volume, to use the terminology with which they are most comfortable.

Doreen Lawrence OBE

Foreword

I REMEMBER READING Bernard Coard's book as a young mother and was shocked by what I read, while wondering why this was happening and what we as Black people could do to change this disrespecting the Black community; because that was what it was. Education is the key element to all children's development and we all have a right to it.

It was scandalous then, when Bernard wrote his book, and it is even more scandalous that, sadly, the British school system is still letting down Black children. There have been many debates on how our young Black children, especially Caribbean boys, are failing in schools. I have attended two of the 'Black Child' conferences, which have been held on the subject, organised by Diane Abbott. At these conferences there have been education ministers talking about the failings, as if the responsibility lay elsewhere and not with them.

In my work, I see these failings and I have seen the struggles that many parents endure on behalf of their children, when they see the persistently widening achievement gap and the high exclusion rates. The children who have experienced the labelling back in the 1960s and 1970s are the parents of today's young Black children who are being excluded from schools in this present time.

This republishing of Bernard Coard's book *How the West Indian Child Is Made Educationally Subnormal in the British School System* has come at a time when many more people are urgently requesting and demanding better education for their children.

We are beginning to see, from the different debates and controversies, that the time has come when not just one or two people, but the whole of the Black community, are demanding higher achievement for their children. Controversy was caused when Trevor Phillips talked about having some separate lessons for Black boys who are failing. Separate schooling has been happening for different ethnic groups, but the mere mention of the same happening for Black children seems to send some people into a frenzy. The British school system has been letting down Black children for generations, so thinking of an alternative could be the way forward.

I have a strong belief that what we are looking for lies within ourselves. We as Black people have it within ourselves to demand more and insist we get it, because for too long we have overlooked our worth. We need to think about our contribution to the economic wealth of this country and what our votes mean at election time. We must consider how we can use this to demand what we are entitled to: the right for decent education for our children. What I am saying is nothing new. Bernard Coard had written about this when his book was first published. He wrote about 'no new provision of housing for our need, despite our contribution to the economy. Thus the society gets us as cheaply as possible to plug a crucial gap in the economy – the need for a sizeable unskilled labour force.'

In America, during the Civil Rights Movement, Malcolm X talked about 'liberating our minds by any means necessary'. Black people refused to ride on the bus and brought the bus company to its knees: Rosa Parks in Montgomery, USA. This means that we as the Black community have the 'Black pound' and our vote. Black people need to collectively decide how strategically we can use what are our 'means' to achieve the rights for our children.

Bernard Coard expressed the injustice over 30 years ago. Now he and other commentators reveal the continuing scandal today and suggest some of the things that have to be done – now.

● Doreen Lawrence is the director of the Stephen Lawrence Charitable Trust and was awarded the OBE for services to community relations in 2003, almost ten years after the murder of her son

Stephen. Doreen and her family fought a long and arduous campaign to get justice for Stephen and to expose the failings of the Metropolitan Police in investigating his murder. The campaign culminated in the Macpherson inquiry into Stephen's death, which fundamentally changed the nature of race relations in Britain, resulting in the Race Relations Act Amendment 2000.

- Established in 1998, the Stephen Lawrence Charitable Trust invests in young people whose aspirations and life chances are constrained by economic, cultural and social hardship, by providing architectural student bursaries. Thereby the trust broadens access to the architectural, planning and associated professions.

Herman Ouseley

Preface

IN 1971, DURING a period of intense action in the African-Caribbean community, the Caribbean Educational and Community Workers Association and New Beacon Books published Bernard Coard's seminal study *The Scandal of the Black Child in Schools in Britain*. The main title of the book was *How the West Indian Child is Made Educationally Subnormal in the British School System*. Though a relatively small volume in size, the work's impact has been far-reaching in that almost every reference to the education of children from the Black and ethnic communities since its publication makes reference to it and its positive approach to the subject. Coard has also compressed the study and expressed his arguments, recommendations and analysis clearly, cogently and in a style easily understood by a wide range of readers.

The book was based upon the campaigning work done in the community to ensure the proper education of African-Caribbean children and upon the direct experiences of Coard himself who, at the time, worked in Educationally Subnormal (ESN) schools, and in youth clubs in the inner city areas of east and south east London. It also relies extensively on the information exchanges and research through which children, parents, black teachers and education activists contributed.

Bernard Coard's work has withstood the test of time because the problems facing African-Caribbean parents and their children have fundamentally remained the same. Racism, race prejudice and social inequalities are crucial factors in the perpetuation of educational policies and practices which cause the system to fail the African-Caribbean communities. These will prevail even though there have been some changes and new developments in the intervening 20-year period.[1]

The need for the Black community to monitor the progress of their children and seek to influence the processes and structures which affect and influence their education is constantly being stressed. The re-publication of Coard's book is a vital contribution to developing an understanding of the issues which faced Black pupils and the nature of those problems in today's environment.

Prior to its abolition the Inner London Education Authority (ILEA) made a contribution towards the publication of the new edition of this work. The basis of that contribution was the need to make available to a wider and different readership the valuable message contained in this work. As a supporter of the initiative of the committee to re-publish (which worked for the publication of the work in the original style and format, as they see that as an education in itself) and a former employee of the ILEA, I can commend enthusiastically the study of Coard's book by all teachers, parents, pupils, education workers and others connected with education.

Note

1   This article was first published in January 1991, to accompany the second edition of Bernard Coard's *How the West Indian Child is Made Educationally Subnormal in the British School System*, published by Kana.

● Lord Ouseley is the president of the Local Government Association and the founding chair of the 'Kick It Out' campaign to rid football of racism. He was the executive chairman of the Commission for Racial Equality between 1993 and 2000, and was the first Black person to hold the post. At the time of writing this preface he was the chief executive of the London Borough of Lambeth. He also held the positions of director of education (1986-88) and chief executive (1988-90) in the Inner London Education Authority.

Ken Livingstone

Introduction

LONDON'S PROSPERITY as a great world city depends on our ability to harness and develop the talents and skills of all of our city's diverse communities – and this can only be achieved if we start at the very beginning with the quality of the education provided to our children.

It has been clear for some years that Britain's education system is failing to give Black boys the start in life which they, and their parents, are entitled to expect. As this report shows, African-Caribbean boys, in particular, start their schooling at broadly the same level as other pupils, but in the course of their education they fall further and further behind so that in 2003, for example, roughly 70 percent of African-Caribbean pupils left school with less than five higher grade GCSEs or their equivalents. This represents the lowest level of achievement for any ethnic group of school children. Though recent DfES figures suggest there has been some small improvement, it is clear that change is not arriving quickly enough.

In national examinations African-Caribbean boys have been the lowest achieving group at practically every key stage for the last five years. Unsurprisingly, the 2001 Census indicated that African-Caribbean men were the least likely of all men to have a degree or equivalent qualification. While

African pupils are generally achieving more highly than African-Caribbean pupils, this is often only marginal.

Gaining good GCSEs is the first stage to securing employability and establishing a skills base for further training and higher education. Deprived of these qualifications, generations of Black youth are effectively consigned to low paid, unskilled jobs and years of unemployment. The effect of years of failure to educate Black children has been catastrophic for those young people and their communities. It will also be a disaster for London as a whole because Black communities make up nearly 11 percent of London's population and an even larger proportion of the school age population. As a city we simply cannot afford to continue failing our Black school children.

Some years ago Diane Abbott MP approached me to enlist my support as Mayor of London, and that of the London Development Agency (LDA), for a programme of research and engagement with Black parents, pupils, teachers and government to work out the root causes of this situation and what should be done to address them. In 2004 the LDA produced a comprehensive report detailing the experiences of Black children in London schools with a number of key recommendations for action.

Of paramount importance among the actions necessary to improve achievement levels among Black children is for the teaching profession, classroom staff and the governing bodies of London schools to properly reflect the diversity of the communities they serve. This is the key to addressing the many factors affecting the education of Black children in London.

Nearly a third of Londoners are of African, Caribbean or Asian heritage. Given that London's school age population is considerably more diverse, I believe that for our schools to fully meet the needs of London's diverse communities the teaching profession must have at the absolute minimum at least this proportion of African, Caribbean and Asian teachers. That means establishing as a key target across Greater London, with a timetable to achieve it, that nearly a third of London teachers should be of African, Caribbean or Asian heritage. At present the figure is only 14.6 percent among teachers categorised by the DfES as Black or Asian.[1] At a borough level, the targets should reflect the different diverse communities of the individual borough. For example, boroughs such as Lambeth and Southwark, which have Black pupil populations of around 50 percent in their schools, only have a Black teaching workforce of nearer 16 to 18 percent.[2]

At the present time we are very far from a teaching profession or body of school governors that adequately reflects London's diversity and at the present pace of change will not achieve this objective in the foreseeable future. In November 2005 I will be publishing a new report on Black teachers in London, following on from the LDA work on this issue, in order to provide a complete picture of education for Black Londoners and pursue this agenda for change.

I continue to have a huge regard for the commitment and professionalism of the teaching profession in London. However, I maintain that a major effort will be necessary to address the under-representation of London's diverse communities in the teaching profession. All of the relevant agencies will have to work together around a programme to achieve the objective of a representative teaching profession for London, and I look forward to working with all bodies to bring about the meaningful change for Black children in London which is so long overdue.

Notes

1   DfES, *School Workforce 2004* (2005).
2   DfES, 2005.

● Ken Livingstone is Mayor of London.

Brian Richardson

Editor's introduction

TELL IT Like It Is is the name of at least three different but outstanding songs released by S.O.U.L, Aaron Neville and George Benson during the era of the great civil rights and Black Power struggles of the 1960s. It is no coincidence that we have decided to use it as the title of this series of essays. Music has traditionally been one of the key mediums through which Black people have expressed both the agony and the ecstasy of their experiences. A brilliant television series, *Soul Deep*, that aired in the UK in the spring of 2005, portrayed how music has played a central role in forging communities and inspiring struggles.

We originally considered using the phrase 'Young, Gifted and Black' which is also of course one of the greatest songs of the civil rights era, before finally settling on Tell It Like It Is. It is not simply a catchy song title but a strong and emotive phrase that means, 'Speak truth to power.' That is, of course, precisely what Bernard Coard did when he wrote his seminal text *How The West Indian Child is Made Educationally Subnormal in the British School System* in 1971. It would be hard to overstate the importance of that book when it was written all those years ago. It had an extraordinary impact both in terms of exposing the scandalous treatment of Black children in education and in galvanising a wide layer of activists and practitioners to do something about it.

For those reasons alone it is a book that deserves not just to be in print, but also, I would argue, on the reading list at every teacher training institution. I say this because, sadly, it is not simply an important and interesting historical read. As Coard himself argued in an essay he wrote in 2004 which we reprint here, it remains relevant today.

As this present publication was being produced, the Department for Education and Skills (DfES) was reporting that Black children are disproportionately excluded from school. An even more recent study for the Joseph Rowntree Foundation, *School Exclusions and Transition Into Adulthood in African Caribbean Communities*, suggested that African Caribbean boys are between four and 15 times more likely to be excluded than their white peers. Depressingly this is even worse than the officially acknowledged figures quoted by a number of contributors to this collection. Admittedly levels of achievement for all ethnic groups apart from Chinese children in the 'Gold Standard' GCSE examinations have improved according to latest statistics. However, 'Black Caribbean' children still lag almost 17 percentage points behind 'white' children, while the deficit for 'Black African' children is 9 percent.

The real impact that this school experience has upon young people's lives is palpable. A Trades Union Congress (TUC) report released at almost exactly the same time as the DfES one suggested that Black and Asian workers are more than twice as likely to be unemployed as their white counterparts. At present rates of growth, it will take 46 years before this disparity is overcome. Such wider social exclusion clearly contributes to a cycle of poverty and deprivation that is transferred from one generation to the next. Within this overall context, therefore, Coard's original pamphlet continues to offer serious critical insights.

It would be wrong, however, to simply conclude that nothing has changed. Much has happened both bad and good in the intervening decades. That is why we have chosen to republish Coard's work alongside a series of other contributions from leading researchers, community activists and commentators, school teachers and teaching unions and young people themselves.

Traditionally education is supposed to concentrate on the three core disciplines of reading, writing and arithmetic. Here we focus on the different – and grammatically correct – 'Rs'. *Tell It Like It Is* is most obviously about race and racism but it also seeks to reflect upon a critical historical analysis and to offer responses to the challenges that remain to be tackled. It is worth re-emphasising the point about racism because all too often in the past policymakers, scholars and schools themselves have skirted around the subject or denied that racism is an issue within the school gates. Even if that were the case – and the essays in this collection overwhelmingly refute that suggestion – it cannot be argued that children's experience of racism in the wider world has no impact upon their behaviour and performance in the classroom.

The book is loosely divided into four sections: Back in the Day, What's Going On, Say it Loud and Seize the Time. Again these are phrases that will be familiar to many readers with echoes of songs, struggles and strategies of the past. The first section focuses upon Coard's original work and its legacy. Section two brings the debate into the 21st century and looks at the situation today. The third section is primarily a series of more personal perspectives, while in the final section a number of writers throw down a series of challenges and suggest a number of organisational, practical and political solutions.

The contributions in this collection seek to analyse and address these issues directly and from a number of different perspectives. Sally Tomlinson, Alex Pascall and Chris Searle place Coard's work in its historical context and describe some of the key developments it gave rise to both in terms of official education policy and the flourishing of community campaigns and publications. These reflections sit alongside a series of responses from contributors such as Gus John, David Gillborn, Heidi Safia Mirza and Stella Dadzie which both challenge the status quo and seek to chart a path forward to progress.

It is simply not possible in a book of this size to include all shades of opinion on race and education. One of the most popular claims is that the responsibility for Black underachievement rests within the Black communities themselves. Central to this claim is the assertion that Black children, particularly boys, lack the necessary motivation to succeed at school. The blame for this lies with the absence of role models, notably fathers who have abandoned their families and their responsibilities. The youngsters meanwhile are, apparently, more interested in the hedonistic, bling bling appeal of Music Television (MTV) than they are in exam success. It is clear from a number of contributions in this collection, including those from young people themselves, that these are real and contentious issues. Incidentally, far from simply rapping about guns, 'girls' and gangstas, questions of racism, education, absent fathers and the pressures on Black women are a common theme in the music of many of the Black role models young people choose for themselves, artists such as Nas, Tupac Shakur, Jay-Z and Kanye West.

There can be little doubt that the 'Ghetto Fabulous' theory has considerable purchase among academics, politicians and within Black communities themselves. However, we make no apology for the exclusion of an extended study on this theory from this collection. As Coard's original pamphlet makes clear, his focus was upon the systemic failure of the institutions of education. Our focus in this book is to critically examine what has happened within the system since then.

It is also timely for us to do this some six years after the publication of the Stephen Lawrence Inquiry Report. Although primarily focused upon the Metropolitan Police Force, that report also acknowledged that there were real, serious and legitimate concerns about the education system. Sir William Macpherson's report is mainly remembered because of its recognition of institutional racism, which he described as:

> The collective failure of an organisation to provide an appropriate and professional service to people because of their colour, culture and ethnic origin. It can be seen or detected in processes, attitudes and behaviour which amount to discrimination through unwitting prejudice, ignorance, thoughtlessness and racist stereotyping which disadvantage minority ethnic people.

There are significant weaknesses in Macpherson's definition. However, it did at least have the merit of dragging the term out of the academic and political ghetto within which it had been trapped, and placed it, albeit briefly, at the centre of political discourse. The real credit for this rests not with a retired, conservative High Court judge but with Doreen and Neville Lawrence who campaigned with such courage, dignity and determination to expose the truth about their son Stephen's tragic murder. Ever since then Doreen Lawrence has dedicated herself through the Stephen Lawrence Charitable Trust to encouraging and promoting achievement among young people. We are especially privileged and grateful to her for providing a foreword for this publication.

We are also pleased to offer young people the opportunity to express their own opinions. Despite the advent of so called citizenship education – one of the legacies of the Stephen Lawrence Inquiry Report – young people are still largely expected to simply accept the authority of adults and speak when they are spoken to. The lively and passionate contributions from members of the Tricycle Group in Brent, and east Londoner Vocalis MC demonstrate that young people are not an indistinguishable mass of hooded tearaways. In a provocative essay Hassan Mahamdallie identifies the shifting nature of racism and asserts that young people of all ethnic backgrounds can be part of the struggle for a better future.

In his 2004 essay Coard issues a rallying call for 'high class education for all'. A number of points are clear from this. Firstly, the demand for race equality should not be at the expense of others. Research evidence shows that a targeted and creative attempt to address the underachievement of one group can provide insights and strategies that can offer benefit to all. Secondly, if race equality is to become a reality, it will require a monumental and united effort by everyone connected with schools, colleges and the education system. Around the UK there are some brilliant examples of good practice in schools. Sharon Geer, coordinator of an award winning Ethnic Minority Achievement programme at Forest Hill School in Lewisham, offers an example of a programme that has achieved considerable success. Meanwhile, David Simon, founder and director of Ebony Supplementary Schools, eloquently charts the 50-year journey from the *Empire Windrush* to the Supplementary Schools of today and the struggles fought with quiet dignity by generations of Black people. Reading his contribution made me reflect upon the sacrifices my own parents Hubert and Evelyn made to provide the best they could for me, and to consider the great debt we owe to that generation. Projects such as these should not be marginal beacons of progress, but part of the mainstream and supported by a considerable injection of resources.

Money matters, but what is also critically important is the attitude, aptitude, confidence and experience of those with responsibility for nurturing young people. Heidi Safia Mirza and Gillian Klein argue that teachers must be given the training, support, time and space to be creative. Julie Hall's contribution sets out some very clear steps that teachers and parents can take to create and sustain a positive learning environment and experience.

It is important that we have included perspectives from the leaders of two of the main teaching unions, the National Union of Teachers (NUT) and the National Association of Teachers in Further and Higher Education (Natfhe). There are some strong sentiments expressed here and many of them are addressed directly at the teaching profession. If real progress is to be achieved, teachers and their representative bodies must seriously grapple with these issues. However, it should be remembered that individual teachers and schools and their unions have often also been at the forefront of the struggle for multiculturalism, anti-racism and progressive education and involved in the fight against racism in the wider society. Those of us who grew up and first became conscious of race and racism in the 1970s will never forget the ultimate sacrifice made by NUT member and activist Blair Peach at Southall in 1979.

Coard originally wrote about the British school system, but in the succeeding decades further education and higher education, notably the post-1992 universities, have played an increasingly important role. For many young Black people they have provided a second chance of success after they have left school labelled as failures. The contributions from Stella Dadzie, Wally Brown and Lola Young are hugely significant, not least because they allow us to accentuate the positive.

Many readers of this book will be unaware of the fact that at the time of writing Bernard Coard remains in prison in Grenada. He was convicted of treason in 1986 as a result of his alleged involvement in the events which culminated in the 1983 political coup in that country, the death of the then prime minister, Maurice Bishop, and the subsequent invasion by United States armed forces. Before deciding to publish this book we thought long and hard about these events which have deeply divided activists for many years. It was concluded that, traumatic though they were and remain for very many people, they did not invalidate the historical and contemporary significance of Coard's work. Collectively, we make no presumption about his guilt or innocence and we do not feel that it is appropriate to discuss those matters at length in these pages. However, it is only right that we declare that one of the organisations that has been involved in this present project is the Campaign for Human Rights in Grenada (UK), a group which campaigns for a fair trial for Coard and the 17 co-defendants with whom he has been incarcerated. We have therefore allowed space in this volume for the committee to provide a brief summary of its work.

Throughout this introduction I have used the word 'we' when referring to the decision-making process which resulted in this publication. This is neither a grammatical error nor a pretentious employment of the so called 'royal' we. The book was conceived and commissioned by an editorial group that included Paul Mackney, Jenna Khalfan, Noreen Scott, Crofton St Louis, Claude James, Hannah Dee, Gillian Klein and Gretchen Cummings which met regularly to discuss ideas and consider progress. They placed considerable trust in me and it has been a pleasure and a privilege to work with them. I hope that I have been able to repay that faith and feel that it is only right that I should take responsibility for any major short-comings or errors.

The great legacy of Coard's 1971 book was that it wasn't simply an academic work that gathered dust on shelves but rather it was a vital instrument that inspired a movement which achieved a great deal. If this small book can help to resurrect such a coalition then this project will have proved worthwhile.

● September 2005

● Brian Richardson is chair of the Communities Empowerment Network, an organisation that works with young people, their families and schools to overcome exclusions and reintegrate young people back into mainstream education. He is also a member of the editorial board of the journal *Race Equality Teaching* and has been an adviser to schools and local education authorities. He works for the Trades Union Congress (TUC) and is secretary of the Southern and Eastern Region TUC Race Relations Committee.

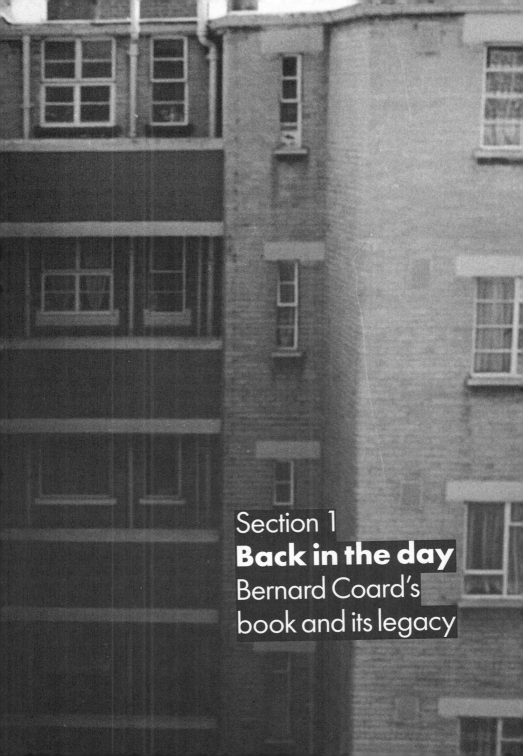

Section 1
Back in the day
Bernard Coard's
book and its legacy

No Problem by Benjamin Zephaniah

I am not de problem
But I bare de brunt
Of silly playground taunts
An racist stunts,
I am not de problem
I am a born academic
But dey got me on de run
Now I am branded athletic,
I am not de problem
If yu give I a chance
I can teach yu of Timbuktu
I can do more dan dance,
I am not de problem
I greet yu wid a smile
Yu put me in a pigeon hole
But I am versatile.

These conditions may affect me
As I get older,
An I am positively sure
I have no chips on me shoulders,
Black is not de problem
Mother country get it right,
An juss fe de record,
Sum of me best friends are white.

© Benjamin Zephaniah, from *Propa Propaganda* (Bloodaxe Books, 1996)

Bernard Coard

How the West Indian child is made educationally subnormal in the British school system: the scandal of the Black child in schools in Britain

THIS BOOK is dedicated to my parents and all Black parents who value their children's education and opportunities in life above all else.

I am indebted to John La Rose and Jessica Huntley for the inspiration and encouragement for writing this book; to Winston Best, Waveney Bushell and Van Rigsby for their criticism and advice; to my wife Phyllis, without whose constant advice, moral support and typing skill this book would have been impossible. Finally I am indebted to the many people and the West Indian organisations who have contributed to the publication and distribution of this book.

Chapter 1: West Indian children in ESN (Special) Schools in Britain

These are five main points I want to bring to the attention of West Indian parents and others interested:

1   There are very large numbers of our West Indian children in schools for the educationally subnormal – which is what ESN means.
2   These children have been wrongly placed there.

3 Once placed in these schools, the vast majority never get out and return to normal schools.
4 They suffer academically and in their job prospects for life because of being put in these schools.
5 The authorities are doing *very* little to stop this scandal.

1 Large numbers

An Inner London Education Authority report entitled *The Education of Immigrant Pupils in Special Schools for Educationally Subnormal Children* (ILEA 657) reveals that five of their secondary ESN schools had more than 30 percent immigrant pupils at the time of their survey in 1967. By January 1968, one of the schools had 60 percent immigrant children!

In the ILEA's ESN (Special) Day Schools, over 28 percent of all the pupils are immigrant, *compared with only 15 percent immigrants in the ordinary schools* of the ILEA. This situation is particularly bad for the West Indians, because three quarters of all the immigrant children in these Educationally Subnormal schools are West Indian, whereas *West Indians are only half of the immigrant population in the ordinary schools*. The 1970 figures are even more alarming, for even though immigrants comprise nearly 17 percent of the normal school population nearly 34 percent of the ESN school population is immigrant. And four out of every five immigrant children in these ESN schools are West Indian! The figures from the ILEA report to substantiate what I have said above are given on page 56 as an appendix.

2 Wrongful placement

The same ILEA report gives figures of immigrant children whom the headmasters of these ESN schools thought were wrongly assessed and placed:

Three of the 19 schools thought that less than 10 percent of their immigrant pupils had been wrongly placed; three thought that between 10 and 19 percent were wrongly placed; a further three thought that the figure was between 20 and 29 percent. One school put the figure at between 30 and 39 percent; two schools thought as many as 40 to 49 percent of the immigrant pupils wrongly placed; and finally, one school estimated that between 70 and 79 percent of its immigrant pupils were wrongly placed!

Thus nine out of 19 schools thought that 20 percent or more of their immigrant pupils had been wrongly placed. This is from Table 9, page 9, of the report. The report states (page 5), 'Where children are suspected as being wrongly placed in the ESN school, this is *four times as likely* in the case of immigrant pupils' (my italics).

3 Permanently ESN
On the question of the number of children returning to normal schools, the report states (page 3), 'The number returning to ordinary schools…is low, and is only slightly higher for immigrants (7 percent) than for non-immigrants (4 percent).' From this we can see clearly that even though massive numbers of West Indian and other immigrant children are being wrongly placed in these ESN schools, only 7 *percent* ever return to normal schools. We must therefore arrive at the conclusion that the West Indian child's frequently wrongful placement in an ESN school is a one-way educational ticket.

4 Why the ESN school is unsuitable for the child who has been wrongly placed
In order to understand why it is so scandalous for large numbers of West Indian children to be wrongly placed in ESN schools – and never get the opportunity to return to normal schools – one must understand the nature of the ESN school, how it is organised, and who it caters for.

ESN schools are designed to assist each child in such a school to realise his *assumed low* capabilities so that he will on leaving school be able to hold down a simple job and be as independent as possible, thereby not being a burden on his family or the state when in adult life. The whole assumption of an ESN school is that the child cannot cope with the average academic requirements of a normal school.

The children are chosen to attend these schools because they are of low intelligence – 50 to 75 or 80 IQ. Children of normal intelligence are supposed to score between 90 and 110 on the IQ tests. The Education Act of 1921 defined ESN children as those who 'not being imbecile and not being merely dull and backward' should be provided for in special classes and schools. Therefore, if a child were an 'imbecile' (ie of under 50 IQ), nowadays referred to as 'severely subnormal' (SSN) he would be placed in a hospital or training centre. If he were 'merely dull and backward', then he would still remain in an ordinary school, with perhaps extra help. To be ESN under the 1921 act, you need to be *very* dull or backward, but not so much as to be an 'imbecile'.

Under the 1944 Education Act, local education authorities were directed 'to the need for securing that provision is made for pupils who suffer from any disability of mind or body by providing, either in special schools or otherwise, special educational treatment, that is to say, education by special methods appropriate for persons suffering from that disability'. It was intended that Special Schools would provide mainly for pupils whose backwardness was due to *limited ability*. Pupils who were not so limited intellectually would need suitable arrangements in ordinary school.[1]

I have run youth clubs for children from six ESN schools in London. I have visited these schools on several occasions, as well as others. I have taught in two ESN schools over the past two years. I have held numerous conversations and discussions with the headteachers and staff of these many schools. The main purpose of an ESN school which emerges from my experience and observation is to 'socialise' the child, rather than attempt academic wonders with him. The child must be provided with a structure which facilitates his learning to live with himself and with other children, and with adults. This seems to be priority number one. If he is to cope with society given his low intelligence, initial sense of failure, and his general lack of confidence, he must be taught, through the provision of the right environment, how to cope with his own emotional problems and how to relate or 'get on' with other children.

This task quite often takes up the best part of the child's years at the ESN school, and so most children hardly get beyond this stage to the stage where they can grasp the 'three Rs' in other than a rudimentary way. Given their low intellectual capacity, this is undoubtedly the right emphasis in their education (always assuming, of course, that the children's intelligence has been correctly assessed, which it hasn't in the case of most West Indian children). The true ESN child can never expect realistically to be given the sort of job which calls for academic qualifications or an average level of intellectual reasoning. Given his limited mental ability, he is placed in a job which is simple, repetitive, requires little initiative, and a minimum of mental effort. Such a job he can manage. A job requiring greater mental skills he would probably fail at, with grave repercussions for his mental health. Once he is given sufficient instruction in the three Rs so that he can cope with signs, notices, simple correspondence, and basic arithmetic, the most important qualification he must possess if he is to hold down a job in society is that of *social adjustment*, namely being able to get on with the boss and fellow workers, and not lose job after job.

Naturally, each school tries to do more than the rudimentary three Rs with children who are capable of more wherever and whenever possible. Some children leave school with the ability to read some books. However, the extent to which this can be done is limited by the fact that the teachers have to concentrate on basic arithmetic, reading and writing, along with woodwork, needlework, cookery, swimming, PE, etc, and cannot teach the whole range of subjects like geography, history, biology, English literature, physics, etc, which would broaden considerably the horizons of the averagely intelligent child. It would be quite impractical to teach all these subjects at an ESN school given the staff size, school library facilities and the intellectual calibre of the pupils who have been specially placed there. It would also be educationally wrong, since, as explained earlier, the major needs of the children are for social adequacy. It is only because ESN schools build up a special library of books to deal with the children's basic reading difficulties, arrange a curriculum which helps these children of low ability, and choose the right staff for the job, that they are at all able to help the educationally subnormal child and prepare him for his role in society. If they were to perform the same duties as a normal school, or do both jobs, they would be unable to do either properly.

Therefore, ESN schools are *not* places where children go for short periods of six months to two years in order to be given intensive and highly specialised help so that they can then be returned to normal schools and function at the normal academic level. Many West Indian parents in my experience have been led to believe that they are, and have therefore been quite happy to let their children attend these 'Special' schools, believing them to be especially good. This explains why many have not protested at their child's assignment to one of these schools. Another reason is that many are never told that they have the right of appeal over the assessment.

If the ESN school did prepare the child through intensive lessons for coping in the ordinary school, then West Indian children by and large would perhaps be rightly placed. Instead, because children are attached to these schools on a *permanent basis*, the curriculum and entire organisation of the school is geared to cope with children who are of below normal academic abilities. It is true that the range of ability in an ESN school is very large, since it copes with 50 to 80 IQ levels. But though the range is large, it is, as a whole, well below average academic standards. The children are being prepared for *survival*, not for *excelling*, or even participating actively in the society as does the average person.

From what I have said so far, it is quite clear that the academic organisation of the ESN school is not geared for coping (and quite rightly) with a child of average or above average intelligence. A Black child of average or above average intelligence who gets placed in an ESN school can be expected to encounter great difficulties. The child who feels he is wrongly placed (and many do feel this way) may become upset or even disturbed and refuse to cooperate or participate fully in the classroom, and so will appear even more retarded – and *become* retarded through mental inactivity – as time goes by. The experience of being removed from a normal school and placed in the neighbourhood 'nut' school, as everyone calls it, is a bitter one. The child feels deeply that racial discrimination and rejection have been practised towards him by the authorities who assessed him wrongly as being ESN. Other Black children, who are young and unsure of themselves, may simply accept the judgement of themselves as being of low intelligence and give up any attempt to succeed academically. The immense influence of other people's expectations in creating the child's own self-image of his abilities and likely performance will be examined, with evidence, in Chapter 3.

On the other side of the coin, the teacher who is told by the educational 'experts' that a child is ESN will obviously *expect* the child to *be* ESN. Therefore the sort of work she will give the child, and the standard she will expect of him, will obviously be much lower than in a normal school. This means the child will learn much less than he is really capable of, and will be very frustrated day by day in the classroom. That such children quite often 'act up' and become behaviour problems under these circumstances is to be expected.

However, even if the teacher had the full range of books and teaching equipment which an ordinary school has, and had the right expectations of the child's intellectual ability, and even if the West Indian child were not in the least bit affected by being taken out of ordinary school and placed in a school with educationally subnormal and in many cases emotionally disturbed children – all highly unlikely assumptions – the problem of keeping one or two children of average intelligence not only just 'occupied' but educationally stimulated, and advancing at a normal academic rate, while at the same time trying to teach 18 or 19 other children at a considerably different academic (and emotional) level, would be virtually impossible.

The implications for the large number of West Indian children who get placed in ESN schools and who can never 'escape' back to normal schools are far-reaching and permanent. As demonstrated above, the West Indian child's educational level on leaving school will be very low. He will be eligible, by reason of his lack of qualifications and his assessment as being ESN, only for the jobs which *really* ESN pupils are able to perform; namely, simple, repetitive jobs of a menial kind, which involve little use of intelligence. This is what he or she can look forward to as a career! In turn, through his getting poor wages, poor housing and having no motivation to better himself, his children can look forward to a similar educational experience and similar career prospects! No wonder E J B Rose, who was director of the Survey of Race Relations in Britain, and co-author of the report *Colour and Citizenship*, states that by the year 2000 Britain will probably have a Black helot class [labouring class] unless the educational system is radically altered.[2]

As Maureen Stone points out in her thesis, *West Indian Children in an ESN School – Why Are They There?*, 'The authorities should realise that by placing these children in ESN schools they are not solving a problem, but creating one, for these same children will grow up to react with hatred and violence against a system that has crippled them by making them in one other respect (education) unable to play their full part in society.'

5 The authorities do nothing

One can appreciate from the evidence presented just how imperative and urgent it is to *stop and reverse* the process by which these large numbers of immigrant and especially West Indian children are being dumped in ESN schools. One would have thought that in the light of their own report on this scandal the ILEA inspectorate would have recommended the reversal of present policy. Instead, the ILEA report (657) states in its first recommendation (page 6), 'Special Schools for ESN children must continue to provide for immigrant children, *even those of relatively high IQ*, until more suitable alternative provision can be made. The recommendation must always be based on the education needs of the child'! (my italics).

The entire report reeks of complacency, and no urgent recommendations are made at all. The ILEA and other local education authorities in Britain have continued to treat the problem with the same complacency, and the numbers of West Indian children admitted to ESN schools continue to soar. But then perhaps it isn't complacency on the part of the authorities, but rather a conscious plan. Perhaps. The evidence for this argument will be presented in Chapter 7.

Chapter 2: Why are our children wrongly placed?

Personal biases in assessment

There are numerous reasons for such large numbers of West Indian children being wrongly placed in ESN special schools. They revolve around the *manner of assessment* by the authorities. In many authorities only the Medical Officer of Health decides, which is farcical, since he has no qualifications in this field. In other authorities, a committee including the headmaster of the child's school and the educational psychologist decides. Usually the opinion of the educational psychologist is decisive. In turn, the single most important indicator to the educational psychologist is the *IQ test*.

Immediately, two problems arise from this. The teacher in the classroom, whose report initiates the assessment proceedings, the headmaster, and the educational psychologist, impose three biases quite often in their assessment of the child:

1 The cultural bias

This normally takes the form of linguistic differences between West Indian English and 'standard classroom' English. The West Indian child's choice of words, usage and meaning of words, pronunciation and intonation sometimes present tremendous difficulties in communication with the teacher, *and vice versa*. This factor, while recognised in a lip-service way by many of the teachers and other authorities involved, is often ignored when assessing and generally relating with the child. Thus teachers often presume to describe West Indian children as being 'dull', when in fact no educated assessment of the child's intelligence can be made under these circumstances. In addition many behaviour patterns and ways of relating to the teacher and to other children which are part of the West Indian culture are misunderstood by the teacher, who usually has no understanding of or inclination to learn about the West Indian culture. The ILEA report (page 10) points out that only three of the 19 schools suggested as a helpful method the training of teachers about the culture of the immigrant's country. While certain initial attempts are being made to educate teachers in this direction, the scope and direction of the programme – and the people running it – make one very sceptical about its usefulness.

One common difficulty, for instance, arises from the fact that the child is not expected to talk and 'talk back' as much in the West Indian classroom as he is here, in the English classroom. English teachers tend to interpret this apparent shyness and relative unresponsiveness as indicating either silent hostility or low intelligence. Many teachers have said to me that only after years of experience have they discovered that often when the West Indian child does not understand what they are saying, he replies 'Yes', because he thinks this is expected of him in his relationship to the teacher. Moreover, many children fear that they may arouse the teacher's anger or be thought stupid if they ask her to repeat what she has said.

2 The middle class bias

In most cases the teacher and the educational psychologist are middle class, in a middle class institution (which is what a school is), viewing the child through middle class tinted glasses, the child being working class in most cases. Both on the basis of class and culture they believe their standards to be the right and superior ones. They may do this in the most casual and unconscious of ways, which may make the effect on the child even more devastating. The child may therefore, not only because of problems with language but also because of feeling that he is somehow inferior, and bound to fail, refuse to communicate or to try his best in the tests for assessment. Evidence to support this statement will be given in Chapters 3 and 4.

3 The emotional-disturbance bias

Many of the problem children, I would contend, are suffering a temporary emotional disturbance due to severe culture and family shock, resulting from their sudden removal from the West Indies to a half-forgotten family, and an unknown and generally hostile environment. They often react by being withdrawn and uncommunicative, or, alternatively, by acting out aggressively, both of which are well known human reactions to upset, bewilderment and dislocation. This behaviour is often misunderstood by these supposedly trained people, as being a permanent disturbance. Despite their training, in my experience many teachers feel threatened by disturbed children, and tend to be biased against them. This accounts for the extremely large numbers of West Indian children who are submitted for assessment by the teachers, not on grounds of intellectual capacity, but because they are 'a bloody nuisance'. And dozens of teachers and headteachers have admitted this to me.

This temporary disturbance of the children due to the emotional shocks they have suffered may well take on a permanent form, however, when the nature of their problem and their consequent needs is misunderstood, and instead they face an educational environment which is humiliating and rejecting.[3] While suffering emotional turmoil they are placed in unfamiliar testing situations, to do unfamiliar and culturally biased tests, with white examiners whose speech is different, whom they have been brought up to identify as the 'master class',[4] and before whom they expect to fail. They then experience the test, only to have their fears confirmed, when they are removed from normal schools – in their mind, 'rejected' – and placed in the neighbourhood 'nut' school. And it must be remembered that the ILEA report states (page 3) that 20 percent (that is, one fifth) of all the immigrant pupils in six of their secondary ESN schools had been admitted to the Special School without even being given a trial in ordinary school first.

The IQ test

All three biases against the West Indian child, cultural, middle class, and emotional-disturbance, apply just as much to the *actual questions asked on the IQ test* administered to the children, and the very nature of *'the test situation'*. The vocabulary and style of all these IQ tests is white middle class. Many of the questions are capable of being answered by a white middle class boy, who, because of being middle class, has the right background of experiences with which to answer the questions – regardless of his real intelligence. The Black working class child, who has different life experiences, finds great difficulty in answering many of the questions, even if he is very intelligent.

The very fact of being 'tested' is a foreign experience to many Black children. The white middle class child is used to tests. The questions that are asked on these tests have to do with the sort of life *he* lives. He is therefore confident when doing these tests. Thus the white middle class child can be expected to do these tests better than the white working class or Black child – and he does. If white middle class people make up these IQ tests, and if they also do the testing, is it really any surprise that their own children score the highest? Does this have anything to do with the real abilities of the children? None.

Similarly, it should be pointed out that an emotionally disturbed child is highly likely to do badly in tests, since the act of sitting in one place for an hour or more, and answering a series of questions and doing a series of different tasks in a special order, is likely to be too frustrating and confining an experience for him.

IQ tests can only be claimed to measure intellectual functioning at *a particular moment in time, without being able to give the reasons why the functioning is at that particular level, or say which factors are more important than which for each child tested.* This point is vital to grasp if one is to understand why the IQ test is meaningless in so many cases.

The child may be functioning below normal because of being emotionally disturbed, or because of being in a bad mood on the day of the test. It could be because of racial resentment at being tested by a white person (see Chapter 4), or the fear of being placed in an ESN school as a result of the test. It could be the result of low motivation to do or succeed on the test; or it could be the fact that the act of being tested is a foreign or unusual experience, and hence the child is nervous and possibly upset. Any or all of these factors is enough to upset his true score by as much as 20 or more points! And all of this is assuming that the questions on the test itself are not culturally biased – which they are!

Now some of the less honest educational psychologists will say that they take account of these factors by stating in their report on the test that the child seemed upset, or disturbed, etc. But this does not 'take account' of these vital factors. *There is no assessment or scoring procedure on the IQ test that can add on points to a child's score to take into account any of the disturbance factors.* What is most disturbing about the use of the IQ test is that *it is the children with difficulties who are on the whole tested.* Therefore the test is being used in an area where the factors discussed above would most distort the test results; in fact, make it a mockery of an exercise. Since 20 to 25 points can in many cases decide a child's future, and the test result is very often wrong by a wider margin when dealing with 'problem children', the test is not only a shambles but a tragedy for many.

Chapter 3: The attitude of the teacher

From what has been said already, it is quite clear that large numbers of West Indian children are failing to perform to the best of their abilities, or even averagely. They are falling behind in their classroom work, and they get low scores on tests, relative to their true abilities. There are many reasons for this, and it is important to know what they are if we are to do anything to alter the situation.

Prejudice and patronisation

There are three main ways in which a teacher can seriously affect the performance of a Black child: by being openly prejudiced; by being patronising; and by having low expectations of the child's abilities. All three attitudes can be found among teachers in this country. Indeed, these attitudes are widespread. Their effect on the Black child is enormous and devastating.

That there are many openly prejudiced teachers in Britain is not in doubt in my mind. I have experienced them personally. I have also consulted many Black teachers whose experiences with some white teachers are horrifying. Two West Indian teachers in south London have reported to me the cases of white teachers who sit smoking in the staffroom, and refuse to teach a class of nearly all Black children. When on one occasion they were accosted by one of the Black teachers, they stated their refusal to teach 'those niggers'. These incidents were reported to the headteachers of the schools, who took no action against the teachers concerned. In fact, the heads of these schools had been trying to persuade the children to leave school when they had reached the school-leaving age, even though their parents wished them to continue their education, in some cases in order to obtain CSEs and O-levels, and in other cases because they thought the children could benefit from another year's general education. Therefore the teachers in this case conspired to prevent these Black children from furthering their education by simply refusing to teach them.[5]

There are many more teachers who are patronising or condescending towards Black children. These are the sort who treat a Black child as a favourite pet animal. I have often overheard teachers saying, 'I really like that coloured child. He is quite bright for a coloured child'! One teacher actually said to me one day, in a sincere and well meaning type of voice, 'Gary is really quite a nice boy considering he is Black.' There are other teachers who won't press the Black child too hard academically, as 'he isn't really up to it, poor chap'. Children see through these hypocritical and degrading statements and attitudes more often than adults realise, and they feel deeply aggrieved when anyone treats them as being inferior, which is what patronisation is all about. They build up resentment, and develop blocks to learning.[6]

When the teacher does not expect much from the child
Most teachers absorb the brainwashing that everybody else in the society has absorbed – that Black people are inferior, are less intelligent, etc, than white people. Therefore the Black child is expected to do less well in school. The IQ tests which are given to the Black child, with all their cultural bias,[7] give him a low score only too often. The teachers judge the likely ability of the child on the basis of this IQ test. The teacher has, in the form of the IQ test results, what she considers to be 'objective' confirmation of what everybody in the society is thinking and sometimes saying: that the Black children on average have lower IQs than the white children, and must consequently be expected to do less well in class. Alderman Doulton of the education committee in the Borough of Haringey has expressed this view, and it is probably fair to say that the banding of children in Haringey for supposedly achieving equal groups of ability in all the schools was really a clever plot to disperse the Black children in the borough throughout the school system. The notorious Professor Jensen, the Enoch Powell of the

academic world, has added credence to the myth of Black inferiority by openly declaring that Black people are inherently less intelligent than whites, and therefore Black children should be taught separately.[8]

In these circumstances, it is not surprising that most English teachers expect less from the Black child than from the white child. The profound effect that low teacher expectations have on the child's actual performance will now be illustrated from an experiment conducted in America.

Two American experts in education[9] conducted IQ tests on the children in a particular school in San Francisco. They did not tell the teachers the true results of the tests. Instead, they picked at random 20 names of children from the school and told the teachers that these were the bright children, even though they were not. At the end of the year the children were tested again, and the teachers were asked many questions about them. The 20 who the teachers *thought* were the brightest did far better than the rest. They got higher scores than the other children in the IQ test. The teachers thought that they were 'happier', more 'curious' and 'interesting' than the other children, and 'more likely to succeed in life than the others'. In Grade 1 the children whom the teachers *thought* were bright gained 27 and a half points (on average) in their IQ scores, compared with an average of 12 points for the others, a difference of 15 and a half points! In Grade 2 the difference was 9 points.

These scores can make all the difference between whether a child gets into grammar school or not; or which stream a child gets put into in a comprehensive; or whether, indeed, a child will be taken out of an ordinary school and placed in an ESN school. And these performances on the part of the children were simply the result of what the *teachers expected* from each child. They had nothing to do with any special help being given to one group, and the teachers and children were told nothing about the experiment. As the experts pointed out, 'In our experiment nothing was done directly for the child. There was no crash programme to improve his reading ability, no extra time for tutoring, no programme of trips to museums and art galleries. The only people affected directly were the teachers; the effect on the children was indirect.' Yet they got these large differences in performance directly related to what the teacher expected of the child. This shows how important it is to get rid of these biased IQ tests, conducted under biased conditions; for the teacher believes in these tests, and the teacher's expectations affect the child's academic progress.

In a study done in London,[10] 118 epileptic children were given an IQ test. Their teachers, not knowing the results of the test, were then asked to give their assessment of the children's intelligence by stating whether a child was 'average', 'above average', 'well above average', etc, from their knowledge of each child. It is important to mention at this stage that epileptic children suffer a lot of prejudice directed against them by the general society, similar to that Black children face – but obviously not as great. Teachers also tend to think of them as being less intelligent than ordinary children – again similar to what the Black child faces.

In 28 cases, the teachers seriously underestimated the child's true ability. This means that a *quarter* of the children were wrongly assessed! In one case a 13 year old girl with an IQ of 120 (which is university level!) had failed her 11-plus examination and was in the D stream of a secondary modern school. Her teacher considered that she was of 'below average' intelligence (average intelligence = 100)! Another child with family problems and very low income got an IQ score of 132 (which is exceedingly high). Her teachers, however, all rated her as being 'low stream' material!

This sort of information is shocking, because now that most schools are either comprehensive or going comprehensive, it is the assessment of the teachers and headteachers which decides which stream a child is placed in – which in turn influences what is expected of him academically. If these teachers who are supposed to know the children make serious mistakes in a *quarter* of the cases concerning epileptic children, against whom there is *some* prejudice, can you imagine how many wrong assessments are made by teachers when Black children are involved?!

Chapter 4: The Black child's attitude – anxiety and hostility

Studies have been done in America and Britain which show that Black children do considerably worse in tests and exams when they are conducted by white examiners and white educational psychologists. In America, Professor Katz proved this beyond all doubt in a series of tests which he conducted with Black children. Whenever a white examiner conducted a test on a Black child the Black child always did much worse than when a Black examiner had conducted the test. Whenever the child believed that it wasn't a test at all, but a game, he always did much better. But the moment the child suspected or was told that it was a test, the child became anxious, nervous, and even hostile, and therefore did much worse on the test. This is because the Black child is only too aware of the uses to which these tests are put by white society. The test has been the main instrument of trying to make Black people believe that they are inferior, and test results are used as an excuse to put children in the lowest streams in schools. The Black child knows this only too well. He knows that the test is rigged in advance (by its cultural bias against him) to ensure his failure, and so he abandons all attempts to do well on it. This can be seen most clearly when a group of Black children were told that the results of their tests would be compared with the results obtained from white children. In this case all the Black children did much worse than when they were told they would be compared with other Black children.

In Britain, Peter Watson,[11] a white educational psychologist, went to a secondary school in east London where there are many West Indian pupils. He took with him a Black assistant. The two of them tested groups of West Indian children separately. The group of West Indian children tested by the Black examiner did considerably better than the group tested by Peter Watson, the white examiner. In other words, they did much *worse* under the white examiner than under the Black one. And the difference in scores was even greater than what Professor Katz found in his experiments in America.

What is very significant to note is that these West Indian children, on returning to their classrooms after completing the test with the white examiner, displayed feelings of aggression and anger which the teachers in the classes noticed. But the West Indian children showed no such emotional reaction after being tested by the Black examiner. Professor Katz had the same experience in America, and so did Dr Baratz.

As Erik Erikson, a world-famous social anthropologist, has pointed out, these IQ tests are influenced by the general state of race relations in the society at the time at which the test is conducted. These tests are not conducted in test-tubes in a laboratory. The child who is doing the test is acutely aware of what white people think about Black people, and how they *treat* Black people. It is no accident that a four year old Negro girl in America told Mary Goodman, a psychologist, 'The people that are white, they can go up. The people that are brown, they have to go down'.[12] For even a four year old Black child understands clearly the role ascribed to Black people by white-dominated society. She knows, even at that age, just how far she can expect to go, socially, economically, and educationally.

The Black child in Britain, facing a white examiner, remembers the white landlord who has pushed Mum and Dad around; he remembers the face of Powell on the television screen, demanding the expatriation of Black people and their 'piccaninny' children; he has seen on the news and heard his parents talk about white skinheads and the white police who have beaten up Black people in the streets at night. More than likely he has encountered a racist teacher in the past; he has certainly been called 'Black bastard' or 'Wog' by many of the white children on more occasions than he cares to remember. If he lives in Haringey he would almost certainly have heard Alderman Doulton of the Haringey education committee stating that Black children had achieved significantly lower IQ scores than white children, the inference being that 'something must be done about these Black children'. He might have put two and two together and realised that this is why he sees so many Black children, including some of his friends, going to ESN schools. The thought will not have escaped him that the test he is about to sit before the white examiner, who is an official of white society, will undoubtedly be used against him, as it has been used against so many of his friends.

Under these circumstances, and in this entire racial context, the Black child feels (and quite rightly) that he is fighting a losing battle. He becomes so consumed with fear, inner rage and hatred, that he is unable to think clearly when attempting the test. Under these circumstances the very bright child does averagely, and the average child does poorly.

Conclusion

The Black child labours under three crucial handicaps: (1) *Low expectations on his part* about his likely performance in a white-controlled system of education; (2) *Low motivation* to succeed academically because he feels the cards are stacked against him; and, finally, (3) *Low teacher-expectations* which affect the amount of effort expended on his behalf by the teacher, and also affect his own image of himself and his abilities. If the system is rigged against you and if everyone expects you to fail, the chances are *you will* expect to fail too. If you expect to fail, the chances are you will.

Chapter 5: What the British school system does to the Black child

Some time ago a white boy of 13 in the school for Educationally Subnormal children where I teach asked my permission to draw a picture of me. I had been his class teacher for one year. I had a very good relationship with him, and he was very fond of me. He enjoyed drawing. The picture he did of me was quite good. He had included my spectacles, which he always teased me about, and he also drew my moustache and beard while he made great jokes about them. When he was finished, he passed me the paper with the portrait of myself, looking very pleased with himself at having drawn what he considered a near-likeness. I said to him, 'Haven't you forgotten to do something?'

'What?' he said, looking curious and suspicious.

'You forgot to colour my face. My face and cheeks, etc – they are not white, are they?'

'No, no! I can't do that!' he said, looking worried.

'Well, you said you were painting a picture of me. Presumably you wanted it to look like me. You painted my hair, moustache and beard, and you painted them black – which they are. So you have to paint my face dark brown if it is to look like me at all!'

'No! I can't. I can't do that. No. No,' he said, looking highly embarrassed and disturbed. He then got up and walked away, finding himself a hammer to do woodwork with in the corner of the room far away from me.

This same boy, along with one of his white school friends, had waited outside the school gate for me one afternoon the previous week. When I approached, one of them said, 'People are saying that you are coloured, but you aren't, sir, are you?' This was a rhetorical question on their part. They both looked very worried that 'some people' should be calling me 'coloured', and wanted my reassurance that I was not. They both liked and admired me, and hated thinking that I might be coloured! I explained to them then, as I *had* done many times before in class, that I *was* Black, that I was from the West Indies, and that my forefathers came from Africa. They obviously had mental blocks against accepting me as being Black.

This white boy, who did not even know who 'coloured people' were, obviously had the most fearful image of what Black people were supposed to be like, even though his favourite teacher was Black, and one of his closest friends in class was a Black child. I happened to know that his house mother at the children's home where he lives has never discussed race with him and does not display any open prejudice to Black people. In fact she has, over the years, been an excellent foster mother to two West Indian boys. Yet he picked up from somewhere a sufficiently adverse image of Black people that he couldn't bear to have his favourite teacher be 'coloured', and could not bring himself to draw me as I was – a Black man. He had to have my face white!

This experience of mine gave me an idea: if this is how two white boys in the class felt about me, then perhaps they felt the same way about their close friend, Desmond, a Black boy of 11 from Jamaica. So I gathered together all the drawings and paintings which the children had done of each other, and sure enough, Desmond got painted white by all the white children! What's worse, Desmond and the other four Black children had painted each other white also!

A week later, Desmond, the West Indian boy, asked me to draw a picture of him. I drew the outline, as he watched, making critical comments from time to time. Having completed the outline, I began shading his face Black. He immediately said, 'What – what are you doing? You are *spoiling* me!'

I said, 'No, of course not. I am painting you as you are – Black; just like *I* am. Black is beautiful, you know. You aren't ashamed of that, are you?'

At that he calmed down, and I completed shading his face Black. Then I did his hair. His hair was black, short, and very African in texture. I drew it exactly as his hair really was. When he saw it, he jumped out of his chair and shouted, 'You painted me to look like a golliwog! You make me look just like a golliwog!' and he was half about to cry, half about to pounce on me for having done so terrible thing as to have drawn his hair like it was, instead of making it long, straight and brown, as he had drawn himself in the past!

After I had calmed him down, again by pointing out that my hair was exactly the same as his, and that *I* liked mine, he decided to retaliate by drawing one of me. He drew my hair Black and African-like, he drew my moustache and beard, but he, like the white boy before, refused to shade my face dark brown or black even though I had done his that way. When I asked him to draw my face the colour it really was, rather than leaving it white, he said very emotionally, 'You do it yourself,' and walked out of the room.

Obviously in an English classroom it is terrible to be Black. The white child is concerned lest his best friend be considered Black, and the Black child is more than concerned that he should be considered Black!

And this is what this society, with the aid of the school system, is doing to our Black children!

The examples I have given above are not isolated ones. There is the Indian girl in my class who wears Indian clothes to school and whose mother wears her caste-marks and sari when going anywhere, and yet this girl once denied she was Indian when speaking to her English friends in the class. Or there is the case of the Jamaican girl in my class who pretended not to know where Jamaica was, and stated indignantly that she was not from 'there' when speaking to some of the other children one day. Both conversations I overheard by accident. I could give case after case, for they are endless. In fact, none of the West Indian children whom I taught and ran clubs for over a period of three years have failed to reveal their feelings of ambiguity, ambivalence, and at times despair, at being Black. Many have been made neurotic by their school experience.

How the system works

The Black child's true identity is denied daily in the classroom. In so far as he is given an identity, it is a false one. He is made to feel inferior in every way. In addition to being told he is dirty and ugly and 'sexually unreliable', he is told by a variety of means that he is intellectually inferior. When he prepares to leave school, and even before, he is made to realise that he and 'his kind' are only fit for manual, menial jobs.

The West Indian child is told on first entering the school that his language is second rate, to say the least. Namely, the only way he knows how to speak, the way he has always communicated with his parents and family and friends; the language in which he has expressed all his emotions, from joy to sorrow; the language of his innermost thoughts and ideas, is 'the wrong way to speak'.

A man's language is part of him. It is his only vehicle for expressing his thoughts and feelings. To say that his language and that of his entire family and culture is second rate is to accuse him of *being* second rate. But this is what the West Indian child is told in one manner or another on his first day in an English school.

As the weeks and months progress, the Black child discovers that all the great men of history were white – at least, those are the only ones he has been told about. His reading books show him white children and white adults exclusively. He discovers that white horses, white rocks and white unicorns are beautiful and good; but the word 'black' is reserved for describing the pirates, the thieves, the ugly, the witches, etc. This is the *conditioning effect* of what psychologists call *word association* on people's minds. If every reference on TV, radio, newspapers, reading books and storybooks in school shows 'black' as being horrible and ugly, and everything 'white' as being pure, clean and beautiful, then people begin to think this way on racial matters.

Several months ago in my class I was reading one of S K McCullagh's storybooks for children, *The Country of the Red Birds*. This author is world famous, and she has written numerous storybooks and reading series for children, used in schools in many parts of the world. She is actually a lecturer in psychology. In this story, these two white children went out to the 'island of Golden Sands'. They got to the 'white rock', where the very helpful 'white unicorn' lives. When they met the unicorn, 'the first thing that they saw was a Black ship, with Black sails, sailing towards the white rock'.

'The Black pirates! The Black pirates!' cried the little unicorn. 'They'll kill us! Oh, what shall we do?'

Finally they escaped from the white rock, which the 'Black pirates' had taken over, and went to the island of the 'red birds'. There, 'a Black pirate stood on the sand, with a red bird in his hand', about to kill it. The white boys and the white unicorn, along with the other red birds, managed to beat off the Black pirate, and the red birds in gratitude to the white boys and white unicorn state, 'We will do anything for you, for you have saved a red bird from the Black pirates.'

For those who may be sceptical about the influence of word association on people's minds, it is interesting to note that when I said 'Black pirates' in the story, several of the white children in the class turned their heads and looked at the Black children, who in turn looked acutely embarrassed.

When the pictures, illustrations, music, heroes, great historical and contemporary figures in the classroom are all white, it is difficult for a child to identify with anyone who is not white. When in addition the pictures of Blacks are golliwog stereotypes, about whom filthy jokes are made; when most plays show Black men doing servant jobs; when the word 'Black' in every storybook is synonymous with evil, then it becomes impossible for the child to want to be Black. Put another way, it would be unnatural of him not to want to be white. Does this not explain why Desmond and the other Black children draw themselves as white? Can you blame them?

But this is not the end of the picture, unfortunately, for the Black children know they are Black. Whenever they might begin in their fantasy to believe otherwise, they are soon reassured on this score by being told they are 'Black bastards' whenever there is a row in the playground – and even when there isn't.

The children are therefore made neurotic about their race and culture. Some become behaviour problems as a result. They become resentful and bitter at being told their language is second rate, and their history and culture is non-existent; that they hardly exist at all, except by grace of the whites – and then only as platform sweepers on the Underground, manual workers, and domestic help.

The Black child under these influences develops a deep inferiority complex. He soon loses motivation to succeed academically, since, at best, the learning experience in the classroom is an elaborate irrelevance to his personal life situation, and at worst it is a racially humiliating experience. He discovers in an amazingly short space of time the true role of the Black man in a white-controlled society, and he abandons all intellectual and career goals. Remember the four year old Black girl in America, mentioned earlier, who said to Mary Goodman, 'The people that are white, they can go up. The people that are brown, they have to go down.' When two other psychologists in America (Radke and Trager) investigated 'Children's perception of the social roles of Negroes and whites',[13] the 'poor house' was assigned to Negroes and the 'good house' to whites by the great majority of white and Negro children aged five to eight years.

Conclusion

The Black child acquires two fundamental attitudes or beliefs as a result of his experiencing the British school system: a low self-image, and consequently low self-expectation in life. These are obtained through streaming, banding, bussing, ESN schools, racist news media, and a white middle class curriculum; by totally ignoring the Black child's language, history, culture, identity. Through the choice of teaching materials, the society emphasises who and what it thinks is important – and by implication, by omission, who and what it thinks is unimportant, infinitesimal, irrelevant. Through the belittling, ignoring or denial of a person's identity, one can destroy perhaps the most important aspect of a person's personality – his sense of identify, of who he is. Without this, he will get nowhere.

Chapter 6: Self-hatred: the Black and white doll experiments

The Black child is prepared, both by his general life experiences and by the classroom, for a life of self-contempt. He learns to hate his colour, his race, his culture, and to wish he were white. He learns to consider black things and Black people as ugly, and white things and white people as beautiful. He believes that since he is Black, he can never be beautiful. Therefore when he draws a picture of himself, he draws himself white. When he draws any picture of a man, it is always that of a white man. Not a single Black child has ever drawn me a picture of a Black man. Of hundreds of drawings done for me over the years by Black children, every one of them is of a white man!

In America, Kenneth B Clark and Maime P Clark did a famous study[14] which demonstrates beyond all doubt the Black child's self-contempt. They interviewed a sample of Black children aged three to eight years old from all parts of America. The children were shown two dolls, one Black and the other white. They were first asked to pick 'the doll that looks like a white child'. Ninety four percent of the children picked out the right doll. Then they were asked for 'the doll that looks like a coloured child'. Ninety four percent got the right doll.

This showed that the vast majority (93 to 94 percent) understood and could recognise which doll looked like each race. They were then asked to pick the doll that they liked to play with best. *Thirty two percent picked the coloured doll, and 67 percent chose the white doll!*

The Black children were then asked, 'Give me the doll that is a nice doll', and 38 percent chose the coloured doll, but *59 percent chose the white doll as the 'nice' doll.*

When they were asked for the doll that looked bad, 59 percent picked the coloured doll, and only 17 percent picked the white doll!

When asked for the doll that was a 'nice colour', 38 percent chose the coloured doll and *60 percent chose the white doll.*

Finally, they were asked, 'Give me the doll that looks like you.' Sixty six percent picked the coloured doll, and *33 percent (one third) of these Black children aged three to eight chose the white doll as the one that looked like them!*

As the Clarks point out with reference to the last question, 'Some of the children who were free and relaxed in the beginning of the experiment broke down and cried or became somewhat negativistic during the latter part when they were required to make self-identification. Indeed, two children ran out of the testing room, unconsolable, convulsed in tears.'

In case anyone is liable to dismiss the above evidence on the grounds that this happened in America and does not apply to the West Indian in Britain, I have bad news for you. The same test was conducted in Britain recently, with the same results!

Chapter 7: Why our children get the worst education – the immigrants' role in Britain

There are two reasons for the presence of Black immigrants in this country: (a) Our countries have been so successfully fleeced that the only employment opportunities open to a very large section of our people have been in England, where all our stolen wealth resides. Therefore we left the West Indies in search of work. (b) The British capitalist needed our services, and actively recruited us in the West Indies because of Britain's shortage of unskilled labour, particularly for dirty jobs.

Immigrants in Britain perform four major tasks:

1 We increase the *supply of labour* through our presence, particularly unskilled labour, relative to the *demand,* thus keeping *wages down and profits up.*

2 We perform many of the menial and unwanted jobs where otherwise there would be a labour shortage.

3 We immigrants, without realising it, serve to divide the working class and dampen their militancy. This is because on the one hand the native worker feels threatened job and social status wise by the arrival of the immigrant, and on the other hand he moves one rung further up the social ladder by the presence of immigrants who form *the* lowest social rung. We have the lowest social status because we are given the worst jobs, the worst housing, and we are never accepted by the society. Both because the English worker feels threatened job-wise and because he has, by our presence here, someone to look down on, he adopts a prejudiced and discriminatory position towards us. The incitement to racial hatred adopted by various members of the establishment, notably Enoch Powell, has the effect of diverting the workers' energies and attention away from the main cause of their low socio-economic position – the establishment itself.

4 The establishment pays cheaply for us in another way apart from wages – in the lack of provision of capital infrastructure, mainly housing, schools, and health and recreational facilities. Both because of low wages and our widespread experience of prejudice, most of us are forced to live in over-crowded, run-down areas, with the least amenities. There is no new provision of housing for our needs, despite our contribution to the economy. Thus the society gets us as cheaply as possible, to plug a crucial gap in the economy – the need for a sizeable unskilled labour force.[15]

But there are contradictions in the Establishment position: through the incitement of prejudice as a diversionary tactic, the white masses have become so insecure that they have demanded the cessation of the flow of immigrants, and many have gone further, following Powell's lead, and suggested the deportation of coloured immigrants. But this is unwelcome to big business, which sees in this the danger of losing their cheap labour market. Thus all three political parties do nothing to remove the immigrant from Britain. The Guianese government has asked the British government to assist in advertising and financing a programme to encourage Guianese and other West Indians living in this country to return to Guyana to help in Guyana's development needs. The British government appears to have done nothing in response.

But there is another threat to big business and the social 'order'. If the children of us immigrants were to get equal educational opportunities then in one generation there would be no large labour pool from underdeveloped countries, prepared to do the menial and unwanted jobs in the economic system, at the lowest wages and in the worst housing; for our children, armed with a good education, would demand the jobs – and the social status that goes with such jobs – befitting their educational qualifications. This would be a very bad blow to Britain's 'social order', with its notions about the right place of the Black man in relation to the white man in society.

Thus the one way to ensure no changes in the social hierarchy and abundant unskilled labour is to adopt and adapt the educational system to meet the needs of the situation: to prepare our children for the society's future unskilled and ill-paid jobs. It is in this perspective that we can come to appreciate why so many of our Black children are being dumped in ESN schools, secondary moderns, the lowest streams of the comprehensive schools, and 'bussed' and 'banded' about the school system.

Chapter 8: Conclusions and recommendations

This booklet has been written for the West Indian community in Britain, though a lot of its message is relevant to the educational problems of Black children in the West Indies and America as well. It is written particularly for West Indian parents, since parents are in a position to do the most for their children, and since West Indian parents are known traditionally for being tremendously sacrificing and ceaselessly ambitious over their children's educational progress and general welfare. It is also written with West Indian teachers, educational psychologists, social workers and community leaders in mind; for through their awareness of the scandalous situation which befalls our children, they can help to galvanise and organise the community for whatever actions are needed to radically alter the situation. The recommendations which follow proceed logically from the evidence presented in this booklet, and are in most cases self-evident. They represent the *minimum conditions* which we as a Black community can and will accept for our children...

Recommendations that we as a West Indian community must insist on in dealing with the authorities

1   No West Indian child (or any immigrant child, for that matter) to be placed in an ESN school unless and until he has had a minimum of two years in a normal school.[16]

2   Moreover, any child considered for placement in an ESN school should receive first a minimum of 18 months to two years of intensive help in 'opportunity classes' in normal school. 'Opportunity classes' should not be full-time classes, but classes which the child attends for one or two hours each day, to get special help. We do not wish to create ESN 'ghetto' streams within the normal school.

3   All West Indian children of 65+ IQ, at present in ESN schools, to be returned promptly to normal schools, where special provisions should be arranged through 'opportunity classes' to return them to normal academic standards. Chapters 2, 3 and 4 demonstrate beyond all reasonable doubt that a West Indian child given a score of 65 on a white, middle class IQ test, conducted by a white Educational Psychologist or Medical Officer of Health, is undoubtedly in the 80-90 range *at least*. Such children have no right to be in ESN schools.

There is also a need for re-examination of the placing of large numbers of West Indian children in the lowest streams of secondary schools. Chapter 3 shows conclusively the profound influence of teacher expectations (of which streaming is a manifestation) on a child's performance.

4   All remaining West Indian children in ESN schools (ie those of 50 to 65 IQ) should be reassessed by Black educational psychologists at the earliest opportunity, with a view to their referral back to normal schools if this proves justified in their opinion.

5   A committee of West Indian educationalists should be set up to look into the possibility of standardising the present IQ tests to West Indian cultural requirements, or constructing a test *or other method of assessment* specifically applicable to the West Indian child, whichever seems necessary in the opinion of that body.

6   In the meantime, all IQ and other tests on West Indian children must be conducted by West Indian educational psychologists *only*. (I would humbly suggest the same for Indian and Pakistani children.) Chapter 4 demonstrates, on the basis of experience, the absolute necessity for this.

7   There should be the recruiting of as many West Indian teachers as possible for schools with large numbers of West Indian children. All 'opportunity

classes' should be Black staffed. Chapters 4, 5 and 6 demonstrate the importance of providing our Black children with adults to identify with and feel proud of, to help to break the vicious circle of self-contempt.

8 Black history and culture, ie the history of Black people throughout the Caribbean, the Americas, Africa and Asia, should be made part of the curriculum of *all* schools, for the benefit of the Black *and* the white children. Chapters 5 and 6 demonstrate the urgent necessity for this beyond any doubt. Indeed, its exclusion from most school curricula constitutes nothing short of criminal negligence (or prejudice) in the educational sphere.

9 Parents whose children are being considered for ESN placement should always be informed of what is happening at every stage in the process of assessment, and of their right to object and appeal against any decision. They should be informed of their rights orally and in writing, and the precise nature and purpose of an ESN school should be explained clearly to them, as it affects their child.

Things we can do for ourselves

1 We need to open Black *nursery schools* and *supplementary schools* throughout the areas we live in, in Britain. Our nursery schools should have Black dolls and toys and pictures, and storybooks about great Black men and women, and their achievements and inventions. Our children need to have a sense of identity, pride and belonging, as well as mental stimulation, so that they do not end up hating themselves and their race, and being dumped in ESN schools. Pride and self-confidence are the best armour against the prejudice and humiliating experiences which they will certainly face in school and in the society.

We should start up supplementary schools in whatever part of London, or Britain, we live, in order to give our children additional help in the subjects they need. These classes can be held on evenings and Saturday mornings. We should recruit all our Black students and teachers for the task of instructing our children. Through these schools we hope to make up for the inadequacies of the British school system, and for its refusal to teach our children our history and culture. We must never sit idly by while they make ignoramuses of our children, but must see to it that by hook or by crook our children get the best education they are capable of! Some supplementary schools have already been started in parts of London. Don't be the last to get your child in one!

2 Parents must make it their duty to visit the schools that their children attend

as often as possible. This will keep the teachers on their toes, and make them realise you mean business where the education of your child is concerned. Find out what 'stream' your child is in, and *why.* If you think he should be doing better, let them know your views. Don't be taken in by the usual statement that 'your child is doing all right.' Show them you are concerned with your child's progress, and let the child know that you care about his progress too. The whole point of this booklet is to show you that it is not always, or only the child's fault, if he isn't succeeding.

3 We should talk and *chat* with our children as often as we can. *Make* the time when necessary. Quite often the child has bad experiences at school, with other children, or with the teacher, or with the sort of work he is being given at school. The only way we can find out about his problems and help him with them is through chatting with him.

4 We should *read* to our children, especially West Indian storybooks and books about Black people throughout the world. See the book list at the end of this booklet for the sort of books you can read with your children. The book list also has the name and address of the West Indian bookshop where all these books can be obtained.

5 Toys such as bricks and other playing materials are *very important* to provide our small children with. Psychologists have proved beyond all doubt that they help to make children more active mentally and think better. If they get bricks, puzzles, drawing and colouring books, as well as dolls and small cars to play with from the time they are one year up, they will tend to be *much* brighter when they start school. (And if we don't want them to hate themselves, we must get them *Black* dolls. Remember Chapter 6?)

6 Finally, if you are a West Indian parent with a child at an ESN school, read over this booklet carefully, take it and show it to the head teacher at the school, and go and see the Chief Education Officer of your borough and demand a reassessment of your child by a Black educational psychologist, in the light of this booklet.

Chapter 9: Questions and answers for parents

What is an ESN Special School? What type of child does it cater for?
Once they were called 'feeble-minded', then 'mentally subnormal', and now the children are called 'educationally subnormal' or 'ESN' for short. As

Chapter 1 demonstrates, ESN schools are really for children who are naturally of very low intelligence. They are *not* remedial schools in the sense of preparing the child for return to normal school. They keep children on a permanent basis. They do *not* therefore cater properly for the child who is of normal intelligence by functioning badly because of language or emotional difficulties, or because he has missed a lot of schooling before coming to this country. In fact, there is some evidence that such children deteriorate mentally at ESN schools.

How and why do children get sent there?

Usually the child's class teacher makes a report to the headteacher, to the effect that the child is far behind in his work, doesn't seem to be catching up, and seems dull. Quite often the real truth is that the child may be giving trouble to the teacher – being a 'bloody nuisance' – and this is one way of the teacher, and the school, being rid of him. Quite often the child may be going through a difficult patch of emotional disturbance, when he can't concentrate on his studies, and this is confused with his intelligence.

The headteacher then makes a report to the education authorities, and then the Medical Officer of Health arranges a medical examination and an IQ test of the child. The Medical Officer of Health then decides, in some boroughs on his own (!), in other boroughs with the help of the headmaster and an educational psychologist, whether the child should be sent to an ESN school.

What is an IQ test?

An IQ test is a test conducted by a Medical Officer of Health or educational psychologist intended to measure the intelligence of a child. It consists of a series of questions (many of them quite stupid, and unrelated to the experiences of West Indian children – see Chapter 2) and tasks for the child to do, lasting about one hour. If the child is upset, emotionally disturbed, unable to understand what the educational psychologist is saying, or if the child is uneasy because of never having done a test like this before, then the score or 'marks' which the child will get on the test will have *nothing whatever* to do with his real intelligence. This is why the test is so absurd and very harmful when given to West Indian children, particularly those with difficulties. West Indian children feel more at ease and do considerably better on the tests when they are conducted by West Indian educational psychologists, so always insist on one if they want to test your child.

Do parents have any say over whether their child is placed in an ESN school? Can parents refuse? Can they appeal against any decision?

Parents must be consulted before a child can be given a medical examination and IQ test. Parents *must* be consulted, also, if a decision to send their child to an ESN 'Special' school is taken. If parents *insist* that the child be given remedial help in the normal school instead of ESN placement, then many authorities will probably agree. However, they can refuse, and place your child in an ESN school even if you object. In such a case, *you have the right of appeal*. If you can bring evidence and arguments to support your case, then the Borough Education Committee or the Secretary of State for Education might reverse the decision. But they have the last word. If you think your child is being wrongly placed, then it is always worth your while to protest and appeal. It might force them to think again.

Can a child be transferred back from an ESN school to normal school?

Yes. But this happens *very* rarely (see Chapter 1). The only cases I know of were cases where the parents kept on putting pressure on the headmaster and the school.

What is the alternative to ESN school for a child of normal ability but who is doing badly at school?

Remedial or 'opportunity' classes in the normal school. These are classes (which only some boroughs have – and you should press your borough to start them if they haven't) where the child can have an hour or two of special help in the subjects he needs help in (like English and arithmetic) from a well qualified and experienced teacher. West Indian children tend to do much better when taught by West Indian teachers, so you must make it your duty to press your education authority to hire more Black teachers for your child's sake.

Appendix I

Table 1: Immigrant pupils in ordinary and ESN day schools, September 1966/1967

Year	School type	No of pupils on roll	No of immigrant pupils	Percentage of immigrants
1966	Ordinary	398,133	52,400	13.2
	ESN	3,876	904	23.3
1967	Ordinary	397,130	59,434	15.0
	ESN	4,109	1,166	28.4

Table 2: Nationality of immigrant pupils in ordinary and ESN schools, Spring 1967 (figures given as percentages)

Nationality	Ordinary schools	ESN schools
West Indian	54	75
Indian and Pakistani	10	4
Cypriot	16	13
Other	21	8
Total number of children	55,161	886

Appendix II

The Caribbean Education and Community Workers' Association

West Indian children are being put in disproportionate numbers in the lowest streams of secondary schools; they have been placed in their thousands in ESN schools where the authorities themselves now admit they do not belong; in some boroughs they are being bussed from their neighbourhood to far distant schools; the children have been banded – or bandied – about the schools in various boroughs, on the assumption that they are of 'low intelligence' and 'culturally deprived', and so must be spread in twos and threes throughout the school system to prevent 'standards being lowered'.

All these actions, and many more that we find out about every day, have been done and *continue to be done* without consulting the children's parents. And in many of those cases where parents have to be consulted by low, they have been deceived – for example, the authorities have described the ESN school as 'Special', rather than a school for the subnormal.

The Caribbean Education and Community Workers' Association consists of West Indian teachers, social workers, educational psychologists and community workers. It has three main functions:

1 To do/carry out research and find out what is happening to our children in the schools – and why.
2 To let all Black parents know what is happening and what their rights are.
3 To help set up parents and youth organisations all over the country to meet the needs of the Black child – supplementary Black schools, youth clubs, nursery schools, playgroups, and so on.

If *you* can help in *any* way, please contact the association. Our address for the time being is: c/o Mr Martin Bart, 24 Willoughby Lane, Tottenham, London N17.

Book list for parents: West Indian literature for children

Books and book lists, with prices, are obtainable from New Beacon Books Ltd, 2 Albert Road, London N4. Tel: 01-272 4889.

Novels
Hurricane, Drought, Fire, Riot. Four adventure novels for children by Andrew Salkey, about the experiences of children from different families during the exciting events of hurricane, fire, drought, and a riot in a marketplace. Set in town and country in Jamaica. Suitable for eight to 12 year olds. *Hurricane* received the German Children's Book Prize in 1968.
The Year in San Fernando, by Michael Anthony. Excellent novel about the experiences of a 12 year old boy who leaves his home in the country for San Fernando, a large town in Trinidad. Suitable for 12 to 16 year olds.

Black Midas, by Jan Carew, a Guianese author.
Anansi Stories and *West Indian Folk Tales*, both by Philip Sherlock.
West Indian Stories, by Andrew Salkey.
Caribbean Narrative, by O R Dathorne.
West Indian Narrative, by Kenneth Ramchand. These last three are selections of Caribbean writing,
suitable for secondary school pupils.
The Sun's Eye, edited by Anne Walmsley. A selection of stories and poetry suitable for 22 to 15 year olds.

Historical novels
Queen of the Mountain, by P M Cousins. An adventure story about the Jamaican Maroons. Very well
written. Suitable for eight to 13 year olds.
Sixty-Five, by V S Reid. The excitement of the 1865 rebellion in Jamaica, as seen by a 12 year old boy.

History
The People Who Came. Book 1 by Alma Norman; Book 2 by Patricia Patterson and James Carnegie.
A good description of the cultures of India, Africa, China, American Indian tribes, and Europe, and
the ways in which they affected the West Indies. For secondary pupils 11 to 14 years.
Marcus Garvey 1887-1940, by Adolph Edwards. The story of the life of the man who preached
Black Pride in Jamaica and America, and opened our eyes.
A Visual History of the West Indies, by Shirley Duncker. Excellent for primary classes.

Plays
Four Plays for Primary Schools, by Edward Brathwaite.
Odale's Choice, by Edward Brathwaite.

Bibliography

C Bagley, 'The Educational Performance of Immigrant Children', Comment on ILEA report, *Race*, vol 10,
no 1, July 1968.
Dr S Baratz, *Journal of Personality and Social Psychology*, 7, 1967, p194.
C Bergman, 'Colonial Colleges', *Times Educational Supplement*, 6 November 1970, p53.
J Bhatanagar, *Immigrants at School* (London: Cornmarket Press, 1970).
Bibby, *Race Prejudice and Education* (Heinemann, 1959).
S Biesheuvel and R Liddicoat, 'The Effects of Cultural Factors on Intelligence', *National Institute Personnel
Research*, vol 8, no 1, September 1959, pp3-14.
G Bowker, *The Education of Coloured Immigrants* (Longman, 1968).
K B Clark and M P Clark, 'Racial Identification and Preference in Negro Children', in T M Newcomb, and
T L Hartley (eds), *Readings in Social Psychology* (New York: Holt, 1947).
W E Coffman, 'Developed Tests for the Culturally Deprived', *School and Society*, no 5, 13, 1965, pp430-
433.
W W Daniel, 'Racial Discrimination in England', based on the PEP Report 1968.
A Davis, 'Poor People Have Brains Too', *The Phi Delta Kappan*, April 1949, 30, pp294-295.
J Derrick, *Teaching English to Immigrant Children* (Longman, 1966).
R M Dreyer and K S Miller, 'Comparative Psychological Studies of Negroes and Whites in the USA',
Psychology Bulletin, vol 57, September 1969, pp361-402.
P C Evans, and R B Le Page, 'The Education of West Indian Immigrant Children', *National Committee for
Commonwealth Education*, 1967.
O M Ferron, 'The Linguistic Factor in the Test Intelligence of West African Children', *Educational Research*,
vol 9, no 2, February 1967, pp113-121.

O M Ferron, 'The Test Performance of 'Colonial Children', *Educational Research*, vol 8, no 1, November 1965, pp42-57.

E Frazer, *Home Environment and the School* (London: ULP, 1959).

R T Goldman and F M Taylor, 'Coloured Immigrant Children: A Survey of Research Studies and Literature on their Educational Problems and Potential in Britain', *Educational Research*, 8, 1966, p3.

M E Goodman, *Race Awareness in Young Children* (Cambridge, Massachusetts: Addison-Wesley, 1952; Collier Books, 1964).

V Leonard Gordon and Kikuchi Akio, 'American Personality Tests in Cross-Cultural Research – a Caution', *Journal of Social Psychology*, vol 69, August 1966, pp179-183,

R E Grinder, et al, 'Relationships between Goodenough Draw-a-Man Test Programme and Skin Colour among Pre-adolescent Jamaican Children', *Journal of Social Psychology*, vol 62, 2nd half 1964, pp181-188.

R C Hicks, *Papua and New Guinea – Journal of Education*, vol 6, no 3, October 1969, pp29-43.

Holt, Reinhart, Winston, *Social Class, Race and Psychological Development*, eds, Jensen, Katz and Deusch, 1968.

V P Houghton, 'Intelligence Testing of West Indian and English Children', *Race*, vol 8, no 2, October 1966, pp147-156.

L R C Howard and W A Roland, 'Some Inter-Cultural Differences on the Draw-a-Man Test: Goodenough Scores', *Man*, vol 54, no 127, June 1964, pp86-88.

L Hudson, 'IQ: The Effect of Heredity and Environment', *The Times Saturday Review*, 7 November 1970.

ILEA, *The Education of Immigrant Pupils in Special Schools for ESN Children*, Report 657, 10 September 1968.

ILEA, *The Education of Immigrants Pupils in Primary Schools*, Report 959, 12 February 1968.

S A Irvine, 'Adapting Tests to the Cultural Setting: A Comment' by P A Schwarz, in *Education and Psychological Measurements*, 2, 3, 1963, pp673-686.

L Kaplan, 'Social Class Influences on Mental Health', section on 'Intelligence and Social Status', *Mental Health and Human Relations in Education* (New York: Harper & Ross, 1959) ch 8.

O Klineberg, 'Negro/White Differences in Intelligence Test Performance', *American Psychology*, vol 18, no 4, April 1963, pp188-203.

G S Lesser, G Fifer and D M Clark, 'Mental Abilities of Children from Different Social Class and Cultural Groups', *Monographs of the Society for Research in Child Development*, 30, (4) (University of Chicago Press, 1965).

A Little, et al, 'The Education of Immigrant Pupils', ILEA, *Race*, vol 9, no 4, April 1968, pp439-452.

M B Loeb, 'Implications of Status Differentiation for Personal and Social Development', *Harvard Educational Review*, Summer 1953, 23, pp168-174.

M Maxwell, *Violence in the Toilets: Experiences of a Black Teacher in Brent Schools*.

W B Munford and C E Smith, 'Racial Comparisons and Intelligence Testing', *Journal of the Royal African Society*, vol 37, 1938, pp46-57.

National Association of Schoolmasters Special Report, 'Education and the Immigrant'.

NUT Pamphlet, *The Ascertainment of ESN Children* (1967).

R Oakley, *New Backgrounds – The Immigrant Children at Home and at School* (OUP, published for the Institute of Race Relations, 1968).

C Peach, *West Indian Migration to Britain: A Social Geography* (OUP, 1968).

J Power, *Immigrants in School* (Councils and Educational Press, 1967).

G P Pritchard, *Education and the Handicapped 1760-1960* (Routledge, 1963).

'Awareness of Ethnic Differences in Young Children: Proposals for a British Study', *Race*, vol 3, July 1960, no 7, pp63-73.

Radke and Trager, 'Children's Perception of the Social Roles of Negroes and Whites', *Journal of Psychology*, 29, 1950.

Schools Council Working Paper 19, *Teaching English to Immigrant Children* (Evan/Methuen).

M A Shuey, *The Testing of Negro Intelligence* (New York: Social Science Press, 2nd edition, 1966), p578.

M Stone, *West Indian Children in an ESN School – Why are They There?* Mimeographed.

A E Tansley and R Gulliford, *The Education of Slow-learning Children* (London: Routledge & Kegan Paul, 1960).

J Vaizey, 'Social Inequality, Democracy and Education', *Education in the Modern World* (London: World University Library, 1967), pp165-189.

P E Vernon, *Selection for Secondary Education in Jamaica* (Kingston Government Printer, 1961).

P Watson, 'The New IQ Test', *New Society*, 22 January 1970, nos 2 and 3.

P Watson, 'Race and Intelligence', *New Society*, 16 July 1970, no 407.

N Wein, 'Compensatory Education', *Race Today*, March 1970, pp72-75.

S Wiles, 'Children from Overseas', IRR Newsletter, February and June 1968.

P Williams, 'The Ascertainment of ESN Children', *Educational Research*, 1965.

Notes

1 For evidence on this, see A E Tansley and R Gulliford, *The Education of Slow-learning Children* (London: Routledge and Keegan Paul, 1960), especially pp1-22.

2 *Times*, 15 May 1970, p11. A *helot* is a modern-day 'hewer of wood and drawer of water'.

3 See chs 3 and 5.

4 See ch 4.

5 For those who need further evidence of open prejudice by teachers, read Marina Maxwell's *Violence in the Toilets, the Experiences of a Black Teacher in Brent Schools*.

6 For further evidence on this and other aspects of the problem, see R J Goldman and F M Taylor, 'Coloured Immigrant Children: a Survey of Research, Studies and Literature on their Educational Problems and Potential in Britain', *Educational Research*, VIII, 3 (1966).

7 See ch 2.

8 See Professor Liam Hudson's excellent article on 'IQ: the Effect of Heredity and Environment' in *The Times Saturday Review*, 7 November 1970.

9 R Rosenthal and L F Jacobson, 'Teacher Expectations for the Disadvantaged', *Scientific American*, April 1968, vol 218, no 4.

10 See C Bagley, *Race*, vol X, no 1, July 1968.

11 P Watson, 'Race and Intelligence', *New Society*, no 407, 16 July 1970.

12 M Goodman, *Race Awareness in Young Children* (Cambridge, Mass: Collier Books, 1964).

13 *Journal of Psychology*, 29, 1950.

14 'Racial Identification and Preference in Negro Children', in T M Newcombe and T L Hartley (eds), *Readings in Social Psychology* (New York, Holt, 1947).

15 For evidence on the economic contribution of the immigrant to the British economy, see *Economic Impact of Commonwealth Immigration* (Cambridge University Press, for the National Institute of Economic and Social Research). See also P Evans, *Times*, 17 July 1970.

16 As the Little, Mabey and Whittacre study on 'The Education of Immigrant Pupils in Inner London Primary Schools', *Race*, April 1968, vol 9, no 4, pp439-452, points out in its conclusions, 'There is a consistent and marked improvement in immigrant performance with increasing length of English education.'

© Bernard Coard 1971

● First published for the Caribbean Education and Community Workers' Association by New Beacon Books Ltd

Chris Searle

A vital instrument

WHENEVER OR wherever the powerful create communities of the excluded, they inevitably provoke those same communities to transform themselves into communities of resistance. Black communities in England have a long history of fighting back and organising against exclusion and racism in education, and they have invariably engaged committed intellectuals and academics within their own ranks in these processes of educational struggle.

When Bernard Coard wrote *How the West Indian Child is Made Educationally Subnormal in the British School System*, a small enough, pamphlet length book with the apex of long titles, he continued the tradition of organic intellectuals being at the centre of their communities' essential struggles. In dedicating his essay to 'my parents and all Black parents who value their children's education and opportunities in life above all else', he not only recognised how educational progress was at the centre of the lives of new immigrant communities, but also how those within these communities who had already achieved academic success – a minority at this stage of their histories – must take an active and central role in these struggles for educational betterment.

And how would such a provocative pamphlet as this ever have been published without the existence of Black community-based publishing initiatives, vibrant Black presses such as John La Rose's north London based New Beacon Books which actually published the work, or Guyana-born Jessica and Eric Huntley's Bogle Ouverture Publications in Ealing, which published many others carrying the same community imperative? No white mainstream publisher would ever have gone near Coard's work, and it was a sign of the rapid development of Black British organs of resistance that at least two initiatives like those of La Rose and the Huntleys existed at this time to take on the essential role of publishing vital documents of Black community struggle. At the time Bogle Ouverture had a shopfront, but Trinidad-born La Rose sold his books from the downstairs front room of his house – a measure of the powerful intellectual and community commitment of this griot of London-Caribbean struggle. Between them La Rose and the Huntleys could slake the cultural thirst of the London Black community's desire for reading and creating the best Caribbean writing and authorship.

I remember the first time I ever visited the La Rose house as a customer after having taught in the Caribbean. A goldmine of reading covered the walls. I walked away having bought Edward Braithwaite's *Islands*, J J Thomas's *Froudacity* and C L R James's *Minty Alley* (both published by New Beacon). I also bought an Andrew Salkey novel, Martin Carter's *Poems of Resistance*, and a batch of Caribbean poetry and political journals including the *Black Liberator*. These were the only emporia in London where one could not only buy Caribbean published works like the Georgetown-produced *Poems of Resistance* but also find the friendly and conscious assistance to know and read more.

The truth is that without such cultural infrastructure as New Beacon Books, Coard's signal book would not have been published. And without Bogle Ouverture Publications neither may Linton Kwesi Johnson's early poems have seen print nor Walter Rodney's pioneering works of political struggle, *The Groundings With My Brothers* and *How Europe Underdeveloped Africa*.

Thus organic intellectuals like Coard and cultural infrastructure like that provided by community presses are essential components of community struggle. That truth has been reinforced by successive campaigns waged around education by Black British communities. Through the 1970s and 1980s the emergence of weekly Black journals such as the *Caribbean Times* added weight and regular information around campaigns for educational progress. Tobago-born Buzz Johnson created Karia Press based in Stoke

Newington and published upwards of 50 titles, including the first reprint of Coard's work in 1991. It was introduced with the preface written by Herman Ouseley, then the chief executive of the London Borough of Lambeth, that also appears in this publication. Johnson's vibrant press had also published another significant educational work by another Grenada-born Londoner, Valentino O Jones. His account of the Josina Machel Black Complementary School in Clapton, *We Are Our Own Educators: Josina Machel – From Supplementary to Black Complementary School* is very much in the spirit of Coard's book and, again, could only have found publication in a Black community-based press. In a publisher's note at the beginning of Jones's work, Johnson declares, 'Karia Press, like Josina Machel Supplementary School, holds the view that, for Black people, education is a vital instrument in our struggle.'

Such a sentiment has spread well outside London of course – as Liverpool educationalist Wally Brown's contribution to this present volume amply shows. The struggle of Black British communities against disproportionate levels of school exclusion faced by Black young people has been a nationwide movement, and many local campaigns have set down their statistics, analyses and programmes for action through local community presses. One such example was the publication revealing the exclusions scandal in the City of Nottingham schools in 1984, *Suspensions and the Black Child*. Again, the spirit of Coard's pamphlet is deeply entrenched inside its sentences.

Of course, *How the West Indian Child is Made Educationally Subnormal in the British School System* would never have been written had its author not only been a conscious teacher within ESN schools and an active youth worker, but also a committed and conscious Black community activist. Teacher-activists who are also organic intellectuals are absolutely essential components of any community campaign concerning education, which is another key reason why the struggle to expand the number of Black teachers in our schools is as vital as it ever was. Reading Coard's words again you realise how essential his inside knowledge of the school system is, as well as how the figures, statistics, educational scholarship and understanding of IQ tests, school culture, teacher attitudes and reactions of the children are to the success of his writing and ultimately to the success of his community's campaign. His concluding section, Things We Can Do for Ourselves, is as relevant now as it was in 1971. Similarly, with a few word changes his five introductory points are still absolutely key to the contemporary struggle against Black exclusions from school. The 2005 government figures on school exclusions reveal another increase in the disproportionate numbers of Black young people still suffering on the end of an exclusive state education. The italics are my amended phrases.

- There are very large numbers of our West Indian children *being excluded from school.*
- These children have been wrongly *excluded.*
- Once excluded from these schools, the vast majority never *regain their places in mainstream* schools.
- They suffer academically and in their job prospects for life because of being put *out of* these schools.
- The authorities are doing very little to stop this scandal.

From 1971 to 2005, the struggle continues still.

- During his career Chris Searle has been a comprehensive school teacher and headteacher and has taught at the Universities of London and Toronto. He has also written extensively. Between 1981 and 1983 he was a teacher trainer in Grenada. Chris is currently employed by the Yemeni Community Association of Sheffield teaching ex industrial workers and asylum seekers. He is on the editorial committee of *Race and Class.*

David Simon

Education of the Blacks: the supplementary school movement

OLD BLACK and white television newsreels show the 'first' generation of West Indians arriving on the SS *Empire Windrush* in 1948, carrying 492 Caribbeans seeking an adventure, employment and better opportunities than they could find in their hot homelands. Many dreams danced to their early calypso and mento beats, and central to this was the education of their children. They believed that their children could become doctors, lawyers, teachers and other professional people – people who'd drink from the fountains of the Western intellectual tradition and build, not as cheap labourers, but as equal architects of modern post-war Britain. Yes, a generation of brown people who believed in fair play, the truth of biblical passages and the power of prayer. But the folklore of old coastguards and lighthouse men said that there was another ship that followed the SS *Empire Windrush*, hidden in the morning mist: according to their pipe-smoked tales, 72 oarsmen and women rowed quietly under tired blown sails and made their way to the shores of England, carrying rebel 'pirates' of Western thought, sailing like smugglers of days gone by. It would be many years later that the journey of this ancestral mythical ship would be understood, for when it came time to hoist the names of supplementary Saturday schools aloft, they would take the names of these men and women who fought for the liberation of mind.

Names such as the Claudia Jones Supplementary Saturday School, the Marcus Garvey Supplementary Saturday School, the Mandela Supplementary Saturday School, the Queen Mother Moore Supplementary Saturday School, the Malcolm X Supplementary Saturday School. It would be then that those of us who would open these schools would realise that this ship's cargo was more than gold bullion – it was the Black radical tradition that went back to Kamit (Ancient Black Egypt), and this radical tradition had to be continued if we were to successfully fight for the education of the Black child.

However, before the Black child could walk to school, the roads had to be made safe, for they, the children, were spat at and cursed in such a way as if to stain their soul. First came the bloody street fights with racist Teddy boys and others – fights with iron bars and knuckle-dusters on street corners, alleys and outside workingmen's clubs. It was never a fair fight. Blows from the government in the form of immigration acts knocked out the naivety of many of these brown blessed people, who had listened to the colonial voice from radios and believed in British government officials like Enoch Powell who had recruited them to come and work in Britain, saying that they would be welcomed. By 1958 there were anti-Black race riots, and in 1959 Kelso Cochrane, a Black carpenter, was stabbed to death in north Kensington by a white racist mob who, like the murderers of Stephen Lawrence many years later, would never be caught. Incidents like these made the Blacks realise that they were on their own. If they wanted to go to church, the doors of Christian churches were closed in their face. If they wanted to buy a house, the building society refused them a loan. If they wanted a room to let, signs of 'No dogs or coloureds' kept them away. So they formed their own churches in living rooms and community halls. They created their own financial institutions by using sous sous hands/partners and bought the big old houses in the inner cities. This generation is old now, or dead. They took the blows of early immigrants, and some tilled the soil so that the seeds of independent education could be planted. Despite everything they tried more than this generation realises. Many ended their last days with twisted arthritic fingers from factory work, or lay in old people's homes with wretched back pain, or travelled back to the Caribbean followed by the cursed smell of bedpans that they cleaned for too little pay. Perhaps one day we'll remember them, raise our glasses of rum and water, sprinkling a few flowers on their grave and memories. Perhaps.

By the 1960s the hurdles of employment and housing had been overcome to some extent. The typical West Indian family gathered in the evenings around precarious paraffin heaters; women pressed each other's hair at weekends, the children went to Sunday school, the men worked long shifts; families attended dances at the local town hall and bank holiday coach trips to the seaside, and there was always rice and peas and chicken. But their children were failing in the British education system. The Black child was being classed as educationally subnormal and sent to special schools. And this failing came amid wicked immigration acts of 1962 and 1968, both aimed at limiting immigration. The educational establishment, when occasionally challenged or questioned, used pseudoscience. They blamed Black speech. A plethora of theories was put forward: 'Patois undermines the Black child's grammar; it causes aggression; it confuses the black child!' So in this decade of realisation and distrust, the Black community began to open up their own supplementary schools, most running on Saturdays, and providing extra classes for children in English, mathematics and culture. These classes took place in homes, local halls, schools and church rooms. The pioneers were Bini Butuakwa, John La Rose and Reverend Wilfred Wood, who opened the first supplementary schools between 1965 and 1969. It was a struggle, and there was opposition and hostility. In 1966 the Afro-Caribbean Self-Help Organisation (ACSHO) opened in Birmingham and established a supplementary school. First, the local education officer claimed that the school taught revolution, then the caretakers' union complained that the school was being let to the Black Power Movement, and amid all these bizarre accusations, a local headteacher questioned whether the school could offer lessons of any real educational value. But it wasn't only the schools that had a battle. Parents, too, had a struggle.

I remember one such case when one cold December a mother walked into our school with a small, round and ungainly child – a little family that were loyal to their local Pentecostal church, and she, the hardworking mother, seemed distraught at the worsening situation of her child's education. The usual interview followed. The mother had a report from her school's educational psychiatrist. In the months to come we would work with this child, not simply teaching her English and mathematics, but social skills, encouraging her to come out of a shell that she had been put in. It was difficult. We hadn't the specialist skills we have now. We stumbled in our helping of her. This little girl, with her stubborn plaits and her knock-knees, was by no means our most challenging case, but her situation was, for she seemed embroiled in educational bureaucracy. A plethora of letters littered her case file. The mother wanted her to go to a 'normal' school, but the authorities wouldn't have it. It was the head-teacher who was intransigent.

After a year or so of her attending the Saturday School, during which time the little girl had stopped dribbling and stopped having a runny nose, the mother again went back to the school, with a plea in her step and our school report on her daughter, to ask that her child be allowed to attend a 'normal' school. Her request was rejected. She was devastated. The church hymns that seemed to accompany her dignified fight for her child seemed to die. We didn't see her again. I like to think that this little family are still together and happy in their home-made church. I like to think that the little girl will share in the optimism of a new day, and be reminded of life's freedom by the play-ful wind that used to trouble her plaits. I like to think that God sent her to us to strengthen our resolve as educators, to make us less romantic and senti-mental, reminding us that we were involved in work that could actually save life. I cannot help but think that we lost this little girl – that she should have remained in our colourful world of learning. It wasn't that the headteacher won: it was that we were too weak. It's these tiny struggles that pile up on the supplementary school, that make those of us who run these projects, on late Saturday evenings, contemplate the education of the Blacks.

In 1971 Bernard Coard wrote *How the West Indian Child is Made Educationally Subnormal in the British School System*. It articulated what was going wrong in the school system, and highlighted the effects of institutional racism on the Black child, by pointing out the lack of expectation that the white teacher had of the Black child. A year later another revolutionary called Walter Rodney would write another book with hidden parallels called *How Europe Underdeveloped Africa* (1972). It was an equally important book. This didn't simply show how the soul of the Black child was being destroyed, but how the race of the Blacks was being devastated by the taking of diamonds, iron ore, uranium, oil, lead, zinc and gold from the ancient African soil, making this once great continent economically subnormal. Both injustices would bring confrontations. In the world of education, the confrontation would be between Black child and teacher, for the Black child would be disciplined and taught within this colonial legacy, and all would pretend that this bloody history was no longer relevant, or had any kind of impact.

Yet the teaching, the curriculum, the discipline, the textbooks, the attitudes and the policies, all stank of this earlier period. Therefore implicit in the teaching and learning of the Black child in the British education system was the indoctrination of white middle class values that was really at the heart of state education. Tragically, in the classroom, this confrontation would reach a climax. The Black child, for so long having sat in this negative learning state, should have felt the blossoms of adolescence, and mapped out their territory of adulthood with a learning mentor to teach them about life. But the years of cultural disrespect, of subtle humiliation, and maybe of weak family support, would result in their rebellion within the school, and the school would react by excluding the child.

Between 1973 and 1976 the rate of unemployment for Black youth rose twice as quickly as it did for their white counterparts. The supplementary schools that opened had to further unearth Black heroes, to use history as a beacon of Black achievement, and in doing so to remind the Blacks that they had a radical tradition that had to be part of the Black child's education if they were to be honestly prepared for the world. Imhotep, Nefartari, Cuffee and Nanny of the Maroons, the Black Caribs of St Vincent and Jamaica, Paul Bogle and the Black Victorians like Olaudah Equiano and Sancho were part of our tradition. They were men and women who were concerned with education and liberty; their example was also an essential part of the training of the Black teacher.

The move for Black History Month that had been born from the American Civil Rights Movement began to take root in Britain. The supplementary movement embraced this history. I, as a young graduate and budding teacher, wanted to know how African gods/principles permeated their curriculum; how Yemaya and Obatala had been part of their mathematical equations of war. I wanted to know what sweet geometry they used to draw secret maps in the sand to plan raids and ambushes.

The 1980s were a decade of blood and tears. The riots of the inner cities lit the skies over British prisons that were full of yesterday's underachieving young Black men, their 'teachers' now uniformed guards. It was the decade that saw 13 black youngsters die in a mysterious fire in Deptford, and which was followed by a march of protest by the Black community. The outlawed Black sailors who had left their ships for a while marched too. Reports rained down on us like confetti: first the Rampton Report (1981) and then the Swann Report (1985) looked into the issue of Black children underachieving. But it was also a time for those who would fight to organise. Groups like the Camden Black Parents and Teachers Association were established.

It was in this decade, in the ripening spring of 1987, that I opened Ebony

Supplementary Saturday School, unaware then that I, young poet and novelist, would serve my apprenticeship as teacher, and later as educationalist in this small project. Now, as I reflect on the decade, and of the maturing Ebony, I realise that it was she that made me into a quiet psychologist to my people. The training that supplementary schools offer is, in my opinion, far greater than the teacher training in universities, for its success is centred around the engagement of culture in the child's learning, and the honest partnership between parent and school. Here the Black teacher performs with greater creativity and innovation even though they have limited resources. Here, in these Saturday Schools, they are not isolated to become victims of brutal discrimination, as they are in the state school system. So, we can say of the supplementary schools, their essence is unity. This is their uniqueness. It stands tall in a disunited community. Its mere existence is a great lesson plan.

And what of the weekly running of the supplementary school? It consists of the preparation of teaching materials, the teaching of children, the managing of resources, the counselling of parents, the motivating of students, the writing of reports, designing assignments: work hampered by limited budgets. Is this the supplementary schools' great work? Yes. It is the constant investigation into the learning of the Black child that unlocks their genius. This builds camaraderie. There is no stronger bond than that between Black women, when the futile love of a man is not there to sabotage this friendship. The supplementary schools movement has been largely built by these women – teachers, mothers and volunteers. Black men cannot leave the education of the next generation, and therefore the defence of their community, to women alone. Who will defend these women? How long do we expect Black women to have babies, work, raise boys and teach? Many women who bring their children to our school are single mothers, who often tell me that they want a Black male teacher, hoping that this will not only address any discipline problems, but hoping that the child will take from the Black male teacher's example. They want a role model. Their home has none. We try our best. How long can we as a community sing Marley's song 'No Woman, No Cry'?

Ebony Supplementary Saturday Schools have served the community for 18 years now. Four thousand children have used our services in England. It has several branches, its own publishing house, a home tuition service, and supports many schools in Africa. Our work has brought us regional and national media attention, and awards (CarAF London Supplementary School of the Year Award 2005), and an even greater vision. If we continue to use the names of the rebels who were teacher-activists, we have to realise that they sought not to copy the system of their oppressors, but to create something that would give dignity to their humanity. This might mean that it's time we dropped the word supplementary from our titles, for are we supplementing something that is already wrong, or are we creating something that is new?

The future of the supplementary movement is uncertain. The schools are diverse. Some seek funding from local government or charities, so their future lies in the hands of a funding officer or committee. Some seek to raise money by their own means, and perhaps ensure their independence more. Perhaps the future of the movement lies in the hands of the Black churches that have a loyal clientele, resources, self-reliance and independence to carry on the movement. If they do then they, like us, must be clear as to what education is. Amos Wilson, in his classic book *Awakening the Natural Genius of the Black Child* (1991), wrote, 'I think it is vital that we understand the major function of education is to help secure the survival of a people… And it's going to require a different kind of education than what is available today.'

This different type of education is what has occupied many of the supplementary schools – certainly at Ebony it has been one of our primary focuses. In 2004 I wrote the book *How to Unlock Your Child's Genius*, which presented an 11-step holistic educational programme for parents, and showed parents how they can become parent-teachers while also improving the learning environment of the home and their community. The book deals with subjects like educational management in the home, diet and learning, e-learning, learning styles, how children learn, thinking skills, financial literacy, education and culture, and more. We launched it at the Black Child Conference staged by the Greater London Authority, and within hours of displaying the book we were overwhelmed by its reception. We sold out within a couple of hours, and ten months on we have sold several thousand at workshops, talks, community gatherings and events. Everyone wanted to promote the book – pirate stations, Black churches, youth clubs, teachers and people who hadn't even been active in education before. Its success is a tribute to the supplementary movement as a whole, for the book has come from this movement, and perhaps could have only come from this grassroots movement.

The supplementary schools must be careful not to restrict themselves to a tiny corner of a city, lost to the wider community and even the community abroad. Earlier this year, one calm Sunday morning, I gave a live radio interview on a community station where the DJ played old reggae classics, that in itself had a scent of mellow herbs. I was asked the usual questions about the book by the slightly languid but genuine host, a Rastaman who'd nod his head to my answers, as if listening to music in an old blues-dance. Towards the end of the interview, the host asked people to phone in to put questions to me. One of them was a woman, a regular to the show, who spoke with urgency in her voice. Funnily enough, I can't remember her question. After the formal phone-in she rang again, and this time asked if she could purchase several copies for schools in Africa. I agreed, and on meeting her later in the week she told me of a project she was involved in helping schools in rural Africa. Things moved fast. I found myself, inexplicably, putting together education packs for these rural schools. Within a few weeks, out of the blue, other representatives from schools in other parts of Africa approached us for materials and possibly training for their schools. A few weeks later we had donated over 100 educational packs and agreed to set up a teacher training centre in Ghana. It took this woman's insistent phone call to give me the vision, to make me see beyond my little corner of London and further, and realise that the expertise, the research and development that goes on in supplementary schools is of value to children everywhere.

It is the summer month of August. A new term will start in the optimism of September, and new faces of children all over the country will appear at supplementary schools; inquisitive faces, all in their various ways wanting to learn, wanting to be somebody in the world, and it will be the noble job of these unsung educational projects to help them. Many years have passed since the SS *Empire Windrush* docked, and the ship of revolutionaries that was also guided to these shores and was/is the inspiration behind many of these Saturday schools. But there is more work to be done. The challenge gets greater, as the Black child's mis-education in the media becomes more awesome and catastrophic. It is time for the Black community to support these seed-schools, to value the tremendous work they do, and for these schools to work together. And in our work, let us remember the Ethiopian proverb: 'If you can't hold children in your arms, please hold them in your heart.'

● David Simon is the author of the novels *Secrets of the Sapodilla* (1986) and *Garvey's Last Soldier* (1999). He is the winner of the 1990 Peterloo Poetry Award. David's play *Mountaintop* was nominated Best First Play by the London Fringe Awards (1993), and was awarded the 100 Black Men Community Award in 2002. David is the founder of Ebony Saturday Schools (1987) which won the CarAF London Saturday School of the Year Award 2005. David is the author of the bestselling book, *How to Unlock Your Child's Genius* (2004).

Wally Brown CBE

The future before us

ALTHOUGH LESS than 50 pages in length, Bernard Coard's booklet[1] is an explosive testament to the treatment of Black pupils in the education system at that time.

Coard cites three obstacles that the Black child in the study faced:

- *Low Teacher Expectation* – if the teacher is unprepared to expend effort on your part because they have a lower expectation of you than a white scholar it is no wonder that the second obstacle –
- *Low motivation to succeed academically by the pupil* kicks in. The first leads to the second which in turn helps develop –
- *Low expectation about one's performance* in the white-controlled hostile education system.

The impact of the booklet led to Black parents and especially Black professionals taking responsibility for their children's education. It led to the setting up of Supplementary Saturday Schools where Black teachers taught large classes of Black pupils in an attempt to support them and to compensate for the damage that schools were causing to them. The Black Parents Movement was also born out of the initiative. The message spread from

London to other conurbations such as Manchester and Birmingham, where large numbers of Black children went to school. In addition, sociologists began to analyse the impact of the treatment of Black pupils in schools. E J B Rose, who was director of the Survey of Race Relations in Britain and co-author of the report 'Colour and Citizenship', stated that by the year 2000 Britain will have a Black helot class (labouring class) unless the education system is radically altered.[2]

We are now in 2005 and in a position to test Rose's theory. Most Black academics would agree that the education system is better for Black pupils, but not radically so. Teacher expectations for Black pupils continue to be low, and we know that Black pupils continue to be damaged by the education system. Gillborn and Mirza, in a study of schools in inner London, showed that although Black pupils in general begin their school career ahead of all other groups of pupils, by the age of 15 they are significantly below all other groups.[3]

It appears that for this cohort the school system has taken them backwards. However, we did not need to wait the 30 years from 1971 to see these results. We could have looked at the future through the eyes of the Black community of Liverpool, a community that had been settled in the city for generations and who continue to suffer disadvantages in education similar to those of Coard's original study. Cultural differences, lack of understanding of English society and systems, and language problems were identified by the government's race relations advisers on why Black immigrants struggled to achieve in England since the 1950s. It was from this false premise that the race relations policy was developed. It was a policy based on 'no blame' to either the host community or its institutions, and placed the main 'blame' for underachievement at the door of the Black person.

Coard presented a different viewpoint, and the experiences of Black people in Liverpool were even more profound in challenging this false premise.

It is well established that Liverpool played a major role in the slave trade, and that the city has had a Black community dating back to at least this time. The Liverpool Black community, at the time of Coard's publication, had origins dating back to 1890-1900 when African seamen who were employed as cheap labour by shipping companies trading with West Africa settled in the dockland areas of the city and married local women.

It is their children and grandchildren who were already settled in Liverpool in the 1970s. This Liverpool Black community had been settled for generations, so there were no cultural barriers. They understood English society and systems equally as well as the white working class, and they spoke with the same 'scouse' accent, in the same way that Black pupils today speak as Londoners, Brummies or Mancunians. Despite this total social integration Liverpool Black people lacked jobs to a much greater extent, and their educational achievement was significantly below their white peers.

Those of us who have been fighting for equality for Liverpool Blacks for the past 40 years and those who came before us continued to tell successive governments that Liverpool's experience is the future before us. Liverpool, in 1971, was a city where its Black community failed to achieve educationally and were invisible in jobs across the city, with the exception of low paid shipping-associated jobs such as boiler scaling or as cheap labour on ships as their fathers had been.

Policy-makers ignored the experience of Liverpool. Teachers and educational policy-makers made many trips to the Caribbean searching for the 'difference' that was affecting Black students in the UK. They only needed to focus closer to home, in Liverpool, Cardiff and Bristol, to get a truer perspective.

The race riots of the 1980s resulted in much analysis and review of race in English cities. There had, however, been earlier major riots in British seaports – in 1918 in Liverpool and Cardiff, and again in Liverpool in 1948, many years before mass immigration into England. It seems that the messages from these incidents fell on deaf ears, or perhaps the messages were understood but ignored because the numbers were small and the problem isolated to one or two cities. By 1980 the problem was much more widespread. It is my considered view – as a person who was born in Liverpool in 1943 to a West African father and an English mother, who experienced growing up in Toxteth and who has been reasonably successful – that Liverpool's experience, if taken more seriously, could have pointed to the pitfalls in the kinds of race policies that were being developed. If this had happened, we would have then addressed the real reasons for Black underachievement.

The underachievement of Black pupils in Liverpool and the marginalisation faced by Black families in the city is well documented. As early as 1930 a report was published that is as equally as explosive as Coard's, but unlike Coard's it placed the blame for the disenfranchisement of Liverpool Blacks with their families. Liverpool Blacks have lived with the stigma of that report ever since.[4]

In 1973, at the same time as the Coard booklet was published, a report from the Race Relations Select Committee, on a visit to Liverpool, criticised Liverpool's education committee system. It found that the Liverpool Black community was discriminated against both inside and outside of the school sector. Liverpool was criticised for its inability to provide a lead to other local authorities with substantial ethnic minority populations. In the words of the committee's report, 'Liverpool left it with a profound sense of uneasiness'.[5]

Furthermore, a report from the Home Affairs Select Committee in 1980/81 expressed similar concerns about education provision and practice in Liverpool: 'Racial disadvantage in Liverpool is in a sense the most disturbing case of racial disadvantage in the UK, because there is no question of cultural problems, of newness of language, and it offers a grim warning to all of Britain's cities that racial disadvantage cannot be expected to disappear by natural causes'.[6]

One of the many pressure groups in the city at the time, the Liverpool Black Organisation, warned the subcommittee, 'What you see in Liverpool is a sign of things to come.' The subcommittee echoed that stark warning.

There is not space in this short piece to explore the way education policy in Liverpool since the Education Act of 1947, but particularly during the 1970s and 1980s, has disadvantaged the Black community in the city. Nationally in 2005 we face major issues in relation to the educational achievement of Black boys. The children and grandchildren of those in the Coard study may not be in schools for the 'educationally subnormal', but this may be because these no longer exist. However, Black pupils' achievement levels, although better than in 1970s, still lag way behind their white counterparts, and perhaps the high exclusion levels we see of Black pupils have the same effect and have the same purpose as that of being banished to an ESN school.

I believe that the present-day parallels to the Liverpool experience should tell us something. Thirty years after Coard, Black pupils are not new to English systems and society, they have no language problems and they are socially integrated, but for some reason they are still not achieving.

I cannot help wondering that if notice had been taken of the Liverpool experience in the 1960s, 1970s and 1980s we would have learnt that the problems and therefore the answers lie with the system and society in general, and not with the individual. But of course to accept that premise is possibly a bridge too far.

In conclusion, the reawakening of Coard's work has been useful in reminding us of how far we still have to travel. It also reminds us of the need to continue to challenge the system. We must not underestimate the size of the problem – Liverpool has struggled with these issues for many generations and, apart from notable exceptions, with little success. It appears that in neither Liverpool nor the UK are we any nearer to addressing the issues of Black underachievement in our education system than we were in 1970.

Notes

1 Bernard Coard, *How the West Indian Child is Made Educationally Subnormal in the British School System* (New Beacon Books, 1971).
2 *Times*, 15 May 1970, p11.
3 D Gillborn and H Mirza, *Educational Inequality: Mapping Race, Class and Gender* (Ofsted, 2000).
4 M Fletcher, *Report of an Investigation into the Colour Problem in Liverpool and Other Ports* (Liverpool University Press, 1930).
5 HMSO, *Report of the Select Committee on Race Relations and Immigration* (July 1973).
6 HMSO, *Fifth Report from the Home Affairs Select Committee Sessions 1980-87: Racial Disadvantage*, vol 1.

● Wally Brown has been principal of Liverpool Community College since 1991. Prior to his appointment at Liverpool, Wally spent two years at the London Borough of Lambeth as head of the Community Education Service. He was awarded a CBE in 2001 for Services to Further Education.

Alex Pascall

British Blacks in educational evolution

THE MASS movement for civil rights and social change in the USA was instrumental in helping the Black community in Britain to deal with the turmoil of hate fomented by the former Tory government minister Enoch Powell's infamous 'Rivers of Blood' speech in April of 1968. Black thinkers, analysts and teachers took strategic measures to implement programmes to inform the Black community of the task ahead for a rising of racial consciousness. We were operating in a climate of race prejudice and right wing politics at feverish extremes; worst of all, the nightmare became real when our children were being misinterpreted, misunderstood and earmarked to bear the label 'Educationally Subnormal'. It was during this period also that the police subjected the Black youth to daily stop and search harassment under the SUS law; tension between Black and Blue then began fermenting.

Programmes for the teaching of cultural studies were crucial; those of us who were engaged in popular culture became part of a taskforce imparting skills and knowledge not as entertainment, but as curricula subject matter, in cultural studies.

Within this period Frank Jeremiah from the Trinidad and Tobago Embassy invited me to assist with an after-school Caribbean cultural studies programme at Thomas Carlton School in Peckham. As a former teacher he understood youth discipline and what was necessary for implementation for the educational benefit of the youth of the race in Britain; as a folklorist he was dedicated to the introduction of Caribbean culture programmes.

Using the medium of storytelling, incorporating poetry, movement and drama, I began my first residency at Thomas Carlton – a school with a sizable population of Black youths finding it very difficult to cope in a British education system strongly oriented against and unrelated to their needs, draining them of self-confidence and self-knowledge.

I went on to teach at St Mary's Primary in Battersea, Creighton Secondary in Muswell Hill (now Fortismere School) and Balham Boys Junior/Secondary in Chestnut Grove and many others. I spent the lengthiest period teaching at the Balham Boys up to 1973; meeting likeminded visionaries, musicians, steel pan technologists/tutors, poets, writers and storytellers. We all shared a common goal – to provide invaluable historical subject matter to motivate the children, and to instil self-confidence which would nullify the label 'Educationally Subnormal (ESN)', that the government and education authorities promulgated.

On the afternoon I arrived at Thomas Carlton School to work with the children, I was equipped with two conga drums. The group of young and energetic Black boys and girls I met were inquisitive about the drums; questions about Caribbean culture flowed as they expressed their worries about what their parents thought about their achievements in school; they were not at all happy about the way they were being viewed by teachers. More than anything else they identified with Bob Marley and his music; they knew about Louise Bennett and her stories; these were children mostly of Jamaican parentage who actually introduced Bob Marley's music to me.

The music, folksongs and folktales were like textbooks introducing Caribbean lifestyle, the cultural environment and the rich variety of cultures from Jamaica in the north, to the southern Caribbean countries.

Phil Sealy, a retired Community Relations officer reflecting on the period decades after the findings of Bernard Coard's study, says:

The school of the extended family which we were accustomed to back home, was not what we met in this country...once we started dropping off in London and other inner cities, we found a society which was like a mother who did not care about her children and to date it remains the same.
Phil Sealey, 2005

As the problem escalated, the unification of Black parents developed into the 'Black Parents Movement'. Parents began organising Saturday School programmes in cities with Black populations, which exerted a positive influence on the educational development of the Black children into the 1970s.

Some parents made sacrifices and paid for private tuition in an effort to ensure that the progress of their children was not jeopardised. Others sent their children back to relatives in the Caribbean countries. Workers within the Community Relations Movement, the Caribbean Teachers Association and the Caribbean Education and Community Workers Association joined forces in maintaining a campaign to highlight to the authorities the need for a re-examination of the policy of placing large numbers of West Indian children in ESN and low stream secondary schools and its effect on those children's academic performances.

The establishment of October as Black History Month is the model which the first visionaries sought to balance the failing educational system of the 1960s, under the heading 'Black Studies'. But then some institutional authorities and right wing groups disrupted the momentum for its entry into the mainstream educational system. In the stream of the movements for change numerous discussions took place; black and white thinkers joined together to call on the BBC for input, for relevant programming and for a Black presence in the media.

1972 saw the advent of Black programming. 'ACCESS' was given for the first broadcast of six half-hour historical programmes entitled *Black Studies*, produced by Sam Uriah Morris, an ex-serviceman, broadcaster and founder member of the Community Relations Commission and Race Relations Board.

The music programme *Reggae Time* followed and in 1974 *Black Londoners* was formatted as a magazine radio programme for London's Black community. This pioneering form of radio remained within the confines of BBC Education, which gave opportunities for Blacks in the media. The programmes captured the ear of both the community and the authorities. I produced and presented the radio series for the following 14 years and during that time educational debates were paramount.

The Thatcher government of the 1980s halted the progress of Black youth, dismantling most of the foundations the Black community had structured for educational, social and economic advancement. Funding for youth clubs and community centres was phased out and Black associations and organisations splintered nationally. Black Londoners' radio programming was also minimised and other efforts ran into frustration. The education debate raged: first we had the Rampton Report and then the Swann Report but all the recommendations were left imprisoned in the archives of hope. It was a time game that killed the appropriate action that should have been instituted and to date it is still the same.

During the years I have spent in the media, I have had opportunities to visit prisons and conduct workshops with inmates. What was missing in the 1960s and what I have continued to discover later in the 1990s in my work educationally have not been very far apart. Most striking were the high percentages of Black disorientated youth of the 1970s who have drifted from the school system into the prison system as inmates still searching for their identity and for cultural and educational fulfilment.

Paul Mackney, the general secretary of Natfhe, asked me about the availability of Bernard's book because of the number of requests he had received. As luck would have it, I was able to introduce him to Crofton St Louis who was managing the War On Want stall at the 2003 TUC Black Workers Conference. From the soundings and support received from others anxious for advancement, the ball started rolling; not only to reprint the book, but to update the publication to include Bernard Coard's educational success with his fellow inmates and to re-examine Black children in the British educational system in the new millennium.

His book is just as relevant in today's educational climate as when his study was first published on the plight of Black children in the British educational system.

Meanwhile Bernard Coard in his imprisonment on the island of Grenada has been successfully addressing the educational needs of other inmates and helping them prepare for their re-entry into society. Given the scale of his observations and success, there must be something which he possesses that we need to examine, to help us tackle the stalemate of the Black and Caribbean children's situation in British schools.

The British educational system, as trends show, is still failing Black youths; therefore it is the duty of all Black and Caribbean parents who want to experience a more just and progressive education system to devise new ways to enhance their children's future for a global society.

Every so often I would come across young men and women who survived the evils of that era. They often reflect on the turning points of their schooldays, the valuable time they shared with some of us who helped to streamline their educational outlook. Today they are high profile business-men and women, solicitors, arts administrators, some in public relations, banking, the music business and the media. They were just victims of the British two-tier educational system and in no way educationally subnormal. They are the ones who may possibly hold the key to address ways forward as the educational dilemma prevails:

The race will free itself from exploiters... No one else can accomplish this task for the race. It must plan and do for itself.

© Alex Pascall OBE

● Alex Pascall is a leading Carnival arts educator and is currently chair of the Black Members' Council of the National Union of Journalists.

Sally Tomlinson

A tribute to Bernard Coard

IN THE late 1960s I was teaching in a primary school in the English Midlands. The children in my class were mainly from the Caribbean and the Indian subcontinent. As with other teachers, I had had no training that might help me understand the backgrounds and lives of the children, or of their parents, who had largely come at the exhortation of the then minister of health, Enoch Powell, to work in the local hospitals. Although our liberal headteacher exhorted us to 'treat them all as children' and teach literacy and numeracy, it was apparent that while the learning problems of the sub-continent children were regarded as linked to second language learning, the 'West Indian' children were subject to damaging stereotyping about their 'natural abilities'. Placement in remedial classes and referral to the then segregated schooling for the 'Educationally Subnormal' was regarded as an inevitable process. In north London a West Indian Association had expressed concern about the ESN issue as early as 1965, and the Inner London Education Authority reported on an over-representation of 'immigrant' – mainly West Indian – children in ESN schools from 1966. However, it was not until 1970, when Bernard Coard gave a powerful speech at a conference organised by the Caribbean Education and Community Workers Association, and published his book *How the West Indian Child is Made*

Educationally Subnormal in the British School System that the damage being done to a whole generation of Black children began to be apparent. His work was a catalyst which gave expression to the anger and bitterness felt by Black parents, who had come to Britain to work and give their children a chance of what they hoped was a decent education, and who found that the school system was not about to change to incorporate their children successfully. The ESN issue had profound symbolic significance for the Black community, as it represented the relegation of their children to a non-education and low social and economic status.

Bernard's work not only articulated and supported the efforts of Black community and parents associations, it also galvanised central and local administrations into some recognition that there was a problem. Evidence to a House of Commons select committee on education in 1973 included comments from 16 official bodies on the ESN classification, and nine to the same committee in 1976, when one witness told the MPs that 'this was one of the very bitter areas' for Black parents. The committee wrote in its report, 'It is clear that the West Indian Community is disturbed by the underachievement of West Indian children at school and seriously disturbed by the high proportion of West Indian children in ESN schools'.[1] However, there was minimal response from the (then) DES, and the Warnock Committee, taking evidence for its influential report published in 1978, managed to ignore the issue.[2] Schools did become more wary of referring Black children for ESN schools and instead numbers of Black children referred into schools for the emotionally and behaviourally disturbed, and into the forerunners of Pupil Referral Units, increased fourfold. Bernard's work was also a catalyst for my own PhD study, as I wanted to explore further what the cultural beliefs of professionals were in that they could over-refer Black children for what they knew was a stigmatised form of schooling, and I duly followed a group of children through their referral and placement process over four years.[3] I was able to conclude that the professionals dealing with the children attempted to rationalise their practices in terms of their cultural beliefs about Black children and by a denial of the pragmatic racism which was increasing in Britain. Despite their beliefs and rationalisations, which included some stunningly racist comments, and a remarkable ignorance of the backgrounds of the children, the professionals did not generally question the assumption that Black and white children start out equal in the assessment process.

Thirty years later it would be nice to report that, as the educational achievements of all young people have improved, the children and grand-children of the 1960s migrants to Britain from the Caribbean are now offered an equal education which would equip them with the qualifications and credentials to live and work in the country and in a global economy. However, this is still not the case. Despite a rhetoric of inclusion, new ways have developed of excluding many Black children from full participation in mainstream education. The school curriculum continues to be Anglocen-tric, and teachers are even less likely to be trained to teach in a multiracial society than in the 1970s. A teacher from Montserrat, studying children displaced by the volcanic activity on the island in London schools, was sur-prised to find teachers asking her where Montserrat was, and another researcher in Birmingham was less surprised to have teachers asking her, 'What language is spoken in Jamaica?' Bernard Coard has continued, as his writing in this volume shows, to be passionately concerned with the fate of young people of African-Caribbean heritage in British schools. I hope, with him, that we can eventually bring an end to the hopeless stereotyping and negative beliefs about the young people, and begin to influence the educa-tional curriculum, teacher education and training, and political attitudes to ensure that all young Black people have a future in Britain as equal citizens.

Notes

1 House of Commons Select Committee on Race relations and Immigration: The West Indian Community (London, 1976).
2 HMSO, *Special Educational Needs* (The Warnock Report), (London 1978).
3 S Tomlinson, *Educational Subnormality: A Study in Decision-Making* (London, 1981).

● Sally Tomlinson is Emeritus Professor at Goldsmiths College, London University, and Senior Research Fellow at the Department of Educational Studies, University of Oxford.

Opposite: Children from Morningside school in Hackney, east London, protesting against league tables. Jess Hurd www.reportdigital.co.uk

Section 2
What's going on
Black children in
our schools today

Another World by Benjamin Zephaniah

Those ships trespassed on my religion
Those hands strangled my life,
Those diseases infected my grass,
Dear teacher,
                I have a problem with Columbus.

Dat sperm put blue in my black
For once I became Capitalism,
You can call it America,
Canada
Or Rhodesia,
I call it Ours,
You can call it free
Democratic
Or the state of something,
I call it Earth.

We went to visit him
We did not steal from him,
We told him Anansi stories
We played Kabaddi with him.
He came to us
He done physical and spiritual burglary
He shared the loot with his family,
My family was devastated.
Dear teacher,
                I am not into Columbus.

Dear teacher,
                Do you know what we are going through?
Have been through,
Or where we have been,
Our wise ones have been assassinated,
Our social services
Are in museums.

Ever heard of the Nubians?
Nubians are we,
Is the price right?
Priceless are we.
We are thirteen months a year
Not cargo,
We are past, present and future
Not His Story,
Look teacher,
         I have a problem with Columbus.

© Benjamin Zephaniah, from *Propa Propaganda* (Bloodaxe Books, 1996)

David Gillborn

It takes a nation of millions (and a particular kind of education system) to hold us back[1]

On 16 March 2002 I took part in the first cross-London conference to address the educational achievements and experiences of Black children. Organised by Diane Abbott MP, and backed principally by the London Development Agency, the conference generated considerable media interest and was attended by around 2,000 black parents, teachers and advocates.[2] Despite its focus on London, the conference had a genuinely national profile, with many people travelling long distances to attend. The Queen Elizabeth Conference Centre has hosted many important meetings, but few have been as lively and committed as the one that day. At one point the doors were locked because there was a fear of overcrowding. *So much for the notion that Black attainment reflects a lack of interest from parents and the community!*

I was fortunate to be part of a session alongside Professor Gus John, long recognised as one of the most outstanding and influential figures in these debates. We jointly addressed the theme 'How the school system is failing Black boys'. The title deliberately echoed Bernard Coard's groundbreaking work and signalled our reading of the issues. The session was held in the main conference hall, and repeated twice during the day. In all, we estimated that about 1,000 people were present.

'Bernard Coard'... 'Bernard Coard'

My part of the presentation drew on research that I'd recently completed with my colleague Deborah Youdell.[3] I spoke about particular aspects of the education reforms that had gone unnoticed by commentators and had not been communicated to parents; about changes in the exam system that literally make it *impossible* for a disproportionate number of Black pupils to achieve the best grades in their GCSEs. As I explained how the system had changed, and the consequences it was having, there were gasps of astonishment from the audience – how could such a system be permitted? Some people shook their heads in disbelief. Several said out loud, 'Bernard Coard'... 'Bernard Coard'... 'It's the same thing that Coard was writing about'. Let me explain.

Tiering and glass ceilings

The dominant examination at the end of compulsory schooling in England is the GCSE, the General Certificate of Secondary Education. In most subjects, GCSE examinations are now 'tiered': that means that instead of sitting a single common examination paper the entrants are separated into different papers, depending on their teachers' assessment of their chances of success. The most frequently used approach is the two-tier model (see Table 1). Here, pupils in the 'Higher' tier can be awarded grades A* to D. Those in the lower ('Foundation') tier can only be awarded grades C to G. In this way, before a young person has answered a single question, the exam system has effectively placed a ceiling and floor on their attainments.

In most cases a pupil entered in the Higher tier who fails to earn a grade D will fall through the tier floor and be 'ungraded'. Similarly, pupils placed in the Foundation tier know that the highest grades (A*, A and B) are literally beyond them – this can rule out the possibility of further studies at A level in the subjects concerned. Additionally, the risk of Higher tier pupils falling through the grade-floor, and being 'ungraded', prompts many teachers to play safe by entering greater numbers for the lower tier. In this way some teachers are treating the Higher tier in a very selective manner so that only those viewed as 'the most able' are permitted entry.

Table 1: Tiering and the grades available in GCSE examinations

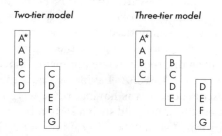

The system in mathematics is even worse – here, a three-tier model applies. Pupils in the Higher tier can be awarded grades A* to C; those in the middle ('Intermediate') tier can win grades B to E; those in the Foundation tier can only attain grades D to G. That means that before pupils even enter the examination room those in the Foundation tier *cannot* attain the all-important grade C (commonly accepted as a minimum cut off by many selectors in education and job markets).[4] Perhaps not surprisingly, schools do not always inform pupils of the full consequences of the system, especially those unfortunate enough to be in the lower tier.

Tiers and tears

Some indication of the devastating effects of such approaches can be gained from the fact that, in two London schools that we studied closely over a two-year period, Black pupils were *under*-represented in Higher tiers and *over*-represented in Foundation tiers: two-thirds of the Black pupils were entered for maths in the Foundation tier. That means that two in every three Black pupils could not possibly achieve a 'C' grade, simply because of the exam that their teachers had entered them for. The decision is solely in the hands of teachers; parents and pupils have no say.

At the 'London Schools and the Black Child' conference a succession of parents, grandparents and other carers spoke from the stage and bore witness to the catastrophic effects of this system. It was the first time that many had understood how it could be that intelligent, apparently hard working sons and daughters had managed to fail their maths exam despite always completing their homework and frequently receiving personal tuition outside the school system. Some wept in frustration and anger.

How is ability determined?

The inequality of attainment that Black pupils experience (or 'under-achievement' as some prefer) is a regular topic for commentators and selected 'experts' in the media. The plethora of opinions that regularly parade as informed insight could lead readers to imagine that there is a lack of research evidence on the matter. In fact there is a great deal of research, and much of it has consistently pointed to a similar range of problems, over several decades and in several different education systems.[5] A consistent finding, in both the US and UK, is that where education systems use some form of internal differentiation (through tracking, setting, banding, streaming), Black pupils are usually over-represented in the lowest status groups. These groups typically receive poorer resources and are often taught by less experienced (and/or less successful) teachers. Of course, these lower ranked groups are not overtly determined on the basis of ethnic origin – they are usually presented as a reflection of the pupils' capabilities, that is, their *ability*. But – as Coard pointed out with such power in the 1970s – we should be incredibly cautious and critical whenever we are told that certain pupils (disproportionately Black pupils) are less able, less well developed, or whatever is the preferred phrase of the moment to describe those pupils who have been deemed to be outside the chosen ranks of those destined to succeed. We need this caution because, despite the facade of value-neutral standardised testing and teachers' 'professional' judgement, in school the word 'ability' is very often another word for what teachers *think/assume* children can do. Let me illustrate with a simple example. During our research, Deborah spoke with a head of department about pupils' reactions when they were told their teachers' predictions for their future exam performance:

> I found that quite strange, that the kids had their estimated grades, because they then came back at you and gave you earache – you know, would challenge you in the corridor, and so you were under threat. You know, 'Why have you only given me that grade,' you know? Because kids, you know, have different perceptions of themselves, they have no understanding, you know, and some of them live in cloud cuckoo land. I mean we've got, we had a whole period where we had Afro-Caribbean kids running around with gold-rimmed glasses on with plain glass in them because they thought it made them look more intelligent, you know, they really had highly inflated opinions of themselves as far as academic achievement, and this is fact. I mean there were a whole group of kids that put

on glasses and wandered round the corridors with gold rimmed glasses on because they really felt that they were sort of A/B...

This quotation is especially illuminating because the teacher *could* have interpreted the situation in a way that shattered common stereotypes. For example, in many quarters a preferred explanation for the lower average Black attainment levels (especially among boys) is that they are somehow afraid to be seen to work hard, that academic effort is uncool. Clearly, elements of this view are at play in all urban centres, among working class pupils in particular, and among all ethnic groups. But the idea that this view is somehow a defining characteristic of Black youth culture ignores both the history of Black community commitment to education[6] and the evidence in front of our eyes. If Black youth are so anti-education, how come they stay in full-time education more than their white counterparts? Similarly, the teacher quoted above is blind to the evidence in front of him. He describes Black pupils who are confident in their abilities, and he even speculates that they change their appearance so as to 'look more intelligent'. And yet this same teacher does not recognise the hunger and commitment before him. He sees only the stereotype – Black young people that embody unrealistic expectations and engender a sense of fear, 'challenge you in the corridor'... 'you were under threat'...'they really had highly inflated opinions of themselves'.

Of course, schools assess pupils all the time, both informally (as above) and formally, including the use of so called 'cognitive abilities tests' – essentially IQ tests by a less discredited name. And yet, amid all this testing, one simple fact is vitally important: there is no measure of potential – every test is a measure of *learned* competencies. Even leading researchers in intelligence testing (a field with an appallingly racist track record) now agree that tests cannot measure innate potential.[7] The racist outcomes that result from supposedly neutral (colour-blind) selection inside schools suggest a wider lesson. Although policy reforms might be conceived (and presented) in colour-blind terms, their effects are frequently anything but blind to 'race'. *Supposedly colour-blind policies often have racist effects.*

Words and deeds
In the summer of 2004 the Department for Education published its 'Five Year Strategy'. Running to 110 pages, the strategy set out the future priorities and policies for education, yet the word 'racism' did not appear at all.

Even the more anodyne terms 'prejudice' and 'discrimination' were conspicuously absent. In contrast, 'business' and 'businesses' appeared 36 times, and 'standards' warranted 65 appearances – prompting an obvious question, *standards for whom?*

This remarkable absence is all the more worrying because one of the key lessons of the Stephen Lawrence inquiry was the importance of facing up to racism (in all its forms), and challenging it openly and honestly:[8]

> There must be an unequivocal acceptance of the problem of institutional racism and its nature before it can be addressed, as it needs to be, in full partnership with members of minority ethnic communities.
> *The Stephen Lawrence Inquiry*, p31

It is difficult to overstate the importance of the fact that the education system's five-year strategy has nothing to say about anti-racism or the need to challenge institutional racism. It is true, of course, that schools now face a tough set of expectations on race equality, arising from the Race Relations (Amendment) Act 2000 – which was a direct result of the courage and tenacity shown by Stephen's parents and their supporters in finally winning a public inquiry. As a result of this new legislation *every* state-funded school in England, Scotland and Wales should:

- Have a written policy on race equality.
- Monitor their activities for signs of bias (especially focusing on achievement).
- They must actively plan to eradicate race inequality.

These new duties are *mandatory* and require schools to be proactive in their pursuit of race equality. This is a major step forward and is among the most radical equalities legislation on earth. Unfortunately, early indications are that the education sector in general, and schools in particular, are lagging behind other public authorities.

Too busy to care?

The Commission for Racial Equality (CRE) recently published an initial report on compliance with the new laws – it paints a discouraging picture in relation to the education sector.[9] First, in a survey of more than 3,000 public authorities, schools were the least likely to reply: only 20 percent of schools replied, compared with an overall rate of almost 50 percent. Of course, nothing substantial can be read into a return rate alone. For example, among countless possible explanations, it might be thought that schools were not interested in race equality, or that they were more fearful of responding to a survey sponsored by the authority that polices the legislation. The most obvious explanation, in the eyes of some teachers with whom I've discussed this, is simply that schools are too busy to fill in questionnaires. Any or all of these might have a grain of truth.

Looking ahead, however, we might assume that since so few schools responded, then at least the ones that *did* participate would be among the most committed. If that is true then the rest of their responses make even gloomier reading. More than half of respondents in the education sector had not identified clear 'goals' or 'targets' for improvement. In relation to differences in attainment, which is especially prominent in the legislation, only one in three schools had set any clear goals for change.

Furthermore, schools were among the least positive about the effects of the changes that they had made: 65 percent of respondents in schools believed their race equality work had produced positive benefits, compared with 74 percent of those in criminal justice and policing, 80 percent in further and higher education, and 89 percent in central government. Perhaps most worrying of all, despite the relatively poor response so far, people working in education were the least likely to express a need for further guidance.

Put simply, early indications suggest that many schools are inactive on race equality: at best they are too busy, at worst, they appear to be complacent about their duties and uninterested in further progress.

Institutional racism: if we can't discuss it, how will we defeat it?

No gains in wider social justice could ever compensate for the loss of a child. Nevertheless, Stephen Lawrence's death and the tireless efforts of his parents Doreen and Neville have led to enormous changes. The scope and potential power of the new race relations legislation is beyond what many would have believed possible just a few years ago. Without action, however, the legislation is worthless. The fact that the Stephen Lawrence inquiry made headlines around the world, and that the law has been changed, means nothing if lessons have not been learned by the powers that be. It is worth reminding ourselves of the inquiry's definition of institutional racism:

> The collective failure of an organisation to provide an appropriate and professional service to people because of their colour, culture, or ethnic origin. It can be seen or detected in processes, attitudes and behaviour which amount to discrimination through unwitting prejudice, ignorance, thoughtlessness and racist stereotyping which disadvantage minority ethnic people.
>
> It persists because of the failure of the organisation openly and adequately to recognise and address its existence and causes by policy, example and leadership.

The Stephen Lawrence Inquiry, p28

This definition requires that we examine the effects of actions and policies, not their intent. Education reforms do not automatically benefit all groups equally – indeed, Black children have usually drawn less benefit from the changes. Notice, in particular, the last sentence of the quotation (which is rarely included when people quote the definition). Institutional racism 'persists because of the failure of the organisation openly and adequately to recognise and address its existence and causes by policy, example and leadership'.

Current evidence suggests that the education system has failed to learn from the tragedy of Stephen's murder and the resultant inquiry. Schools have been slow to respond to their new duties and most appear content to take no further action. At a national level, in the education department's 'Five Year Strategy' for radical educational change, the issue of institutional racism is notable by its total absence. Several possible explanations present themselves: first, the education department may think that institutional racism has been eradicated from the system (despite the continued inequalities in attainment and despite the persistent over-exclusion of Black children); second, the department might assume that this is wholly a matter for schools that it can wash its hands of; or perhaps the Department for Education is simply content to ignore the issue. You decide.

Conclusion

A lot has changed in the education system since the initial publication of Bernard Coard's book. A national curriculum has been imposed; the examination system has been changed; published league tables (based on crude scores) dominate discussion of educational 'standards'; and education has moved from the margins of political debate to become one of the most hotly contested areas of policy. But much has remained unchanged. We have more research than 35 years ago and we have more academically successful Black children – and yet we still endure a system that fails disproportionate numbers of Black children, excludes many from mainstream schooling altogether, and channels others into second-class courses deemed more appropriate by a teaching force that continues to be unrepresentative of the community it serves. The need for radical change is as pressing today as it ever was.

Notes

1 Title inspired by Public Enemy, *It Takes a Nation of Millions to Hold Us Back* (Def Jam Recordings, 1988). This is an expanded and updated version of a paper prepared for the Stephen Lawrence Charitable Trust.

2 Greater London Authority, *Towards a Vision of Excellence: London Schools and the Black Child: 2002 Conference Report* (London, 2003).

3 D Gillborn and D Youdell, *Rationing Education: Policy, Practice, Reform and Equity* (Buckingham, 2000).

4 In the spring of 2005 the Qualifications and Curriculum Authority announced plans to remove the three-tier model in mathematics from 2006 onwards. The restrictions and inequities built into the two tier model, however, will remain unaltered.

5 There is insufficient space for a detailed review of the evidence here, but longer treatments are available in D Gillborn and H S Mirza, *Educational Inequality: Mapping Race, Class and Gender – A Synthesis of Research Evidence*, Report #HMI 232 (London, 2000); and D Gillborn, *Racism, Policy and Contemporary Schooling: Current Inequities and Future Possibilities*, Sage Race Relations Abstracts, 29(2) (2004), pp5-33. Excellent sources on the US situation are J A Banks and C A M Banks (eds), *Handbook of Research on Multicultural Education*, Second Edition (San Francisco); and L McNeil, *Contradictions of School Reform* (New York, 2000).

6 See, for example, D Reay and H S Mirza, 'Uncovering Genealogies of the Margins: Black Supplementary Schooling', *British Journal of Sociology of Education*, 18 (4) (1997), pp477-499.

7 For a discussion of the evidence see D Gillborn, 'Ability, Selection and Institutional Racism in Schools', in M Olssen (ed), *Culture and Learning: Access and Opportunity in the Classroom* (Greenwich, Connecticut, 2004), pp279-297.

8 W Macpherson, *The Stephen Lawrence Inquiry*, CM 4262-I (London, 1999).

9 Schneider-Ross, *Towards Racial Equality: An Evaluation of the Public Duty to Promote Race Equality and Good Race Relations in England and Wales* (London, 2003).

● David Gillborn teaches at the Institute of Education, University of London. He is also the founding editor of the international journal *Race, Ethnicity and Education*, which has quickly established itself as an arena for critical research and debate on racism and ethnic diversity in education.

Professor Gus John

Parental and community involvement in education: time to get the balance right

Foreign is not best

Early in 2005 Trevor Phillips, chair of the Commission for Racial Equality, visited the East St Louis School District in Missouri and saw how the school administration and schools there were tackling the problem of under-achievement among Black school students, boys in particular. Phillips was especially impressed with the methods used to keep Black boys focused on learning and to help them build upon their achievements. Foremost among those methods was the practice of teaching Black boys in their own teaching groups, ie separate from girls, since the school population was virtually 100 percent Black.

On his return to Britain, Phillips intimated that a similar method of working with underachieving Black boys might be adopted here. The media reported Phillips as proposing that Black boys should be taught in segregated groups, thus sparking a massively irrelevant debate about segregated Black schools or segregation within schools. Throughout the last four decades education and schooling as well as that historical by-product of theirs, underachievement, have become increasingly racialised. It is that racialised discourse that the media fuelled in response to Phillips's enthusiasm for what he had seen in East St Louis. The fact that Black supplementary schools and voluntary education projects had been working in similar ways with school students who voluntarily attended those sessions seemed not to matter to the media. Among those catered for in those community schools were many of that vast number of Black boys the mainstream schools permanently excluded. It is a measure of the marginalisation of our efforts by the schooling system itself that no real attention has been paid to the many successful methods the supplementary schools have employed over the years to build the self-esteem of young Black boys and help them become confident and successful learners as well as socially competent people.

Having been so grossly misrepresented in a bizarrely distorted debate, Phillips organised a seminar at the CRE on 1 June 2005, bringing together academics and non-government organisations with an involvement in the issue to try and establish the factual situation and see what might work best for Black school students in Britain, England in particular. What follows is the text of the presentation I made at that seminar.

Where we were then
For at least the last four decades Black parents and communities have been actively concerned about:

- the quality of education on offer to Black school students
- levels of educational attainment as between Black boys and Black girls and as between Black boys/girls and other ethnic groups, including white ethnics
- access to and progression in employment by Black male school leavers in comparison to Black female school leavers
- the rate of exclusion of Black boys from school and the correlation between that and levels of Black male unemployment and the percentage of Black youths and adults in custodial institutions

Voluntary and community education projects, including the now well established Saturday and Supplementary Schools movement have attempted since the late 1960s to make meaningful interventions in respect of those concerns. There are an estimated 1,500 Supplementary and Saturday Schools in England and Wales, some 300 of which are in London alone. Those schools and the parents, teaching staff and community activists associated with them have a record of intervention in relation to the four key concerns highlighted above, and more. Indeed, their activism and remedial, supplementary and complementary education activities predate by at least two decades any serious interest in these matters, let alone concerted action to deal with them, on the part of the state.

The key issues in parental and community involvement in education, I suggest, are:

- What has been the result of those 40 years of community activism in response to our experience of the schooling and education system?
- How, in spite of that activity, has the condition of being Black, young and particularly male in the schooling system led to so many casualties among two generations of British born Black people?
- Why has the cumulative experience of the schooling and education system led to 'the abandonment of hope and the death of aspiration' for so many of our young people?
- Crucially, how can Black parents and communities learn from the advances and failures of the past and refocus our activities both in relation to our own responsibilities and in challenging what schools continue to do?

Time does not allow me to drill down into each of these key issues in any detail. Let me therefore make a few observations about the state we are in and what we as parents and communities need to be doing about it.

Until comparatively recently it was impossible to get mainstream schools to take seriously what Black communities were doing about the quality of the schooling experience of Black children. When we sought to make the school curriculum more relevant and provide Black children with an understanding of themselves and of the contribution to knowledge and the humanising of societies Black people have made throughout history, we were roundly accused of political indoctrination and teaching Black kids to hate whites. Well, now, we couldn't have done too great a job there, for 55 percent of all African-Caribbean males and 35 percent of all Caribbean females in the UK have white partners. Those who have children are having to deal with a more insidious and visceral form of racism than that suffered by Black individuals as part of Black communities.

With royal and imperial British arrogance, the state schooling system refused to heed the messages that were coming forward from our interface in the community education projects with the same students they were writing off as unteachable or ill disciplined.

For decades, 1960s to 1990s at least, successive governments operated structures which suggested that the problem lay with us as Black people because of our immigrant status and our backward language and backward ways. Remember Section 11 of the 1966 Local Government Act? Section 11 funding gave way to Ethnic Minority Achievement Grants, followed by Ethnic Minority and Traveller Achievement Grants and special funding programmes to deal with the deficits that Black learners were presumed to have. Needless to say, those operating these highly questionable programmes were mainly Black people themselves. We were and are always put in charge of our own assumed pathology, not unlike the colonial arrangements of yesteryear.

Sadly, however, the supplementary schools movement was not a mass movement of black people in education, nor did it give rise to one. While many individual parents got involved in the work of the schools and supported their and other children's learning, most were content in the knowledge that the supplementary school was limiting the damage the mainstream system was most likely to inflict upon their children, rather than being concerned about taking collective action to make the mainstream schools adopt approaches to teaching, learning and curriculum that would give all children a greater zest for learning and a chance to excel.

What is more, the issues that exercised Black parents were not shared by the majority of white parents, let alone white teachers and teaching unions. For example, when some of us attempted to get the then Council for National Academic Awards, the precursor of the Qualifications and Curriculum Authority, to stipulate the knowledge, understanding, skills and core competences teacher graduates should have in order to teach in inner city schools with their growing numbers of Black children, not only did we encounter resistance from the CNAA and the teacher training institutions, but Black parents on the whole felt that that was asking too much of teachers and that our aim should be to get more Black teachers in schools.

There was an automatic assumption that, just by virtue of being Black, a teacher would be able to deal with all the issues Black students were bringing into the classroom from home, peer group and community, irrespective of the age of the teacher, their ideological position or whether they were progressive or downright reactionary. That assumption was also predicated on the suspect notion that Black students would automatically welcome and respect a teacher simply because they were of African-Caribbean or West African heritage like themselves. Grandparents and some first generation migrant parents might have had residual knowledge of the contours of the relationship between children and teachers, based on their own experience. The situation is clearly considerably more complex now, impacted as it is by sharp contradictions of class, image, professional versus marginal status, and all the rest of it.

As important, of course, is the fact that if Black student teachers are subjected to the same training as whites, with all the underpinning pedagogical values, the assumed ideological neutrality of the teaching and learning process and the like, their training would not have addressed the central issue of the place their Blackness has in the teaching and learning relationship and in negotiating power relations within the school.

Where we are now

There is an increased level of self-organised and self-directed education activity within our communities. However, unlike the 1960s to the 1980s, let's say, the focus of that activity is much less on issues of character building, Black identity formation, the curriculum mainstream schooling ignores, the potential of Black school students that is not being developed, etc, and much more on performance in relation to test and examination results.

For example, since the Labour government in the last administration set aside just over £1 million to support the supplementary schools, schools in receipt of that money are being routinely inspected by Ofsted to ensure that the quality of teaching and learning matches the government's raising achievement agenda.

Yet, despite two full scale reviews of the National Curriculum, the government is still requiring schools to deliver a curriculum that is essentially geared to preparation for life in a principally mono-racial and mono-cultural environment. In other words, despite the fact that in many urban centres we number anything between 25 percent and 55 percent of the population overall, we are still not considered mainstream enough to have the curriculum reflect British society as it is rather than how some would prefer it to be.

The state we're in

Meanwhile, of course, the education project has become contaminated for far too many of our children. The malaise is indeed characterised by 'the abandonment of hope and self-belief and the death of aspiration'. To put it even more bluntly, it is characterised by an implosion within our communities to the extent that the mainstream schooling agenda is a massive irrelevance for many Black students, boys and girls, who are dealing with issues in their homes and communities that make what goes on in the average classroom sound like a catechism class.

The consequences of that for Black communities, for the future of Black people in the economy of this nation, for the nature and quality of Black parenting and for social order generally are immense.

The government's own report on Ethnic Minorities and the Labour Market (produced by the Strategy Unit in the Cabinet Office in 2004) identifies African-Caribbean, Pakistani and Bangladeshi groups as having the lowest educational attainment and lowest occupational status. The report notes that African and Asian people make up one in 13 of the UK population and that over the past 20 years they have accounted for two thirds of the growth of the total UK population.

Similarly, in the coming ten to 20 years, the British labour market will be dependent, increasingly, on the supply of labour from those communities. That knowledgeable and skilled labour force will not be available if the current pattern of underachievement, school exclusions and youth offending within African and Asian communities persists

In 1998, for example, Black school students aged six to 16 were 12 times more likely to be excluded than their white counterparts. That trend has continued, albeit the government's targets for reducing school exclusions have led to a marginal decrease in the number of Black students being excluded.

In the last five years the Youth Justice Board has highlighted the correlation between school exclusion, youth offending and the high number of Black young people in youth custody:

The 13,000 young people excluded from school each year might as well be given a date by which to join the prison service some time later on down the line.
Martin Narey – Director General of the Prison Service, 2001

Of 400 young people in a Young Offender Institution (YOI), 200 had been excluded from school.
Martin Narey

Two-thirds of the population of YOIs had left or been put out of school at age 13 or under.
Home Office Research

Speaking about the link between school exclusion and social exclusion, Lord Warner of Brockley, former chair of the Youth Justice Board, noted:

> 80 percent of young offenders of school age are out of school, either through exclusion or refusal to attend...mainstream schooling is not willing and not able to deal with children with challenging behaviour.

A famous sociologist remarked over half a century ago that for many socially excluded groups:

> Crime results from exclusion from legitimate means of achieving success.
> **Robert Merton, 1949**

As I observed in a public meeting in 2004 of the organisation which I chair, Parents and Students Empowerment (PaSE):

> Social exclusion is a process. It is a dynamic process. It is the systematic and structural deprivation of the individual's opportunity to participate in society and consequently a denial of dignity, self-esteem and self-worth.
>
> It is a process that creates a cumulative set of circumstances in which the individual is unable to achieve the quality of life to which s/he aspires, and that is consistent with dignified living.
>
> As Black communities we encounter it in both its passive and active forms. Parents and communities must intervene proactively to tackle both forms, especially active social exclusion, ie 'the form of exclusion that comes about when young people lay claim to particular identities and make choices about lifestyles which compound their disadvantage and their existence on the margins of the society'.
>
> Social exclusion (passive and active) for a growing number of young people results in 'the abandonment of hope and the death of aspiration'. It is a condition in which shared values cannot be taken for granted and where conduct becomes so amoral that young people pose a huge risk to themselves and to others. No amount of moralising about gun violence, the cheapness of life, the endgame philosophy of, 'I have nothing and therefore I have nothing left to lose, so show respect or I'll blow your brains out', no amount of moralising about any of that will alter the situation.
>
> What is more, is that despite the fact that a new generation of young Black males is being socialised into that culture, schools and education authorities

are still conducting their business as if young people of that disposition have forfeited the right to their education entitlement, as if it is not the business of school to engage with those challenges to their self-development, their life chances and their functioning as responsible social citizens.

Sadly, and understandably in many respects, the state and our communities are much more focused on manifestations of that implosion than upon the growing number of African heritage young men who are high achievers, who are faithful partners and exemplary fathers, and who occupy elevated positions in the professions. But we dare not forget them.

We need to constantly remind ourselves that that profile is not an aberration but in fact a true reflection of the range of capacities and of family organisation in our communities here and elsewhere.

Parents and communities need to engage them in forums for young people to share experiences of surviving schooling and becoming high achievers, despite coming from the same social background and neighbourhoods and being faced with the same challenges as those who are failed by the system.

There is a tendency among us to adopt a pharisaic attitude and celebrate the fact that our children are not like 'dem dutty bwoy dem, all ah dem so damn wicked and bad', as one frustrated parent put it to me recently, rather than giving thanks and saying, 'There but for fortune go mine.' We cannot consider ourselves or any of our offspring to be safe until we ensure all our boys are safe and do not represent some kind of grenade waiting to go off indiscriminately.

What is to be done
So where do we go from here?

First, we must acknowledge and mobilise widespread support from within our communities and the wider society for the view that the whole schooling project is increasingly arse about face, not just for our children but for a growing number of children of all ethnicities. It is futile to keep on complaining about the lack of discipline and the anti-academic stance adopted by some Black boys and girls.

Yes, there are girls who routinely see fit to plait one another's hair throughout a lesson, chatting among themselves as the teacher tries to deliver a carefully prepared lesson plan. And there are boys who spend the entire lesson messing with their mobile phones and honing their text language development skills.

Yes, there is an unacceptable level of bullying by Black boys and girls of their peers who are bright, focused and are working to their potential.

What is clear is that such conduct is never a true reflection of the ability of those students, let alone of their capacity to cooperate and be focused learners. So we need to deal with the issue of internalised negativity and the effects of the constant refrain that Black students, boys in particular, do not achieve.

Second, we need to challenge the 'one size fits all' approach to the structuring of schooling that makes such unrealistic and futile demands on some young people, however much Mr Blair might protest that his is 'not a one size fits all' formula.

It is perverse at worst and politically cynical at best to persist with a system that is patently producing massive casualties in every succeeding generation of Black British citizens. In order to do that, you must have decided that that section of the population is much more expendable than others, capable of bearing more collateral damage in peacetime.

Third, if we accept that parents have a legal duty to ensure that their children attend school up to the age of 16, unless they opt to educate them themselves as more and more are now doing, if we accept that those children are entitled to an education and that the more dysfunctional their attitudes to their self-management and to schooling, the more need they have for education for self-development, then the question arises: why should their emotional, spiritual and self-development needs not be met in school as part of the teaching and learning process?

Why can schools not be organised in such a manner that where children's needs require them to work in much smaller teaching and learning groups the school has the flexibility to facilitate that?

In the broad scale of things, given all the rhetoric about choice, about combating social exclusion and promoting community cohesion, what is wrong with class sizes of no more than eight for some learning groups? And why should not those learning groups be of Black boys specifically or of Bangladeshi boys specifically if their learning and developmental needs warrant it? Surely, the fact that few schools actually give themselves the space or pay students the respect to discover how and in what circumstances they learn would imply that a deeper level of engagement might be necessary with students who stand in opposition to the regime of schooling or plainly derive very little from it, however regular their attendance.

Why can parents of school students with challenging behaviour at home and at school not join activity in the school that seeks to support the transition from disruptive and self-destructive behaviour to becoming students who have purpose and for whom learning at their own pace is meaningful and enjoyable?

Part of that activity must of course be 'talk'. Students must be allowed to see conversations with teachers, especially, as the norm. The student's right to be heard and to express an opinion in relation to issues affecting them, including the dynamics of schooling, is one that is not always respected. That single fact accounts for more of the aggravation that results in school exclusion than just about any other factor. The citizenship curriculum addresses itself to, among other things, the teaching of democracy. Pity it does not engage with the issue of how sensible it is to teach democracy in schools without democratising schooling itself.

What might be the role of school in helping to support parents in their parenting role and thus empower them to be better partners in their children's learning?

Fourth, we need to support parents and young people in devising strategies for surviving schooling, acknowledging the fact that this or any other government is not about to hurriedly reform the organisation of schooling in the manner I suggest. On the contrary, government appears to believe that you could legislate for respect and that by shouting, 'Zero tolerance!' you actually frighten young people into conformity.

And what about communities?
We need to acknowledge that seeking private solutions to these deepseated public ills that put our entire communities under threat is counterproductive in the long run. I may send my child to a private school. I might even pack him off to relatives in the Caribbean so he could hopefully do better in an entirely different education culture. I may send him to the supplementary school and thus give him extension classes for a very modest fee. But until we act collectively to tackle the appalling experiences so many young people have at home, in school and in our communities, we run the risk of being in fear of our bright and successful children's lives.

As one very distressed parent in a mainly white suburb put it to me recently:

> You make the sacrifice and move to places like this because of all the gun crime and horrendous things these Black boys are getting up to, and then you find yourself face to face with some very nasty racists threatening you with all sorts. I suppose it's a case of who you would take your risks with, your own kind in the city or vicious racists who want to force you back into the inner city.

In summary, then, I am calling for collective action by Black parents and communities:

- to find ways of discharging our own responsibilities and supporting one another to save our children
- and to apply pressure on the government to ensure that so many of our children are not written off by schools but are facilitated to become confident learners and responsible social citizens, demanding and safeguarding their own rights and having due regard for the rights of others

I am interim chair of a national organisation called PaSE, Parents and Students Empowerment. PaSE operates as a partnership of parents and young people, bringing together school and college students and those not in education, training or employment from across the country:

- to debate the issues confronting them
- share experiences and strategies for positive engagement with school, community and society
- and to work towards the formation of a national organisation of young people committed to working together to tackle those issues, share good practice and influence government policy at local and national levels

PaSE has been working across the country in collaboration with the Communities Empowerment Network (CEN) and targeting young people, their parents/carers, learning mentors, counsellors and other significant others in the lives of those young people. Some of that work has involved casework in relation to school exclusions, strategies for avoiding conflict and for focused, disciplined learning, as well as work around involvement in gangs and dealing with bullying by members of gangs.

I believe that that process of engagement which enables young people and parents to share experiences, discuss challenges and work towards solutions is necessary across the country and we need to make full use of the new technology to network nationally and internationally.

- Professor Gus John is visiting professor Faculty of Education, University of Strathclyde, and chief executive, The Gus John Partnership Limited

Diane Abbott

Teachers are failing Black boys

THERE IS a silent catastrophe happening in Britain's schools in the way they continue to fail Black British school children. When African and Afro-Caribbean children enter the school system at five they do as well as white and Asian children in tests. By 11 their achievement levels begin to drop off. By 16 there has been a collapse. And this is particularly true of Black boys – 48 percent of all 16-year-old boys gain five GCSEs, grades A to E. Only 13 percent of Black boys in London achieve this standard. In some boroughs the figure is even worse.

This is not a new issue. As long ago as 1977 a House of Commons select committee on race relations and immigration reported that 'as a matter of urgency the government should institute a high-level and independent inquiry into the causes of the underachievement of children of West Indian origin in maintained schools and the remedial action required'. But in 1999 Ofsted, in its publication, *Raising the Attainment of Minority Ethnic Pupils*, said: 'The gap between Afro-Caribbean pupils and the rest of the school population continues to widen.'

But it is an issue no one wants to address. Ministers and advisers talk endlessly about social exclusion and the problems of children for whom English is a second language. You can discuss the underachievement of boys, but not how the system fails Black boys. Research both in this country and the United States shows that Black boys need men in the classroom. They simply do not see reading or educational attainment as masculine or 'cool'. Although this also applies to white working class boys, strategies designed to address male underachievement in general are not working with Black boys.

It may be the demonisation and marginalisation of Black men in British society which makes some young Black boys hold fiercely to a concept of masculinity which is about bravado and violence. But with Black boys there are the added factors of racism and the extreme unwillingness of teachers and educationalists to face up to their own attitudes.

Black boys are often literally bigger than their white counterparts and may come from a culture which is more physical. Primary schools, in particular, are almost entirely staffed with women and, while some white women teachers achieve excellent results with Black boys, it would be remarkable if all white women teachers were free from the racial stereotypes that permeate this society about Black men. Groups which work in the Black community are seeing increasingly younger Black boys being excluded and it seems a Black boy doesn't have to be long out of disposable nappies for some teachers to see him as a miniature gangster rapper. Yet experienced Black teachers describe how the most unruly and obnoxious Black schoolboy can melt given firm but loving handling. It is important to stress that there are models of success. For a generation, Britain's Black community have run self-help Saturday Schools specifically to compensate for the failures of mainstream schools. Traditionally they had a strong emphasis on formal education together with a positive Black identity.

The Claudia Jones Saturday School is a successful one in my own borough of Hackney. The Seventh Day Adventist schools in London are de facto all Black, the best known being John Loughborough in Tottenham, north London. The children wear uniform and there is a strong emphasis on discipline and high standards. They have had success in raising the achievement of Black boys whom mainstream schools had written off. What all of these schools have in common are highly motivated Black teachers, involved parents, strong discipline and boundaries, and a celebration of the children's cultural identities.

We all have a role to play. Black parents need to become engaged in a constructive way with the school system. Teachers need to examine their attitudes. Most teachers, and their trade unions, see themselves as liberals on race matters and they react badly to any suggestion that they are failing Black children. But, as the 1985 Swann Report pointed out: 'Teachers' attitudes towards, and expectations of, West Indian pupils may be subconsciously influenced by stereotyped, negative or patronising views of their abilities and potential, which may prove a self-fulfilling prophecy, and can be seen as a form of unintentional racism.' In 2001 most Black parents would say nothing much has changed.

Above all the government needs to give a lead. Ministers need to push it up the agenda. In 1996 Ofsted said: 'The question of race and equality of opportunity has fallen from the prominent position it once held.' Time to put it back up there. We have a generation of Black children to save.

- This article first appeared in the *Observer*, 6 January 2002.

- Diane Abbott is MP for Hackney North and Stoke Newington.

Heidi Safia Mirza

'The more things change, the more they stay the same': assessing Black underachievement 35 years on[1]

Introduction

Thirty five years ago Bernard Coard's[2] seminal pamphlet brought to light the scandal of disproportionate numbers of Caribbean children being labelled as Educationally Subnormal (ESN). But this scandal seems so long ago, a lifetime for those of us of Caribbean heritage born in that generation. Much research and political debate has taken place about the value of Britain as a multicultural society since the 1970s.[3] We now have the Race Relations (Amendment) Act 2000 which positively monitors and promotes racial equality in our schools. Our British social discourse is underpinned by the importance of equality and diversity, citizenship and human rights, social cohesion and inclusion.[4] In this climate of democratic liberal enlightenment we think and say to ourselves, 'Surely such scandals could not be happening now, not in the 21st century, not when we understand the dynamics of racial injustice, and have learnt, through the death of Stephen Lawrence, the lessons of race hate?' But there is a saying, 'The more things change the more they stay the same', and while racist treatment of our children may not be so blatant as 35 years ago we are still plagued by the problem of racial differentiation in educational treatment and outcome for Black Caribbean young people. The question for us three and a half decades on is, why do these racial inequalities still persist and how is racism in our educational system expressed in new and different times? A historical mapping can be revealing.

1960-1970 : Patterns of assimilation

Forty years ago there were many theories as to why Black children may not do well at school. In 1960s Britain Black children from immigrant communities were bussed out to cool out and water down white fears whipped up by Enoch Powell, the racist Smethwick by-election, and the Notting Hill Riots. It was believed the children of migrants needed to assimilate, lose their cultural markers and blend in. It was believed they were not only culturally and socially deficient, coming from less civilised societies, but also that they were inherently intellectually lacking. The now discredited pseudo-scientific IQ tests of Jensen and Eysenck claimed to show black children were racially different and as such had lower intelligence.[5] But 'natural ability' is still an issue. In what Gillborn and Youdell call the 'new IQism',[6] the pressures of educational policy, such as league tables, cause the sifting and sorting of pupils into tiers and streams by perceived ability. The patterns are often racialised with Black children locked into the lower streams.

The theory of low self-esteem was a popular explanation to challenge explanations of low IQ in the 1970s. Milner's scientific doll studies[7] suggested that if you chose a white doll rather than a dark one like yourself you were exhibiting negative self-esteem and low self-concept. The self-fulfilling prophecy of low self-esteem leading to low pupil aspirations, which in turn fed into low teacher expectations, was seen as the key mechanism to explain Black underachievement. Indeed it was a central tenant of Coard's thesis. But his focus was not on any intrinsic lack of positive Black identity and Caribbean cultural inferiority as others suggested.[8] He argued that in a white-controlled and oppressive educational system where the cards are stacked against you, it is easy for young Black people to become alienated and lack motivation.

But do these ideas of the self-fulfilling prophecy and notions of negative self-esteem have any currency now? Work on raising the achievement of young Black people through raising self-esteem is still very much with us today, though in its more sophisticated form of positive role models and mentoring. While it has been a lifeline to many Black Caribbean and Asian young people whom the effects of racism have damaged, we still need to acknowledge its roots in the cultural deficit model of negative self-esteem and understand its limitations.

English as a Second Language was also seen as a problem then, not just for those who spoke English as a foreign language such as Pakistani and Bengali children, but also for those who spoke Patois and Creole. As Coard's research showed, children who came from cultures that spoke non-Standard English, whether born here or in the Caribbean, were assessed and put into special units infamously called 'Sin Bins'. The Black Parents Movement[9] was an important grassroots political response by the Black community to the criminalisation and the wanton discarding of their children in this way. But 35 years on we still have segregated schooling disproportionately populated by young Black pupils. No longer called 'Sin Bins', they are now called PRUs (Pupil Referral Units). The issue that drives the impulse for segregated schooling now is the discourse on discipline and antisocial behaviour. As Tony Sewell[10] has shown in his research, there is no doubt that Black masculine peer pressure to be 'cool', urban youth culture, and inter-racial gangs are issues for schools. This clearly relates to underachievement. However, there has been no attempt to decouple these issues of social control from the issues of 'race' and racism. David Gillborn's[11] research shows we have effectively criminalised generations of Black children, particularly boys, by not recognising the subtle consequences of stereotyping, particularly what he calls the 'Myth of the Afro-Caribbean Macho' which has seeped into the classroom and the consciousness of teachers. It's an epidemic, a *real* crisis for the children and the parents.

1980-1990: Mapping multiculturalism

Barry Troyna, one of our important educational theorists, called this period of multiculturalism the 3 S's – 'samosas, saris and steelbands'.[12] It was an apt description of the day to day interpretation of Roy Jenkins's famous call for multiculturalism as 'not a flattening out process but one of equal opportunity and cultural diversity in an atmosphere of mutual tolerance'.[13]

In the 1980s, 25 years ago, there were the Brixton Uprisings. The hate was consuming, but this explosion of anger and frustration was also a watershed. The Scarman report that followed uncovered the racism of criminal justice system. The Rampton and Swann reports on multiracial education showed educational underachievement had taken root, and for the first time linked it to socioeconomic concerns of race and class. At this time dedicated scholars saw the visionary potential of multicultural education and engaged in radical, expansive and inclusive scholarship.[14] In a critique of existing theories and the limitations of the 1988 Educational Reform Act they called for a more coherent approach to multicultural education. They showed that many complex factors make a difference. Schools make a difference, as do the curriculum, poverty and class inequality, home-school relations and regressive colour-blind government policy.

The anti-racist teachers' movement also identified institutional and structural racism in the school system. Teacher expectations had always been at the core of theories on the self-fulfilling prophecy of how educational underachievement operates in a cycle of low expectations followed by low pupil outcomes. But 20 years on there is still no integral anti-racist training for teachers. Seventy percent of Newly Qualified Teachers say they do not feel equipped to teach pupils from different ethnicities.[15] They may get one hour's class on diversity in their whole training.

In the 1980s the right wing backlash against multicultural education was all-consuming. From the USA to the UK they ridiculed any attempts at cultural inclusion as 'political correctness' and 'dumbing down'. Now, after the 2001 summer disturbances in Bradford and Oldham, Trevor Phillips, the head of the CRE, too, has declared, 'Multiculturalism is dead'.[16] It is argued it has led to segregation and caused ethnic enclaves, particularly in schools which have held young people back. Many British born Black and Asian young people are now seen to be alienated and unintegrated into a common sense of shared Britishness.[17] But now in the government's sophisticated language of Social Cohesion and Social Inclusion – which embodies the notion of interfaith and intercultural understanding, citizenship and community engagement – we see again that communities must integrate, lose their cultural markers to become viable. Is this a return to assimilationism? Has the wheel turned full circle? Are we back where we were 40 years ago? Is this just a new take on the same old problems? What is our vision for a *real* multicultural Britain?

2000-2005: Postmodern difference and diversity

We have entered a new era in 'race talk'. Now we talk of 'diversity and difference'. As Kenan Malik[18] powerfully argues, we no longer focus on old fashioned ideas of equality and the universal qualities that make us, humanity, the same. Now, in the wake of the Identity Politics of the 1980s, we celebrate our differences: being a woman, being Black, being Muslim, being gay. Discrimination based on gender, sexuality, race, disability, and age and religion is now on the legislative agenda.

This politics of recognition enabled those who had been marginalised to find a voice. It was a liberating time, but not without its problems. It has been translated into a bureaucratic approach to diversity, which monitors our progress and tracks our differences. We now have glossy brochures with our multicoloured faces and wonderful policies and institutional statements that promise inclusion and change. But in reality, as a recent London Development Agency report shows, there has been little progress towards racial equality.[19] Good intentions remain locked in an institutional paper trail, unable to translate to hearts and minds. Now we hear of diversity as 'good business sense'. We can expand the market more effectively by embracing difference. Diversity, we are told, opens up human potential and enables the best to excel. Ironically in the marketplace difference and diversity has led to the 'declining significance of race'. Now in a colour-blind approach we are told we are all the same. Fair treatment is based on merit. But what if we don't all have the same equal opportunities to get that merit?

In our education system how does this notion of merit translate? Underpinning the Aiming High[20] programme to raise achievement for Black and minority ethnic young people we see graphs that chart hierarchies of difference between ethnicities.[21]

Table 1: Pupils with five grades A to C GCSE examination results

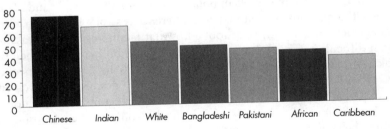

DfES, GCSE results, England 2004, National Statistics First Release SFR 08/2005 (24 February 2005)
www.dfes.gov.uk/rsgateway/DB/SFR

Here we rank ethnic groups in order of ability. It is seen as a good thing, with Indian and Chinese (the so called 'model minorities') at the top and

Africans and Caribbeans (the so called 'failing' minorities) at the bottom. But what does this tell us? Some are gifted, others are not? Are Asians docile and hardworking (like coolies of the past)? Do Blacks have a chip on their shoulder and rebel (like uppity slaves of the past)? What do you think? What do we think? What do teachers think? We can ask, 'What about class, gender and regional difference in attainment?' We know these make a difference, but this complexity is rarely highlighted in the 'race' and achievement debate.[22]

Now, as this graph shows, ethnicity and cultural difference have become signifiers for 'race'. This is the new racism. We have moved from biological notions of innate differences in the 19th century to religious, national and cultural notions of innate differences in the 21st century. It is as if cultural and religious differences are embodied in nature. In the new cultural construction of 'race', cultural and religious difference is played out when we say '...Blacks are good at sport, not so good at school. Chinese are good at maths, and make good food. Asians are good at business and love family life. Muslims cannot be trusted: they are aggressive, sexist and, under all those clothes, usually a bit wild eyed.' Racism in this cultural and religious guise seems less overt. We understand these differences. Recently a student said to me, 'What do you mean by "We"?' What I mean is the pervasive way We all talk about race, as if cultural and religious differences are fixed and immutable. It is a racialised way of being that infiltrates our daily language, personal interactions, professional practice and, what's more, our social and education policies.

There has been some excellent policy research on diversity. Maud Blair[23] at the DfES has shown what makes a difference is strong leadership, clear management and a positive school ethos that facilitates open discussion about difficult issues, such as racism, sexism and bullying. But when we look at the evidence of raising achievement projects under the initiatives of EIC (Excellence in Cities) and EMAG (Ethnic Minority Achievement Grant), what we find is not a focus on the 'hard' structural issues identified by Maud Blair and her team. We find instead a 'soft' approach focusing on culture, behaviour and the home. There are schemes for motivational and personal development, schemes for counselling and pastoral support, mentoring and role models. There are projects on parenting skills, translation services and summer schools; homework and breakfast clubs, writers' workshops, and exam techniques.

It could be argued that these schemes are making a difference, and I am sure special provision, such as Trevor Phillips has recently advocated for Black boys, can and does make a difference. The most recent figures show Bangladeshi, African, Caribbean and Pakistani pupils' GCSEs results are up by nearly three points.[24] But the approach to raising achievement is still located in the old multicultural palliatives of the three S's, with concepts of negative self-esteem and cultural deficit. The new cultural racism has slipped in by the backdoor.

Conclusion

If we look at the racialisation of education in Britain over the last 35 years we see patterns of persistent discrimination, both blatant and subtle. The outright segregation and exclusion which Coard found in the ESN 'Sin Bins' can still be seen in the PRUs and educational practices which lead to the disproportionate levels of exclusions and examination failure by Black boys at school. We can also map trends in our more subtle theories and approaches to Black educational underachievement. Both then and now we can see policy responses based on low or differential ability and intelligence, such as testing, setting and streaming. There are many schemes that still address beliefs about cultural confusion, negative self-esteem, alienation and bad behaviour among Caribbean youth and their parents. While we like to think we have progressed in terms of sophisticated debates and progressive legislation on equality, diversity and human rights, our solutions to the problems remain limited. 'Raising Achievement' funding initiatives focus on short term policies which lead to inherently safe, conservative 'do-able' practices which just keep reinventing the wheel with weak woolly institutional responses to the causes of real racism.

The persistence of Black underachievement for nearly four decades is a scandal. Bernard Coard's ground-breaking work revealed shocking educational injustice for Black pupils in 1971, but the journey to find justice is still not over. Since then more than three generations of young Black people have been failed by the educational system in Britain. This is a travesty of wasted lives. We must continue to expose the illusive chameleon nature of racism in education as it changes its mantle over time, for in the end, as the evidence shows, in a racist society, 'the more things change the more they stay the same'.

Notes

1 This paper is based on edited extracts from my Inaugural Professorial Lecture, 'Race, Gender and Educational Desire', delivered on 17 May 2005 at Middlesex University www.mdx.ac.uk/hssc/research/cres.htm

2 B Coard, *How the West Indian Child is Made Educationally Subnormal in the British School System* (New Beacon Books, London, 1971).

3 Runnymede Trust, *The Parekh Report: Commission on the Future of Multi-Ethnic Britain* (Profile Books, London, 2000).

4 R Bhavnani, H S Mirza and V Meetoo, *Tackling the Roots of Racism: Lessons for Success* (Policy Press, Bristol, 2005).

5 H S Mirza, 'Race, Gender and IQ: the Social Consequence of Pseudo-Scientific Discourse', in *Race, Ethnicity and Education*, vol 1 (1) (1998), pp109-126.

6 D Gillborn and D Youdell, *Rationing Education: Policy, Practice, Reform and Equity* (Open University Press, Buckingham, 2000).

7 D Milner, *Children and Race* (Penguin, Harmondsworth, 1975).

8 A Little, 'Schools and Race', in *Five Views of Multi-Racial Britain* (Commission for Racial Equality, London, 1978).

9 For archives documenting the civil rights struggle for a multiracial Britain see the Runnymede Collection at Middlesex University (www.mdx.ac.uk/www/runnymedecollection) and the George Padmore Institute Archives (http://www.georgepadmoreinstitute.org/archive.asp)

10 T Sewell, *Black Masculinities and Schooling* (Trentham, Stoke on Trent, 1997).

11 D Gillborn, *Race, Ethnicity and Education: Teaching and Learning in Multi-Ethnic Schools* (Unwin Hyman, London, 1990).

12 B Troyna, 'Can You See the Join? An Historical Analysis of Multicultural and Antiracist Education Policies', in D Gill, B Mayor and M Blair (eds), *Racism and Education ; Structures and Strategies* (Sage, London, 1992).

13 Roy Jenkins speech to the National Committee for Commonwealth Immigrants, 23 May 1966 (quoted in Runnymede Trust, 2000).

14 See, for example, S Tomlinson, *Ethnic Minorities in British Schools* (Heinemann Educational Books, London, 1983); P Figueroa, *Education and the Social Construction of Race* (Routledge, London, 1991).

15 Multiverse, *Exploring Diversity and Achievement Newsletter*, issue 1 (London Metropolitan University IPSE, London, February 2004).

16 A Andrews, 'Multiculturalism Is Dead', *Guardian* (8 April 2004).

17 A media debate on the failures of multiculturalism has raged since some Muslim British born young men bombed London in July 2005. See, for example, N Klein, 'Racism is the Terrorists' Greatest Recruitment Tool', *Guardian* (13 August 2005); and M Howard, 'Talk About The British Dream', *Guardian* (17 August 2005).

18 K Malik, 'The Dirty D-word', *Guardian* (29 October 2003).

19 LDA, 'The Educational Experiences and Achievements of Black Boys in London Schools 2000-2003', The Education Commission (London Development Agency, 2004).

20 DfES, *Aiming High: Raising Achievement of Ethnic Minority Pupils*, consultation (London, March 2003), DfES/0183/2003.

21 DfES, National Statistics First Release SFR 08/2005 (24 February 2005). www.dfes.gov.uk/rsgateway/DB/SFR

22 D Gillborn and H Mirza, *Educational Inequality: Mapping Race, Class and Gender – a Synthesis of Research Evidence* (Ofsted, London, November 2000), www.ofsted.gov.uk

23 M Blair and J Bourne, with C Coffin, A Creese and C Kenner, *Making the Difference: Teaching and Learning Strategies in Successful Multi-Ethnic Schools* (Department for Education and Employment, London, 1998).

24 DfES, *Minority Ethnic Pupils Make Further Progress at GCSE* (24 February 2005). www.dfes.gov.uk/pns/display

● Heidi Safia Mirza is professor of Racial Equality Studies at Middlesex University. She is known internationally for her work on ethnicity, gender and identity in education with bestselling books such as *Young, Female, and Black* and *Black British Feminism*. As a member of the Labour government's Schools' Standards Task Force she helped shape many initiatives to do with raising standards in education for Black and minority ethnic pupils. She has established the Runnymede Collection at Middlesex, a unique race-relations archive and library documenting the late 20th century civil rights struggle for a multicultural Britain. Her most recent book co-authored with Reena Bhavnani, *Tackling the Roots of Racism: Lessons for Success*, is published by Policy Press.

Gillian Klein

When will they ever learn?

EVERY ONE of my students learned two things about Bernard Coard's book: the title, and the fact that it described precisely what he saw happening in schools in England. This was in the days of teacher education in the 1990s, when they were students, not trainees, and when the implications of psychological and social factors on children's development and learning were a valid part of the curriculum of undergraduate or postgraduate student teachers.

Issues of equality – generally race, gender and class – could be planted in the hospitable beds of reflective and non-mechanistic initial teacher education. But when the way teachers are prepared changed, the beds were dug up. Learning to teach focused on how to survive in the classroom and how to deliver the national strategies and curriculum. In the target strewn arena that replaced the garden, there was neither space nor time to consider the nature and needs of pupils, or to cultivate reflection in the future teachers.

So who was surprised when the Teacher Training Agency's (TTA) research in 2003 found that 70 percent of newly qualified teachers felt that their training had not prepared them to teach in culturally diverse schools? Apparently only the TTA, who presented the figures at the launch conference of Multiverse (about which more later) in October 2004. And maybe the new teachers who wondered why they couldn't respond appropriately to their classes. Few had heard of Coard, or Rampton or Swann, or of the vast literature that has since accrued on equality and education. It wasn't among the targets. And there were fewer and fewer teacher educators who had read the books themselves and could inspire and enlighten the trainees.

I'm not saying that all was well in the 1970s and 1980s after Coard's hugely influential book was widely read. Many teachers continued to problematise black pupils (see, eg, Gillborn 1995 and following; Sewell 1997, and other chapters in this book) and most attempts at multiculturalism were, as Mirza says here, 'shallow'.

But bussing stopped, Saturday Schools gave Black children and parents additional support, organisations like NAME spread the word, and in-service education regularly focused on social issues. Pressure from librarians and teachers sent publishers scurrying back to their texts – they scrapped some, like Giles Brandreth's *Here Comes Golly* and the *Oxford Junior Book on Africa*, and re-edited others – the 'greasy Greeks' vanished from Dahl's *The BFG* and the gollys from Noddy. Books that were inclusive were eagerly sought as a market was perceived for them (Klein, 1985). Now textbooks are more inclusive and authors like Malorie Blackman and Benjamin Zephaniah are mainstream.

For sections of the school population, however, little changed, as attested by the decades of commentary and the contributions to this book. In 2005 the DfES tells us that Caribbean boys are more than three times more likely than their peers to be excluded from school. They are still disproportionately in the bottom streams in a system which is now so driven by league tables that in some schools streaming starts in Reception. We learn from the Commission for Racial Equality that schools have been the slowest of all public institutions to fulfil their statutory duties under the Race Relations (Amendment) Act of 2000.

In its 2005 survey the TTA finds it 'encouraging' that the percentage of newly qualified teachers perceiving that 'their training had prepared them to teach pupils from minority ethnic backgrounds' has crept from 30 percent to 35 percent. But, like the Department for Education and Skills (DfES), it expresses concern about the issues. Initially the TTA focused on recruiting more ethnic minority teachers. Research (eg Callendar, 1997) suggests that Black teachers can indeed make a difference because of their teaching style. The TTA successfully met their target in 2004. But recruitment is only half of it – what matters as much is retention. And in this they have been less successful. The explanation may lie partly in career progression – ethnic minority teachers are disproportionately on the lowest pay scale, and remain there longer (Osler, 1997).

Even were there many more Black teachers, their job is to teach, not to act as role models – although this may be a plus – and certainly not to be the sole advocates for giving Black pupils the same opportunities as white pupils. That is the duty of all teachers, even though white teachers often try to put the responsibility for anything to do with race on the shoulders of Black colleagues (see Pearce, 2005).

Most training institutions deal with equality in a day, or just one session, or not at all. There are exceptions, and not all of those have high proportions of minority students. But the body of knowledge that built up in the 1980s, the cascade of knowledge created by Professor Maurice Craft's Training the Trainers programme set up in the wake of the Swann report, *Education for All* (1985), and the Eggleston report, *Education for Some* (1986), melted away under the shifts in education instigated by the New Right in the late 1980s and still largely informing government policy now.

The past 34 years have seen two changes which we now need to build upon. One is the documented knowledge about what improves the educational provision and therefore the life chances of Black children. Race and education feature regularly in professional and academic journals, and two are devoted entirely to the subject. The General Teaching Council has used its Connect network to set up ACHIEVE, a network for Black professionals promoting race equality in schools.

In her chapter here, Heidi Mirza singles out Maud Blair's work on 'Making a Difference', which informed the DfES Aiming High programmes recently rolled out across England. And that is the second significant change: the pilot interventionist programmes supported by the DfES's Aiming High, and local initiatives such as the City Challenge. Excellence in Cities – now ended – had a measurable effect and was important in putting learning mentors into schools (see Cruddas, 2005). That such projects have had some success is borne out by the DfES figures published in 2005. They show that rather more Black children are obtaining good grades – 27.3 percent of Black Caribbean boys got five or more passes at GCSE compared to 21.9 percent in 2002. But this is still shocking when we compare it to the national average – which is 47 percent.

This statistic suggests that interventions which in one way or another make more appropriate educational provision for Black pupils do indeed raise their attainment at school. But the statistic also shows up the initiatives as being too scattered and too sporadic to change the culture of all the schools attended by Black children. Short term interventions allow teachers to default after a project finishes, to a culture of low expectations and stereo-typed views – as identified by Coard in 1971 and confirmed in this collection. And to expect newly qualified teachers coping with the demands of their first job to delve for information in the welter of literature and government information is unrealistic, if not ridiculous.

It is all too little and it starts too late. To employ a medical metaphor, it treats a few of the patients lucky enough to be in the care of the right NHS Trust – where many do get better – while the epidemic of inadequate provision continues the demise of decent life chances for the rest. Measures such as the 'catch-up coaching' for Black boys mooted for 2005-2006 (*Times Educational Supplement,* 26.8.2005) are just the latest example of this approach, tackling the boys and not the system.

We have some understanding of what happens when white trainees and beginning teachers are not given relevant training, thanks to the research of Russell Jones (1997) and others (eg Gaine, 2005, Pearce, 2005). They are likely to take a position that 'I treat all children the same'; 'They're all children to me – I don't see their colour.' Jones researched white student teachers, all of them convinced that their intentions were of the best and that they themselves were certainly not racist. But they filled the vacuum in their training in various unhelpful ways. A student who looked to the class teacher for guidance on how to help a Black pupil who appeared not to be learning told Jones that 'he's as thick as pigshit', because that's what the teacher told her. Another student informed him that there were no ethnic minority pupils in her placement class, and when he said he had noticed at least three, she explained that their parents were 'professional people', conflating, as is so common, 'colour' and 'problem'.

Can students be blamed for these views? We all have to make sense of our world, and these students had no preparation for teaching a diverse population. Race equality was dealt with in, at best, a half day. Mostly it was glossed over as part of a general lecture on equality. It seems that tutors were either insensitive, inadequately informed or hampered by the brevity of their slot, as some students found the session 'counterproductive' (as above). For whatever reason, it left a vacuum in the new teachers' understanding of their job. And if they found themselves in schools that fail to respect and nurture Black children, they were left with nothing but stereotypical views of their Black pupils. Nothing in their training had taught them to think otherwise.

The TTA needs to start putting this right. It even has a good idea of what beginning teachers need to know. Its document of 2000 identifies the areas in which teachers need to become informed and/or take action – areas that have scarcely changed since the Multi-Ethnic Inspectorate of the Inner London Education Authority created an *Aide Memoire* in 1981 to help them clarify the issues they should be looking at in the ILEA's schools. The same issues feature in a book in a series for student teachers published in the 1990s. They are: policies; whole-school issues and school ethos; curriculum; pedagogy – teaching and learning styles; home-school liaison; learning resources; assessment (Klein, 1993). These were taken further in the book that sold 24,000 copies, developed under the auspices of the Runnymede Trust when Robin Richardson was its director, *Equality Assurance in Schools: Quality, Identity, Society* (1993), and Richardson and others are still publishing new insights and wisdom on education and racial equality.

The sections of the TTA's *Raising the Attainment of Minority Ethnic Pupils: Guidance and Resource Materials for Providers of Initial Teacher Training* (2000) follow the familiar, useful model:

1 including all pupils: setting the context
2 the ethos and practices of the school
3 an inclusive curriculum
4 effective language and learning support for pupils for whom English is an additional language
5 understanding social, cultural and religious issues
6 the Early Years
7 teaching refugee pupils
8 effective liaison with parents and other carers
9 effective links between the school and the wider community
10 good practice in the recruitment, retention and support of minority ethnic trainee teachers
11 useful references and organisations

Five years later this could still stand as the framework for a compulsory and assessed unit on race equality to be taught by all ITT providers across Britain. But there is no such unit.

The reasons can only be guessed at: overcrowded curriculum; lack of will; lack of knowledge among teacher training providers; lack of assessors...What is certain is that when the TTA first invited bids for a programme of provision of knowledge about race to be provided in all teacher training institutions, some of the bids were based on offering a team who could effectively teach these matters in institutions across the country.

This did not happen. Instead the DfES and TTA opted for a web-based programme, Multiverse. Multiverse is not under criticism here – my concern is that the TTA has offered it *instead* of specific training at initial level. It seems to be claiming that making relevant information accessible is all that is needed to put an end to decades of teacher training that sells Black pupils short. But Multiverse can never be more than a useful and accessible resource for teachers and trainees who wish to inform themselves on a range of relevant issues, perhaps to do with Traveller pupils or racist bullying – or racially differentiated exclusions.

However strongly it develops, Multiverse does not fill the vacuum in initial teacher training. And until that is done, white beginning teachers will mostly fill it with stereotypical thinking in place of understanding and professionalism. Only a fortunate few pupils will benefit from the informed and targeted programmes that do indeed raise Black children's academic attainment – in certain schools in certain areas. For the rest, the majority, it will be just as it has been for over 34 years: Black pupils and students will continue to be failed by 'the British School System'.

References

M Blair and J Bourne, *Making the Difference: Teaching and Learning in Successful Multi-Ethnic Schools* (Sudbury, DfES and Open University Press, 1998).

C Callendar, *Education for Empowerment: the Practice and Philosophies of Black Teachers* (Stoke on Trent, Trentham, 1997).

L Cruddas, *Learning Mentors in Schools: Principles and Practice* (Stoke on Trent, Trentham, 2005).

DES, *Education for All – the Education of Children from Ethnic Minority Groups* (London, HMSO, 1985).

DfES, *Aiming High: Raising the Achievement of African-Caribbean Pupils* (London, DfES, 2003).

DfES, *Ethnicity and Education: the Evidence on Minority Ethnic Pupils* (RTP01-05) (Nottingham, DfES Publications, 2005).

J Eggleston, D K Dunn and M Anjali, *Education for Some: the Educational and Vocational Experiences of 15-18 Year Old Members of Ethnic Minority Groups* (Stoke on Trent, Trentham, 1986).

C Gaine, *We're All White Thanks* (Stoke on Trent, Trentham, 2005 forthcoming).

R Jones, *Teaching Racism – or Tackling it? Multicultural Stories from White Beginning Teachers* (Stoke on Trent, Trentham, 1999).

G Klein, *Reading into Racism: Bias in Children's Literature and Learning Materials* (London, Routledge and Kegan Paul, 1985).

G Klein, *Education Towards Race Equality* (London, Cassell, 1993).

A Osler, *The Education and Careers of Black Teachers: Changing Identities, Changing Lives* (Buckingham, Open University Press, 1997).

S Pearce, *YOU Wouldn't Understand – White Teachers in Multiethnic Classrooms* (Stoke on Trent, Trentham).

R Richardson, *Here, There and Everywhere: Belonging, Identity and Equality in Schools* (Stoke on Trent, Trentham, 2004).

Runnymede Trust, *Equality Assurance in Schools: Quality, Identity, Society* (Trentham Books with the Runnymede Trust, 1993).

T Sewell, *Black Masculinities and Schooling: How Black Boys Survive Modern Schooling* (Stoke on Trent, Trentham, 1997).

TTA, *Raising the Attainment of Minority Ethnic Pupils: Guidance and Resource Materials for Providers of Teacher Training* (London, TTA, 2000).

www.multiverse.ac.uk

www.teach-tta.gov.uk

● Gillian Klein is co-founder and director of Trentham Books and editor of the termly journal *Race Equality Teaching*. During her 20 years with the ILEA she also worked to further racial equality in education. In the 1990s she lectured at Warwick and Middlesex Universities' initial teacher education departments. Gillian has written widely for children, and for teachers and librarians. Her latest book, which she co-edited with Penny Travers, is *Equal Measures: Bilingual and Ethnic Minority Pupils in Secondary Schools*.

Terry Wrigley

A common struggle

MANY CONTRIBUTIONS to this book have rightly focused on issues specific to African-Caribbean communities. Of course we need to investigate solutions that address the specific needs of African-Caribbean boys. Yet clearly there are some issues which interact with the way our education system is failing other sections of society, notably Asian Muslims and also many children of white manual working class parents. Understanding common problems can help us engage with others in a common struggle over shared issues. These include:

- segregation into 'lower-ability' classes and different schools
- attitudes to language
- the marginalisation of community culture
- a standardised curriculum
- patterns of teaching and learning
- exclusions

It is important to recognise that all of these occur in a context of government policies which are standardising schooling at the expense of diversity, speeding it up in the name of improvement, and increasingly subordinating it to the demands of employers rather than community needs.

Segregation

Bernard Coard made many of us realise that schools were actively producing 'subnormality' by labelling Black students and dumping them in special schools. The situation was a disgrace. Racial discrimination was disguised as a psychological problem – a classic case of institutional racism while blaming the victim.

We can see similar patterns at work with other minorities. For many years Pakistani and Bangladeshi students were segregated into special language units, which actually delayed them in learning English. When reintegrated into the mainstream school, they were often placed in 'low ability' classes and fed a dulled-down curriculum leading to minimal qualifications.

Segregation on the pretext of providing a more fitting education has been the traditional fate of working class students. Before comprehensive schools were set up, most were placed in low-status secondary modern schools, and then sent off to work at 14. Many of the early comprehensives were organised into streams and bands which largely coincided with divisions of class and colour.

Teachers, unions and enlightened education authorities struggled to overcome these forms of segregation. They were never fully abolished, but Blair's government is actively restoring them. It is supposedly more efficient, but the research evidence is contradictory: in general, it shows little effect either way on the majority but a risk of demoralisation for lower groups.[1] Nowadays even five year olds are being divided up like this under pressure to push up school test scores. New Labour has perpetuated the competitive market between schools, established under Thatcher, allowing parents who can exert the most influence to get their children into higher-performing schools, and building a concentration of poverty in other schools.

Such practices trap the majority of African-Caribbean and Asian students – and most children of manual and unemployed workers, however white their skins – in a steep-sided hole. Wherever children are divided by 'ability', teacher prejudice of one kind or another – clothing, behaviour, accents, and more seriously religion, colour and class – begins to play a part in the selection process. Any cultural gap between children or teenagers and their teachers can lead to misplaced judgements about intellectual inferiority.

In fact, such divisions actively produce low ability, reinforcing the stereotypes and therefore seeming to justify them. They isolate struggling pupils from those who have travelled more, read more books and acquired academic styles of English. Lower classes endure a more tedious curriculum with less challenge, less discussion, less problem-solving and more dull exercises. No wonder they are more likely to produce sullen and discontented or disruptive pupils.

Language

The notion of 'language deficit' appeared in the 1960s as an explanation of underachievement in schools. It was first applied to Caribbean Creoles, but soon after to white urban working class dialects. Crude judgements were made based on linguistic ignorance. For example, sentences with double negatives (I didn't see nobody), or with 'is' or 'are' omitted, were declared not only bad grammar but also *illogical* – though nobody made these comments about French or Russian, which do the same. Wiser linguists understood that Creoles and Cockneys also have grammars, only different ones.

Some concerned white liberals argued that Black students and manual workers' children didn't have a language for rational thinking. William Labov[2] in New York, interviewing young people on the streets of Harlem, proved that they did, while Harold Rosen[3] in London pointed to the rich political debate of the Docklands and the mining towns.

For many years it had been normal for schools to keep anything but Standard English strictly outside the gate. Fierce debate arose when radicals in the 1970s insisted that Creole and Cockney were just as valid, and Standard English was only one dialect among many. John Richmond and his colleagues in Lambeth[4] agreed but equally realised the force of prejudice: Black and white working class students would face serious disadvantage without competence in Standard English, both spoken and written. He argued, however, that this could only be achieved on the basis of respect for their other forms of speech and encouraging its use for school learning.

Building on this, more enlightened teachers encouraged bilingual Asian children to discuss in pairs in Punjabi or Bengali before presenting their ideas to the class in English. More progressive schools in the USA showed that Hispanics make most progress when Spanish and English are both used in the classroom[5] – an arrangement which the Bush government is desperate to stop.

Marginalisation of cultures

As Heidi Mirza argues elsewhere in this collection, multiculturalism has often been shallow – a tokenistic celebration of 'steelbands, saris and samosas' and a show of religious symbols. Traditional culture was frozen and dynamic fusions were overlooked. More than this, multicultural education often stopped short of challenging racism.

The marginalisation in schools of family patterns and lifestyles, neighbourhoods, jobs, music, interests, skills, stories – the rich complexity of popular culture – has long affected working class communities. Richard Hoggart, Terry Eagleton, Tony Harrison[6] all tell, in their different ways, how they were offered school success only if they turned their backs on neighbourhood and friends. We do not even have a word equivalent to *multicultural* to describe a curriculum with respect for English working class life. Its history, culture and concerns are simply not considered. For Black communities it was even more extreme: it amounted to wiping out their entire cultural history at precisely the moment in young people's lives when questions of identity are of paramount importance. When schools shut out their students' culture, whether this is brass bands or bangra, reggae or rock guitar, in the name of a higher learning, students quickly pick up the message that they are worthless. Many fight back by rejecting school learning altogether.

There are sufficient examples of community schools and projects to show that learning is enriched and achievement rises when schools build on the lives and interests of the neighbourhood. There is a rich harvest when parents bring into the school their cooking, drumming and gardening, their travels and their songs, their stories and their struggles. This is the challenge whenever communities are at a distance from the orthodox school curriculum.

The standardisation of the school curriculum

The issues described in the previous section were around before the National Curriculum was imposed, but many teachers, especially in London and other larger cities, were beginning to develop a more relevant and responsive curriculum. African history, the Indian and Islamic heritage in mathematics, songs and stories from diverse cultures entered the mix.

At a deeper level, teachers began to raise questions about power: Columbus and his 'discovery' of America; the slave trade and the struggle to end slavery; the Irish potato famine. They began to realise that it is the victors who write history, and started to challenge dominant accounts by providing alternative perspectives. This challenge of perspective equally applies to class power.

The school curriculum is only ever a selection from knowledge and culture – but the selection is heavily influenced by the most powerful and highest status sections of society. The Thatcher government imposed the National Curriculum to reassert the dominance of a ruling class vision: its view of history, national heritage, the empire. At the same time, science and technology were taught without considering their impact on our lives. Other voices were unheard.

New Labour has in many ways tightened control, but it is up to teachers and communities whether it stays that way. It takes time and energy, but it is possible to subvert the government's intentions. This desire led to the successful inaugural conference, in March 2005, of Rethinking Education (www.rethinkinged.org.uk). For this movement to succeed, an alliance is needed of teachers, students, parents and communities. We should insist on a wider view of what is worthwhile knowledge, and the need for young people to engage in critical debate about the troubled world they live in.

Teaching and learning

Instead of building up active and engaged forms of learning, New Labour has promoted methods which require energetic young people to sit and listen endlessly. Recent studies of the Literacy Hour, for example, show that pupils rarely speak except in answer to questions – they never ask questions themselves – and usually only for one or two words.[7]

This style of learning fails to develop the voice and judgement of young people. For others, the enforced passivity leads to frustration and rage. Increasingly, those who cannot stand this environment are labelled hyperactive and drugged on ritalin.[8] It is not surprising that teenagers who enjoy the most vibrant street culture are most often excluded.

Meanwhile government advice insists on discipline and order. Education secretary Ruth Kelly has called for 'zero tolerance' – the policy which, on America's streets, has resulted in young Black men being jailed for petty offences. Schools clearly cannot work well if they are in chaos, and violence brings misery for all, but a good working atmosphere can only be sustained where there is respect, not repression. All marginalised young people, whether African-Caribbeans, Asian Muslims, or white working class adolescents, need learning which engages their interest and makes heavy discipline redundant. There are many ways of learning which give young people a sense of voice and agency: drama and role play, writing and presenting to real audiences, solving real-life problems, using video to highlight all kinds of injustice and demand a change.

Exclusions

Statistics show beyond a doubt that African-Caribbean students are the most likely to suffer exclusion from schools. Racism is a key explanation for exclusion of Black boys. It means that Black boys are more likely to be expelled for things that many white boys can get away with. At the same time, we have to understand the wider context in which this is happening.

The introduction of national testing and a competitive market between schools led to a dramatic increase in school exclusions. Permanent exclusions among all young people increased 450 percent from 1990 to 1995.[9] This was not because behaviour suddenly got worse, but because head-teachers felt under pressure to get rid of low performing students or those whose problems were taking up too much time.

The rate of exclusions is not spread evenly across all social groups, and African-Caribbean boys suffer particular discrimination, but it is part of a wider pattern of inequality. In Scotland, in a mainly white population, fixed-term exclusions are very high among pupils on free meals (a rough measure of social class). Exclusions increase fourfold between the last year of primary and the first year of secondary. This should lead us to question the way schools are organised. Is it really sensible for adolescents, many with unstable home lives, to be herded from room to room between a dozen different teachers? Many secondary school teachers see so many faces in a week that they can scarcely remember their names. Research in the USA has shown the benefit of smaller schools that are organised so that a class faces fewer different teachers, particularly for Black, Hispanic and poorer students.[10]

Respect and resistance

This book celebrates the publication of Bernard Coard's provocative and challenging pamphlet. Sadly, we are also nearing another anniversary. It is almost 20 years since Gus John, an African-Caribbean community education worker in Manchester, was asked to investigate[11] the murder of a Pakistani schoolboy by a white teenager in their school playground. Though the city council tried to suppress it, the report was published as *Murder in the Playground*. It put blame, of course, on the pervasive racism which this troubled white boy had picked up. It also blamed the school, and the education authority, for a tokenistic multiculturalism, rather than a policy to challenge racism and other forms of discrimination. A school culture had been allowed to develop in which it was common for African-Caribbean students to gang up with whites against young Asians. Finally the report blamed the city's equal opportunities policy which had identified various kinds of disadvantage but failed to recognise the needs of poor white working class boys!

The situation we face today is even more dangerous than then. Poverty is greater, and communities have suffered chronically. Schools are less free to design a curriculum which will engage young people. Youth drinking and drug abuse are more widespread. On top of this, since the Iraq war, Muslims feel particularly threatened but there is a serious risk that xenophobia and racism will blight other communities.

We cannot allow this situation to go unchecked. We need to build up a resistance to the way this government is running education, and the country overall. The long history of struggle of African-Carribbean communities has much to teach all of us who desire to build that resistance. We will stand together, or we will fall separately.

Notes

1   J Ireson and S Hallam, *Ability Grouping in Education* (London, Chapman, 2001).
2   W Labov, 'The Logic of Non-Standard English', republished in P Giglioli (ed), *Language and Social Context* (1969), and various other collections.
3   H Rosen, *Language and Class: a Critical Look at the Theories of Basil Bernstein* (Bristol, Falling Wall Press, 1972).
4   S Eyers and J Richmond (eds), *Becoming our own Experts: Studies of Language and Learning* (The Talk Workshop Group, Vauxhall Manor School, 1982).
5   J Cummins, *Language, Power and Pedagogy: Bilingual Children in the Crossfire* (Clevedon, Multilingual Matters, 2000).
6   R Hoggart, *The Uses of Literacy* (Chatto and Windus, 1957); T Eagleton, *The Gatekeeper: a Memoir* (Allen Lane, 2001); T Harrison, *Selected Poems* (Penguin, 1984).
7   See, for example, M Mroz et al, 'The Discourse of the Literacy Hour', *Cambridge Journal of Education*, 30(3) (2000).
8   G Lloyd et al, *Critical New Perspectives on ADHD* (RoutledgeFalmer, 2005).
9   National Children's Home, 'NCH Factfile 2000', in P Mittler, *Working Towards Inclusive Education* (Fulton, 2000).
10 The best starting point is probably www.schoolredesign.net
11 As well as Gus John, the inquiry team consisted of Lily Khan, Reena Bhavnani and Ian Macdonald QC. The Burnage Report was published as *Murder in the Playground* (Longsight Press, London, 1989).

●   Terry Wrigley is a senior lecturer in education at the University of Edinburgh. He edits the journal *Improving Schools*, and is author of two books, *The Power to Learn* (2000) and *Schools of Hope* (2003). He is a member of the Scottish Socialist Party and active in the anti-war movement. Following the establishment of the Rethinking Education network, he has just written *Another School is Possible*, to be published by Bookmarks.

Peter Hick

Still missing out: minority ethnic communities and special educational needs

Introduction

In 1971 Bernard Coard exposed the disproportionate placement of immigrant children in special schools for the 'Educationally Subnormal' (pupils with 'moderate learning difficulties' in today's terminology). Today's issues of institutional racism in the ways children from Black and minority ethnic (BME) communities are identified as having special educational needs (SEN) are different. But many children from a number of BME communities are still missing out on important educational opportunities – either by being disproportionately labelled as having SEN, or by having their needs overlooked.

Ethnicity and SEN: the issues today

In what ways are children from BME communities still missing out in terms of special educational needs? The Department for Education and Skills (DfES) recently started collecting data on individual pupils' attainment, using particular categories of ethnicity and SEN. A preliminary analysis of the first year's data[1] highlights a number of key findings, for example:

- Permanent exclusion rates are higher for Travellers of Irish Heritage, Gypsy/Roma, Black Caribbean, Black Other and White/Black Caribbean pupils.
- Black Caribbean and Black Other boys are twice as likely to have been categorised as having behavioural, emotional or social difficulty as 'White British' boys.
- Pupils with English as an additional language are slightly less likely to be identified with SEN and are less likely to be classified as having a specific learning difficulty [eg dyslexia]. However, they are more likely to have an identified speech, language or communication need.
- Pakistani pupils are two to five times more likely than White British pupils to have an identified visual impairment or hearing impairment.
- Gypsy/Roma pupils and Travellers of Irish Heritage have very low attainment through Key Stage assessments and also have much higher identification of SEN.

These findings are based on special educational needs identified by schools, a process called 'School Action Plus', or by local authorities, through 'Statements' of SEN.

Background

How does it happen that children from some BME communities are discriminated against, or treated less favourably, when their teachers are not racist? In order to understand how a process of insitutional racism can lead to an over- or under-identification of SEN in BME communities, we need to recognise the role of special educational needs categories in an administrative process for rationing resources.

Some children do experience difficulties in learning, and parents and teachers may seek to identify them as having SEN in order to access additional resources for them. But SEN are defined in relative terms: a child's needs are 'special' if they require more support than is usually available to other children.[2] But how much is more? In practice this can vary between schools, and between local authorities, influenced by local policies, resources and patterns of provision, together with levels of social disadvantage. There may be variations between schools in the level of needs they support within their own resources, and when they access outside agencies as 'School Action Plus'; and between local authorities in the proportion of children with 'Statements' of SEN and the criteria used to progress from 'School Action Plus' to 'Statements'. The legal definition of

SEN is not based on an objective, uniformly applied measurement or diagnosis of 'need'.

It is important to understand that the various categories of SEN are assigned to individual children through a social process. For example:

At what point does the disaffection and underachievement of a Black Caribbean boy at a secondary school, who is increasingly resisting schooling (possibly as a result of what he sees as a racist experience), become an emotional or cognitive need, recognised as a special educational need meriting necesary additional resources organised by the SENCo [SEN Coordinator]?[3]

A 'social model' of disability describes SEN categories such as 'moderate learning difficulties', or 'behavioural, emotional or social difficulties', together with medical diagnoses such as ADHD (Attention Deficit Hyperactivity Disorder) as labels that serve to pathologise children.[4] They tend to focus attention on individual children's difficulties rather than on how well schools support them, or on social disadvantage. The way in which individual differences between children are defined, so that some are categorised as having 'special educational needs', is socially constructed.[5] Assessment tools such as IQ[6] tend to reflect social and educational inequalities, based on social class and ethnicity.

SEN and school exclusion

The issue of school exclusion is dealt with elsewhere in this book, so I will discuss it only briefly here. Black Caribbean boys who are identified as having SEN are particularly vulnerable to being excluded from school. Pupils with 'Statements' of SEN were nine times more likely to be excluded from school than those with no SEN in 2002/3. Figures for the same year show the highest exclusion rate by ethnic group was for Black Caribbean pupils, at 37 per 1,000, over three times the rate of white pupils excluded.[7]

However, there was a sharp decline from 1997/8 (76 per 1,000) for Black Caribbean exclusions, while figures for other BME communities remained relatively stable.[8] The evidence shows that some schools exclude at much higher rates than others with comparable populations, and that those that exclude more children tend to exclude disproportionately more BME children.[9] Recent research has highlighted examples of more positive approaches.[10]

Pupils with English as an additional language

There is evidence of a tendency among professionals to overlook specific learning difficulties[11] such as dyslexia in pupils with English as an additional language, and to misinterpret literacy difficulties as signs of general (moderate) learning difficulties. Equally, some children with English as an additional language may be incorrectly identified as having speech and language difficulties.[12] In the first case, children may be denied access to the specific support they need, as a result of ethnicity or language heritage. In the second case, pupils may be labelled as having SEN and denied access to appropriate support for their language development in English. In both cases, learners from minority ethnic communities are missing out on important educational entitlements and opportunities. These outcomes seem to reflect a lack of resources allocated to the needs of pupils with English as an additional language, which can be seen as a consequence of institutional racism.[13] There is a need for sustained research to develop culturally appropriate and locally referenced assessment instruments, together with much better training for teachers and other professionals.

Sensory impairments and learning difficulties in South Asian populations

There is a higher incidence of learning difficulties and sensory impairments among some communities of Pakistani and Bangladeshi descent in the UK, that is sometimes thought to relate to inter-family marriage practices. However, a recent authoritative literature review for the Department of Health pointed out that 'in the case of learning difficulties consanguinity [first-cousin marriages] has effectively been ruled out as a single explanation',[14] and concluded:

> The prevalence of learning difficulties in South Asians aged between five and 32 is up to three times higher than in other communities... The evidence points to a well established link between socio-economic deprivation and the prevalence of mild or moderate learning difficulties...The link is reflected in lower income, poorer housing, higher unemployment and a greater reliance on welfare benefits. Some evidence of a link between severe learning difficulties and poverty has been reported...[15]

The cumulative impact of poverty and multiple disadvantage on South Asian families caring for a child with a disability has been well documented, and is often compounded by reduced access to specialist health and social services.[16] Both communities and professionals may make ill-informed assumptions that can create further barriers to accessing support. There also seems to be a higher proportion of Pakistani pupils in special schools for children with severe learning difficulties, and one explanation for this is that some parents are less well placed to negotiate more inclusive provision. Yet there is evidence that parents from some minority ethnic communities tend to take a relatively strong interest in their children's education.[17]

Towards inclusive schools

There are a number of government initiatives that are currently beginning to address some of the issues highlighted here. For example, the DfES does recognise institutional racism as an issue[18] and Ofsted has highlighted examples of good practice in schools.[19] Yet the statistical evidence relating to disproportionality or underachievement, for example, cannot be fully understood in isolation from knowledge of the social, historical and cultural legacies of particular minority ethnic communities. The solutions lie not only in supporting more inclusive practices in schools and local authority services, important though such initiatives are.

Institutional racism is a reflection of the society in which the institutions develop, and a society with deeply embedded social inequalities cannot hope to achieve equality in education without broader social change. A competitive education system in a society divided by social class plays a part in the reproduction of social inequality by ethnicity and by special educational needs. It may be that only a fully comprehensive education system can begin to address the roots of racism experienced by children from BME communities with SEN. An education system that is fully inclusive of children described as having special educational needs will be a truly comprehensive education system.

Notes

1 DfES, *Ethnicity and Education: The Evidence on Minority Ethnic Pupils* (London, DfES, 2005), p2.
2 DfES, *Special Educational Needs: Code of Practice* (London, DfES, 2001).
3 L Gerschel, 'Connecting the Disconnected: Exploring Issues of Gender, "Race" and SEN within an Inclusive Context', in C Tilstone and R Rose (eds), *Strategies to Promote Inclusive Practice* (London, RoutledgeFalmer, 2003), p53.
4 M Oliver, *The Politics of Disablement* (London, Macmillan, 1990).
5 G Thomas and A Loxley, *Deconstructing Special Education and Constructing Inclusion* (Buckingham, OU Press, 2001).
6 M J A Howe, *IQ in Question: the Truth About Intelligence* (London, Sage, 1997).

7   P Babb, J Martin and P Haezewindt, *Focus: Social Inequalities* (2004 edn) (Office of National Statistics, London, TSO, 2004).

8   As above.

9   A Osler, *Exclusion from School and Racial Equality* (London, CRE, 1997).

10 M Blair, 'The Education of Black Children: Why do Some Schools do Better than Others?' in M Nind, J Rix, K Sheehy and K Simmons (eds), *Curriculum and Pedagogy in Inclusive Education* (Abingdon, RoutledgeFalmer, 2005)

11 T Cline and T Shamsi, *Language Needs or Special Needs: The Assessment of Learning Difficulties in Literacy Among Children Learning English as an Additional Language: a Literature Review* (London, DfEE Publications, 2000).

12 K Winter, 'Communication Equation: Under- and Over-Representation of Bilingual Children in Speech and Language Therapy Provision' (unpublished PhD thesis, University of Birmingham. 1999).

13 F Diniz, 'Race and Special Educational Needs in the 1990s', in *British Journal of Special Education* 26(4) (1999), pp213-217.

14 G Mir, A Nocon and W Ahmad, with L Jones, *Learning Difficulties and Ethnicity* (London, Department of Health, 2001), p7.

15 As above, p10.

16 W Ahmad (ed), *Ethnicity, Disability and Chronic Illness* (Buckingham, Open University, 2000); R Shah, 'Learning Disability and Ethnic Minorities', guest editorial in *Learning Disability Bulletin*, no 132, Spring 2004 (Kidderminster, British Institute of Learning Disabilities).

17 DfES, *Ethnicity and Education: The Evidence on Minority Ethnic Pupils* (London, DfES, 2005).

18 DfES, *Aiming High: Raising the Achievement of Minority Ethnic Pupils* (London, DfES, 2003).

19 Ofsted, *Managing the Ethnic Minority Achievement Grant – Good Practice in Primary Schools* (London, 2005, Ofsted); Ofsted, *Managing the Ethnic Minority Achievement Grant – Good Practice in Secondary Schools* (London, Ofsted, 2005).

● I wish to acknowledge my debt to Deirdre Martin at the University of Birmingham in developing my knowledge of the literature in this field.

● Peter Hick is a lecturer in Inclusive Education at the University of Birmingham. He has taught at the University of Manchester, the Open University and Bolton University. After teaching young people with special educational needs in a further education college, he worked as an educational psychologist, often with children from minority ethnic communities. He has been involved in a campaign against racism in Oldham (p.hick@bham.ac.uk).

Stella Dadzie

Further education: a prescription for progress?

When society fails one generation of children, it lays the foundations for similar, even worse, failures in the generations to follow.
Bernard Coard, quoted by Polly Curtis in the *Guardian*, 1 February 2005

SINCE THE 1970s, further education, traditionally the destination of less academic school-leavers seeking vocational qualifications, has attracted growing numbers of Black students who, though not labelled 'ESN', are still euphemistically described in policy documents as 'marginalised', 'underachieving' or 'educationally disadvantaged'. The sector's intake, once predominantly 16-19 year olds, has changed dramatically since the days of the traditional technical college, and now includes adults of all ages as well as young people who are still (officially, at least) in school. So it is arguably the same children who caused Bernard Coard such concern – and their children and grandchildren – who have been walking into colleges ever since, seeking the proverbial second chance.

Some inner city colleges have been grappling with the challenges this presents for decades. Although there are many success stories – Black students who overcame the odds and went on to become chefs, actors, social workers, graphic designers, engineers, nurses, teachers, you name it – it is undeniably true that countless others have been failed as abysmally by FE as they were originally failed by the schools.

It was Coard's contention, back in 1971, that the three factors that cause Black boys to fail were 'low expectations on his part about his likely performance in a white-controlled system of education; low motivation to succeed academically because he feels the cards are stacked against him; and low teacher expectations, which affect the amount of effort expended on his behalf by the teacher and also affect his own image of himself and his abilities.' It would seem that, in the intervening years, little has changed. The fact that there are today more Black men in Britain's jails than in its universities, or that Black women, at most 4 percent of the population, constitute around 40 percent of women in UK prisons,[1] cannot be blamed on colleges alone. Yet these damning statistics suggest that the FE system, originally intended to encourage those who leave school with nothing to achieve something meaningful with their lives, still has a long road to travel where Black people are concerned.

The enlightened college manager would probably argue – and not without justification – that the failure of colleges to dismantle the barriers to Black achievement is not through want of trying. Initiatives targeted at adult learners such as access courses, flexible learning support and the provision of creche facilities have all helped to ease the progress through the system of people who might otherwise have remained an unemployment statistic. Indeed, adult-friendly developments in FE through the 1980s were typically a response to demographic and economic changes that made attracting more 'non-traditional' learners an imperative if colleges were to survive. Falling numbers of 16 to 19 year olds, acute skills shortages in the labour market and the impact of information technology helped to create a new market for those who had previously found their access to FE barred.

The new mantra – entitlement of all to lifelong learning – sounded philanthropic at the time, but its motives were primarily market-driven. The country was in dire need of a skilled workforce, and if this meant encouraging women, ethnic minorities and older adults back to college, colleges would need to learn to accommodate them. Witness the long roll-call of those that failed to see the proverbial writing on the wall, and succumbed to closure or merger as a consequence of their resistance to change. The call for employers, colleges and other learning and skills providers to 'embrace diversity' has similar economic imperatives to this day.

In the context of race relations, there were social incentives, too. The inner city uprisings of the early 1980s created a climate of fear, debate and self-examination, post-Swann, that named institutional racism as a key contributor to Black underachievement years before Macpherson reiterated this finding. The result, in more diverse colleges, was a proliferation of equal opportunities and anti-racist policies, ethnic monitoring requirements, targeted access provision, community outreach and other LEA-sponsored initiatives intended to woo Black adult learners who had been failed by the schools. But as colleges began opening their doors to this strange new breed of student, they were also forced to look afresh at themselves.

It was soon apparent to all but the colleges involved that for the ostriches to be accommodated in chicken houses, so to speak, the roof would need to be raised. The roof, in this context, symbolised not only the structural and procedural inequalities that were built into the fabric of college life, but also the Eurocentric assumptions that permeated the curriculum, and the negative stereotypes that influenced the attitudes and expectations of a predominantly white lecturing staff. Progressive colleagues, still enthused by the heady days of the 1980s when the ILEA and other like-minded education authorities had resourced a plethora of initiatives designed to dismantle the prevailing barriers, saw this kind of overhaul as long overdue. Discrimination was often blatant, both in the classroom and the staffroom. For the majority, however, institutional change proved too challenging and, frankly, not worth the effort. Pleading too few Black students in mainly white areas, or blaming cultural rather than organisational deficits in colleges where there were 'too many', it proved easier to overlook the harsh realities of institutional racism or pretend they didn't exist.

In some respects, the 1990s represented a few years of reprieve. The impact of incorporation, when the 1990 Education Act freed colleges from the constraints of LEA funding and effectively privatised them, meant that race and equality policies could gather dust as managers focused on the only thing that mattered to their college's survival – placing 'bums on seats'. FEFC[2] funding formulas rendered access, ESOL,[3] outreach, childcare and other low earning or non profit making provision particularly vulnerable to cuts, while the Black staff who had found work in these areas were typically last hired, first fired. Effectively abandoned in all but a handful of far-sighted colleges with a genuine commitment to change, the rhetoric of race equality began to sound increasingly hollow. Despite the damning findings of the 1990 *Labour Force Survey* which showed Black unemployment to be up to 60 percent higher than for whites in some areas of the country, courses that were deemed to be economically unviable were closed, while guidance and support services that 'non-traditional' students relied on were withdrawn. Inevitably Black students, who by the early 1990s were disproportionately represented within the FE sector, were also disproportionately affected.

The term 'bums on seats' remains FE-speak for a plethora of cash-related recruitment, retention and achievement incentives that boil down to this: if colleges want to secure a comfortable level of government funding, they must not only attract enough students but also retain them for the duration of the course, ensure maximum attendance and make sure they achieve a meaningful outcome, typically defined as a qualification, a job or progression to HE. This tick-box approach to educational achievement, which the Learning and Skills Council has since perfected, has rarely lent itself to the innovative and sometimes costly responses needed to address the barriers that may impede Black learners. Nor does it encourage recognition of the kind of achievements that are not readily quantified or measured, namely the subtle transformations in confidence and self-esteem that occur when people choose to engage with learning on their own terms.

Black students were not the only casualties of incorporation, yet it is easy to see how these quality assurance mechanisms, designed to eliminate waste and rationalise provision, impacted on their life chances. For a tutor whose very job would sometimes depend on recruiting students who would stay the course and succeed, the risk involved in enrolling anyone who was not a safe bet was often too high. Why consider someone with (according to the stereotype, at least) a poor academic record, no funds, inevitable housing, childcare or language needs, and (if school records are to be believed) a less than helpful attitude to learning, at the expense of a more traditional middle class, white student with a less challenging profile?

With the publication of Helena Kennedy's report *Widening Participation* in 1998,[4] a kind of schizophrenia set in. Despite the funding constraints imposed by the FEFC, colleges were once again being urged to widen their client base and embrace the predominantly market-driven case for doing so. To address their reluctance to do so, a student's postcode became one of several arbitrary criteria for student selection, as complex bureaucratic incentives were introduced to widen participation by attracting punters from the other side of the tracks. Yet keeping hold of these students was problematic, for all the reasons outlined. The ostriches were still being crammed into chicken houses.

There would always be those who survived *despite* rather than because of the system. For them, it seems, the fundamental belief in education as a route out of poverty prevailed, despite the hurdles. Nevertheless Black under-retention and under-achievement, as evidenced in colleges and schools where ethnic monitoring was taken seriously enough to warrant analysis, were embarrassing facts of life – this despite years of fine-sounding policies that claimed to offer *all* students equality of access, opportunity and outcome, regardless of their race, culture, ethnicity, nationality or citizenship.

In the wake of Macpherson's report with its revival of far from new debates about institutional racism in the public sector, many colleges could no longer ignore the fact that they were failing in their mission to provide their Black students with the promised second chance. Indeed, FE was the only public sector body to take Macpherson on the chin and initiate an immediate commission of inquiry into the extent of institutional racism within the sector. The Commission for Black Staff in FE spent the next two years gathering witness evidence and commissioning research. Its findings, published in November 2002, were only too predictable. Perhaps it was fear of what would be unearthed if it focused on learners that led the decision-makers to restrict the commission's investigations to the area of employment. Nevertheless its report revealed widespread racial discrimination across the sector, and proved a damning indictment of 25 years of race equality policies in UK colleges (see Appendix).

Although the commission's remit was to look at the situation of Black staff, it did manage to highlight some significant findings for students. Among them was LSC data showing that, despite a significant improvement in recent years, 'minority ethnic students are still underachieving in comparison to their white counterparts, with all minority ethnic groups attaining lower grades...' Unpacked, this confirmed what had hitherto been mostly anecdotal evidence that, 30 years after Coard, a disproportionate number of Black students previously failed by their schools are continuing to underachieve in colleges.

It would be wrong to suggest that the picture is uniform, or that the fault lies entirely with the colleges. Alongside institutional and structural racism, worship of the material, peer pressure and the impact of a popular culture that promotes the ugliest of racial stereotypes all play a role in the complex picture of Black under-attainment that emerges. Some colleges have recognised this. They may be the exception to the rule, but they are evidence that it is possible to establish dynamic community partnerships, and bring about the changes in ethos and delivery that encourage Black students to excel.

So is there a prescription for progress? Post-the Race Relations (Amendment) Act, the official line is impressive. The impact of the new legislation, with its specific duties on colleges to declare their anti-racist colours and conduct regular monitoring and impact assessment has certainly elevated race equality to the realms of strategic planning, if only to comply with the law. Inspection and review both focus on the expectation that it is college governors and senior managers who are ultimately responsible for the delivery of this elusive dream. Although it is a far from uniform picture, colleges are learning the language, if not the delivery, of race equality. Staff training days are abuzz with activities designed to challenge stereotypical attitudes and encourage more positive attitudes towards ethnic diversity. Many hours are now spent developing race equality policies, action plans, targets and performance indicators.

Yet curiously some managers, skilled as they are in quality assurance, insist that in this area alone they remain novices. Their excuses – cultural and language barriers, curricular and resource constraints, the lack of suitable BME candidates for jobs, etc – are well rehearsed and repeated ad nauseam. In some boardrooms – not to mention classrooms and workshops – it is almost as if the debates about institutional racism that have plagued education since Coard's seminal publication had never occurred. Meanwhile, a whole body of good practice that has been built up in the intervening years is ignored.

A quarter of a century of race relations legislation has made only the smallest of dents in the vicious circle of low expectations and underachievement that Coard and subsequently Swann and Macpherson helped to expose. It remains doubtful whether laws alone will initiate the changes that are needed for this scenario to be permanently reversed.

If the law is a paper tiger, other responses may be called for. But why reinvent the wheel? The necessary changes – and by implication, the components of any prescription for progress – are much the same as they were when Coard spelt them out in the early 1970s. Arguably, they involve the same radical reassessment of what is taught; the same far-reaching attitudinal changes in those who teach and manage the curriculum; and the same structural changes in society that would enable Black students who do achieve to access the jobs they are qualified for. With Black graduates twice as likely to be unemployed as their white counterparts, there may be little incentive for Black people without degrees to choose the FE route. Like their embattled tutors, they may wonder whether it is worth the investment of time and effort. In 2005 they are still more likely to encounter Black catering and security staff than Black principals and lecturers, and to be disciplined or excluded when they are deemed to have misbehaved. Yet their numbers continue to grow, and according to recent LSC data twice as many go to college as enter the job market on leaving school.

Whether the new legal context has given rise to cosmetic or profound changes remains to be seen. Colleges are learning the rhetoric of race equality by heart, but they have yet to demonstrate that they have embraced its practice. This will occur when they have understood the importance of moving beyond policy statements to engage in a genuine dialogue with their Black staff and students. Despite the persistent labels, they are better placed than anyone to suggest what needs to be done. Should this dialogue ever take place, they will undoubtedly reiterate Coard's observation that, however well intended, any solutions to the deep-rooted, structural problems that prevail in the FE system will not be resolved until college managers, entrusted in law with the task, learn to act 'in tandem with those from below'.

Appendix:
Commission for Black staff in FE – summary of 2001 findings

Leadership and management

- A survey of 270 members of the clerks' network revealed that, of the 134 colleges responding, only 8 percent of governors and one corporation clerk were Black.
- 58 colleges (43 percent of those surveyed) had no Black governors at all.
- There were only four Black principals of mainstream colleges, constituting less than 1 percent of the cohort.
- At senior managerial level, fewer than 3 percent of staff were from ethnic minority groups.
- The Further Education Funding Council revealed that in 2001 there were only two full-time Black inspectors (3 percent) and no senior Black inspectors.

Staff qualifications and status

- 55 percent of minority ethnic staff in further education had been educated to first degree level compared with 49 percent of white staff.
- 6 percent of minority ethnic staff had no formal qualifications compared with 8 percent of white staff were similarly unqualified.
- In contracted positions, Black staff were three times more likely than white staff to be employed in security posts.
- Black lecturers are concentrated in continuing education, including basic skills and English for speakers of other languages and, to a lesser extent, in maths and science.

Employment policies and procedures

A specially commissioned national survey showed that:
- Fewer than half (42 percent) of further education colleges always used formal recruitment procedures when appointing part-time hourly paid teaching staff.
- Fewer than one in five of colleges nationally use target setting to address the under-representation of Black staff.
- Only 15 percent of colleges set targets for the employment and progression of Black staff.
- Only 53 percent of colleges were making use of ethnic monitoring data
- Fewer than half of all colleges (45 percent) had organised specific equality training programmes for staff.
- 6 percent of colleges nationally did not have an equal opportunities policy and only 6 percent of colleges had a specific race equality policy
- Only 18 percent of colleges have specific equality policies or criteria relating to redundancies and/or restructuring.

Student numbers

- The percentage of minority ethnic students in further education in England increased from 12 percent in 1997-1998 to 14 percent in 1999-2000.
- Four fifths of young people from minority ethnic groups remain in the education system compared with just over two thirds of white young people.
- 22 percent of white FE students live in deprived areas. The proportion of students from minority ethnic groups living in disadvantaged areas is far higher – 76 percent for Black Africans, 73 percent for Bangladeshis and 67 percent for African-Caribbeans.

Student achievement

LSC data showed that minority ethnic students were still underachieving in comparison to their white counterparts, with all minority ethnic groups attaining lower grades despite a marked improvement in achievement for all minority ethnic groups.

Notes

1   See *Home Office Crime Survey*, 2001.
2   The Further Education Funding Council, which was replaced in 2000 by the Learning and Skills Council.
3   English as a second or other language, now more likely to be referred to as English as an additional language (EAL).
4   See H Kennedy QC, *Learning Works: Widening Participation in Further Education* (FEFC, 1997).

- Stella Dadzie is a well known writer, historian and equalities consultant whose work takes her into schools and youth clubs across the UK. She is co-author of *The Heart of the Race*, published by Virago, and *Toolkit for Tackling Racism in Schools* published by Trentham Books.

Lola Young

Accentuating the positive

IF WE continually tell one section of the community they can only fail, then there is a danger that they will come to believe it, as all of us will. Instead, let's try to tackle the problems by accentuating the positive, as well as always articulating the negative.

Participation in higher education (HE) is actually proportionately higher among Black and minority ethnic (BME) communities, as more go on to study post-18 than their white counterparts. A team based at the Institute for Employment Studies which included Professor Tariq Madood undertook research on BME participation in higher education which brought into the open some interesting and multi-layered findings. The report concluded that:

> ... There is a tendency...to focus mostly on the least successful, and on difficulties, rather than on successes. Some minority ethnic students are doing much better than comparative white groups... This should be given greater recognition, along with the success 'drivers'.[1]

Among the difficulties it noted that:

- Although well represented in HE, BME students do not do as well in terms of degree performance.
- They also do less well in terms of employment.
- They are more likely to go on to further study or training.
- BME graduates are still under-represented in the graduate intakes of many larger organisations.

This last point is in part explained by the recruitment strategies of some of the prestigious businesses that seek to recruit graduates. These organisations are inundated with applications for employment from new graduates each year, and one of the ways they filter applications to make them manageable is to consider only those who have attended Russell Group universities or, at best, pre-1992 institutions. BME students are most likely to attend post-1992 universities. As the research shows, 'Old universities are most likely to accept white candidates, and to a lesser extent Chinese candidates, from among a group of similarly qualified applicants'.[2]

This is in turn related to earlier educational attainment and background. The patterns of academic achievement established from secondary school in terms of level of attainment are repeated at university with Black Caribbean and Bangladeshi students gaining less first class honours and 2:1s than other groupings. This is hardly surprising given that all BME students achieve lower grades over fewer GCSEs, and lower grades at A level. This makes it more likely that they will attend those establishments that operate a more flexible approach to A level grades and academic record. This is what makes the achievement of many post-1992 universities all the more significant, and it is frankly disappointing that the former polytechnics are seen as second choice, and are spoken of as such in public. In my view they do a fantastic job in working with students who have had negative educational experiences and helping them to achieve academically.

BME students can and do achieve, and our message should be that everyone has their part to play – this is not simply about placing blame. Parents, students, schools, employers and FE and HE all have to work really hard together on this – and that includes working class and middle class parents, BME and white parents, to improve our schools and motivate our children, encourage the broadening of horizons and the raising of levels of aspiration. But in this partnership, there are those who have the power to make really significant changes happen. Those who have that power and who don't exercise that appropriately will have to take responsibility for lack of progress. Those in leadership roles in further and higher education establishments and agencies should take on a vocal, public leading role in promoting equalities beyond the rhetoric of policy statements, and beyond the confines of the institution.

Note

1   M Shiner, and T Madood, 'Help or Hindrance? Higher Education and the Route to Ethnic Equality', *British Journal of Sociology of Education*, vol 23, no 2, 2002.
2   As above.

● This extract is taken from the John Baillie Memorial lecture for Natfhe that Lola Young delivered at the House of Commons on May 23rd 2005.

● Lola Young is an advocate, activist and adviser in the field of culture, heritage and diversity. She leads the arts and heritage consultancy Cultural Brokers. In 2001 she was awarded an OBE and was appointed a life peer in the House of Lords in 2004.

Section 3
Say it loud
Experience and
perspectives
across the
generations

Yout Rebels by Linton Kwesi Johnson

a bran new breed of blacks
have now emerged,
leadin on the rough scene,
breakin away,
takin the day,
saying to capital nevah
movin fahwod evah.

they can only be
new in age
but not in rage,
not needin
the soft and
shallow councilin
of the soot-brained
sage in chain;
wreckin thin-shelled words
movin always fahwood.

young blood
yout rebels:
new shapes
shapin
new patterns
creatin new links
linkin
blood risin surely
carvin a new path,
movin fahwod to freedom

From *Mi Revalueshanary Fren: Selected Poems* (Penguin, 2002)

Linton Kwesi Johnson

The problem of the colour line

I WAS CONSIDERED very bright as a child. In the elementary school system the class you were in would be dependent on how well you were doing. So by the time I was leaving Jamaica I was in fifth class. All my contemporaries were 14 and 15 year olds and I was 11, and I used to get lots of sweets from guys for doing their homework and stuff like that.

I didn't know hardly anything about England. We had these little books in school, stories about an Eskimo boy from Canada, a boy from Borneo, a boy from Canada, a boy from London. And you know, as a child I used to think literally the streets of London were paved with gold. So I was in for a rude awakening when we arrived and I saw all these grey buildings with smoke coming out of the chimneys and so on. It was a November day, the 8th of November, and it was grey and cold and horrible and I just wanted to get back on the plane and get back to Jamaica.

School was initially a traumatic experience for me because that was my first confrontation with racism. You know, kids would be calling me 'Black bastard', 'You people live in trees', and all kind of racial abuse. At the time, the thing that was being said about us was that black people eat Kitekat. I don't know how that story got around. At school the comprehensive system had three streams. You had an A stream, a B stream and a C stream and myself, and 95 percent of all the other Black kids were in the C stream. I gradually worked my way up into the B stream but for all intents and purposed we weren't supposed to be having any academic aspirations and so on. We were supposed to leave at 14 and go and do an apprenticeship or go to join our fathers and mothers in hospitals or on the buses or whatever. I remember when I was 14, Mr F Harris, our careers teacher, called me in for an interview and he said, 'Johnson, you'll be leaving school in a couple of years – what do you intend to do?' So I said, 'I want to become an accountant, Sir', because at the time my best subjects at school were accounts, commerce and economics. He said, 'Accountant! A big strong lad like you! We need lads like you in the forces. Do you realise you have to serve a five years articleship? You have to get two A Levels and then you have to serve five years articles', blah blah blah. 'And anyway, you people are always complaining about the police. Have you ever considered joining the police?'

Mind you, there were at least two or three teachers I had tremendous respect for. My First Form tutor was a guy called Chris Harbon who taught at the Royal Academy for Dramatic Arts and he used to take us up to the BBC, all kinds of things, to the radio and stuff. And my Sixth Form tutor was a man called Mr Winkler and he thought I had great potential. He kept on telling me about Michael Manley and how he had been to the London School of Economics and how I could do the same thing. And then there was another teacher called Mr Woods, a Jamaican teacher, and he was excellent. I did CSE English and it was because of him I got Grade One. I didn't have to bother with the O Level afterwards. So that was schooling for me.

At school I became involved in the Black Panther Movement. As a youth, growing up in Britain, I would see these people on the streets every Saturday with their newspaper *Black People's News,* or something it was called, I can't remember. And then one of the leaders of the organisation, Althea Jones, had come to our schools to take part in a debate. I can't remember what the debate was about but I was very impressed by her, and I decided to go to one of their meetings. And I eventually became a member of the Black Panther Youth League and then a member of the Black Panther Movement.

It was in the Panthers that I discovered literature, Black literature, because we were encouraged to read. In fact there were books that we studied, chapter and verse, going through them systematically. One of them was *Capitalism and Slavery* by Dr Eric Williams. The other was

Frantz Fanon's *The Wretched of the Earth*. And the third one was *The Black Reconstruction* by W E B Du Bois. We had a little library and we were allowed to borrow books, and one of the books that I borrowed was a book called *The Souls of Black Folk* by W E B Du Bois. That was a book. It was one of the most beautiful things I ever read. It just, it just blew my mind. It was about the experiences of Blacks in America after slavery had been abolished; and the language, I was struck by the language, the poetic language of Du Bois' writing. I remember one phrase from the book. He talked about 'The Colour Line'. The problem of the 20th century was the problem of the colour line. And after I read that book I just wanted to read more and to write and to express my own ideas and my own feelings and my experiences growing up in England.

● This is an excerpt taken from 'Linton Kwesi Johnson in Conversation with John La Rose', first published in *Changing Britannia – Life Experience With Britain* (New Beacon Books and George Padmore Institute, 1999).

● Linton Kwesi Johnson is widely acclaimed as the world's first dub poet. He set up his own recording label in 1981 and has produced numerous albums including *Forces of Victory* and *Bass Culture*. His latest selection of poems, *Mi Revalueshanary Fren*, is published by Penguin.

Benjamin Zephaniah

Over and out

I HAVE TOLD this story many times while on stage and maybe because I tell it on stage nobody believes it, people tend to think that I've made it up for show business reasons. So now I want to set the record straight, this is all true.

St Matthias School does not exist any more but it used to be on Farm Street, Hockley, Birmingham B19. At this school for some strange reason the boys only played football, the girls played hockey, rounders and netball, but we only had football.

In assembly one morning our headmaster told the school that because the school now had an Afro-Caribbean pupil (that's me), he would now like to change things a little. Words like multiculturalism weren't used very much then, but he made it clear that at this school there should be something for everyone. He then proclaimed that the school was to have a cricket team and that I was to be the Captain.

In 2004 it may seem obvious that not all Black people love cricket but back then in 1960 something, this headmaster just failed to believe that I couldn't stand the game, he insisted that I was a 'born cricketer'. Well let's face it, sometimes people do play down how good they are at a sport in the hope that the opposition will be unprepared and this is what the headmaster and many others thought that was what I was doing. Every time I repeated my hatred of the game people smiled, when I told my fellow pupils that I had never handled a cricket bat I was told to 'stop messing about', I felt well and truly stereotyped.

It took one bowl to get me out forever. I remember it well, as I stood waiting for the ball to arrive I shook with nervousness, I wanted to go home. The ball bounced in front of me and almost flattened an ant, as it came up I went to strike it but it came up so fast I couldn't see it, the ball hit my right hand and broke my longest finger. I ran to the medical room shouting things like, 'I hate cricket' and 'Mom' and I've never played cricket again.

Some weeks later I was approached by the headmaster as I was drinking my free school milk and he asked, 'Are you any good at boxing, lad?' I replied, 'No', trying not to look Afro-Caribbean, 'but I am very good at formation flying...sir', I said.

● Benjamin Zephaniah was born in Birmingham where, during his school years, he was sent to an approved school for being rebellious and a 'born failure'. Millions of people now know Zephaniah for his hard hitting poetry against injustice. As well as publishing several volumes of poetry, he has written novels, broadcast on radio and television, and released several albums including his latest, *Naked*. Benjamin hit the headlines in 2004 when he refused an OBE.

● www.benjaminzephaniah.com

The Tricycle Group

THE FOLLOWING contributions are from people involved in the Tricycle Group, 'the voice of young people', established in 2003. It is a partnership of Genesis community and the Tricycle theatre and is a youth-led project involving young people from across Brent.

To date one of the group's most successful ventures has been to write and perform a thought-provoking piece about anti-Muslim racism in the wake of 9/11. The group is about giving young people a say in a society where they are often denied this most basic of rights. In 2005 they began filming a documentary about Anti-Social Behaviour Orders and issues such as homelessness and education.

The pieces by Elrica Senior and Craig Cameron came out of discussion about education organised by the group in the summer of 2005. At the time a moral panic was being whipped up by the media with daily and increasingly hysterical reports of anti-social behaviour by young people. Top of this list of shame was a phenomenon known as 'happy slapping', random and apparently unprovoked acts of violence against an unsuspecting victim, recorded and circulated to friends via their mobile phones by the assailant.

Had they been out on the streets, there can be little doubt that the young people here would have been treated with disdain and suspicion by the police and the authorities. Dressed, as many of them were, in baseball caps and hooded tops, they may well have found themselves excluded from shopping centres and other traditional downtown gathering points. I must point out that this is not mere speculation. Shortly before the session took place one of the biggest and newest shopping centres on the outskirts of London announced it would be banning those wearing hooded tops from its centre (though of course the Nike shop inside continued to sell the offending items).

Yet the young people I met were bright, articulate and passionate.

Most admitted they were no angels and that they had 'got up to a few things' at school, but it was equally clear that most of them felt a sense of injustice at the way they had been treated in the education system. One or two could think of nothing positive at all to say about their schooldays, but most had mixed feelings. They enjoyed being with their friends and had fond memories of favourite subjects and teachers, both Black and white. But overall there was a feeling of frustration at what they regarded as racist stereotyping and a stifling of their freedom of expression.

These comments were not restricted to their experiences in the classroom. Instead one participant argued that he felt 'like society is set up to make you sweat tears and cry to get a little bit that's gone the next instant'. Another argued with regard to racism that 'things haven't got better. They just know how to mask it more. It's more undercover.'

These contributions are a reminder to educationalists, the press and politicians that, far from simply being an indistinguishable mass of tearaways, young people are complex and challenging with thoughts and opinions that we must find time and space for and seriously take into consideration when planning our, and their, future.

Elrica Senior
Not just a statistic

I am a Black British woman born to Jamaican parents who grew up in Willesden, Brent, a small, deprived area which borders onto a richer area, Brondesbury. I was educated at Copland Community Science Specialist College in Wembley, Middlesex. Wembley is a busy area and is central to a lot of neighbouring areas. It is a diverse community but the majority of the students at Copland, a comprehensive school, were Black and Asian.

I had many different experiences at school but they were mainly negative. I am a very confident and opinionated young person and was not intimidated by the staff at my school, and this got me into trouble. Teachers called me arrogant and disruptive because they didn't understand how I could be young, female and Black with so much to say.

A teacher once told me that there was no point in me doing well at school, because when 'my kind' finish school we have five children for five different men and go on benefits. I had teachers tell me I would never pass any of my exams, and they always gave me low expectancy grades compared to the white or the Asian children. An Asian teacher told me I didn't belong in her class and told me to look around the room. When I did, I could see that there were hardly any other kids from my background in the class. Another thing that teachers didn't like about me was that I was smart academically and also had a lot of common sense. Because of this I was never suspended from school. I remember one particular occasion when a teacher threatened to have me suspended. I had confronted him in the classroom because he used to spend more time talking on his mobile phone than teaching the class. I have also threatened to sue my school, report them to the education board and speak to the newspapers.

Although I had many negative experiences there were also a few positive ones. I had a drama teacher, a white man, who would always push me and see that I did my best. He had a lot of time for me, always helped in everything, and he would also let me know when I was making improvements. That's how teachers are supposed to be.

All these negative experiences at school moulded me and helped me understand how society sees Black people, especially young Black females: as baby machines, illiterate and always on benefits. They gave me a personal drive, and made me eager to become successful and not a statistic. I understood that there was still racism and discrimination, it was just in different forms, and that I always had to work twice as hard as the other pupils from other ethnic backgrounds. Although people are not as direct with racism and discrimination any more, the government has legalised it in different ways. For example, teachers have the power to throw young people out of school without giving them substitute education. The statistics show that a disproportionate number of young people that are excluded are Black males. Education empowers people and gives you the skills to become successful. Young people who are thrown out of school and denied their education are not empowered for the business world, so they are discriminated against while trying to get a job. This is just one form of institutionalised racism and discrimination.

I come from a single parent home, but I have never been deprived of anything – in fact, my experiences opened my eyes and made me understand how strong Black women are and how much I admired my mum. My mum was educated in Jamaica and wasn't familiar with the British education system, but she was eager to learn and she always supported me at school. She wanted to know what I was doing, how it would help me and what she could do to help. She would approach my teachers and ask them to show her/explain to her how to do the work so she could help me. She always encouraged me to do well and explained how hard life would be for me because of my colour. She taught me about my history and we learned about other things together. The automatic assumption that children from a single parent home are deprived is complete rubbish – you can have both parents and your home could still be broken.

Middle class people and people in authority don't understand young people and regard youth culture – our clothes, music and daily struggles – as negative. Young people dress in hoodies, tracksuits, trainers and hats because it is our identity. In deprived areas a lot of young people dress the same because we are all going through similar things. We listen to music about robbing, shooting and reputation because those are things that happen on a daily basis, and I believe the government is to blame.

There is no relationship between young Black people and the police. The only time the police want to talk to us is when a crime has been committed. The government tries to put restrictions on how we dress and never sees things from our point of view. Why would we want to dress like people that don't respect us? The government also gives the police too many powers – they believe they are above the law. I remember hearing about a police officer who was let off for speeding because he was testing his new car. If that had been a Black boy he would have been sent to prison.

Whenever a crime happens in a deprived area such as Harlesden it takes the police 20 minutes to get there. If it happened in Maida Vale, a rich area, they suddenly become telepathic, there on the scene before you call them, and they catch the criminal within minutes. Police also harass young people and it is seen as OK, because it is automatically assumed that we are about to do something bad simply because we are young and Black.

The government introduces measures such as Anti-Social Behaviour Orders but never wants to deal with the real problems. They are just a way of keeping Black people trapped and fighting each other. If everyone is kicked out of school with no education and is forced to sell drugs, eventually someone will go on someone else's patch. This then leads to conflict, and that's what the government wants to see – us killing off each other so they don't have to.

Craig Cameron
Personal experiences of my time at school

I was born in Kingston, Jamaica, and came to London when I was four years old. I came to Brent, to an area called Kingsbury. Brent is a very diverse and multicultural borough – a very poor borough which is on the borderline to some very rich areas.

I enjoyed my time at my first school, Fryent Primary School in Kingsbury, Brent, and made many friends. My mother paid a keen interest in my schooling and had a good relationship with my teachers.

I then moved on to Kingsbury High School (KHS), which was a top grant maintained comprehensive school and was the second biggest high school in the UK. The school has a lot of heritage and history, and within this there is a certain amount of elitism with the teaching.

I was always a very bright student, but I felt that I was treated differently because I was a Black male while the culture and the atmosphere at KHS, and the majority of the teachers, were middle class and white. Although my overall experience at school was positive, whenever I was in trouble or the school was trying to sanction me I found that I was being treated more harshly than others. I feel that this was a reflection of how society generally stereotypes Black men. Afro-Caribbean boys are seen as aggressive and confrontational, with a constant negative attitude.

Within my culture people can express themselves in a loud and enthusiastic, passionate way. This is how my parents are, and that's how I know how to be. At school I mostly had Black friends from the same ethnic and social backgrounds, so we had the same interests and things in common. The way we behaved was misunderstood at school and regarded as rudeness, agression and bad attitude.

I gradually began to understand how I could be seen by others in society. As my mother always said to me, I had to work harder than other kids because within society as a Black person I had less value than others. I did my bit to challenge this prejudice and the discrimination I experienced at school, and I always made sure that my opinion was heard all the time. Because I was intelligent I didn't really get as hard a time from teachers as others, but I had drive and was encouraged at school by my parents – not all my friends were like this. They could be treated differently and were more at risk from institutionalised racism, as schools have the power to throw kids out from schools if they are deemed unteachable. Because of their treatment at school a lot of young Black males have low self-esteem and confidence, and developed mistrust for general authority and the schooling system which affected their overall performance at school.

I felt that there was a disproportionate amount of Black boys that were expelled from KHS. My time at KHS helped me to understand how contemporary society saw the Black male – it helped me to assign my own identity despite people stereotyping me and not trying to understand who I was. This pushed me to be strong and determined, better able to challenge prejudices, and gave me the ability to be a good judge of character.

Throughout school my mum was very aware of what I have and would experience, as she knew about the prejudices and ways of society that I would grow to know. My mother was a very good role model – she was strong and had a lot of wisdom. I believe that she felt that she needed to be, because she had to do her best at showing me as best as she could how to be a good man.

Although my mother did a great job, I feel that I had a lack or a void in my life, and that this void was a positive male role model, like a dad or an older brother. There were many young Black boys at my school who did not have this. I feel that I was lucky in terms of how my mum compensated for this, but a lot of others filled that void by becoming involved in gang culture. For them it was almost like having the family that they never had at home, and it is a reaction to how they were treated at school and how society generally sees them. This gang culture encourages all the negative things that make you fail within the systems of contemporary society, such as not doing well at school and gaining no training so you have no skills to make you succeed at work. The way that your speech becomes restricted and not elaborated, which make others think that you're not smart.

Youth and gang culture didn't really affect me when I was at school – well, not the negative part of it anyway, as I knew it was the wrong way to go. I knew life had a lot more to offer than that and knew I had options, as I understood the system of society and how to succeed. Others didn't understand and didn't feel they had options in life, and went the wrong way in life to gang culture. Many of my Black friends didn't have confidence in school and got into gang culture. They assigned themselves their own male role model, which was usually a drug dealer with a big car, girls and a lot of money. This is what they would aspire to be.

I felt with Black boys that there was a self-fulfilling prophecy – because their confidence in the education system was low and the confidence of teachers in them was low, they didn't bother trying at school. This ultimately affected their ambition and what that thought they could be in life. Most felt that they could only make it as footballers or DJs and even hustlers. The image that hip-hop stars portray as role models for Black men does not help either, as this was a very strong external influence on young Black males when I was at school.

• The members of the Tricycle Group who participated in the discussion are Angelo Frederick, Faisal Dhondee, Jason Crichlow, Sade Shamon Stephens, Jermaine P Nelson, Kirstie Jane Wendy Romeric, Yanick Francois Greene, Teizeai Levy, Aleem Egunjobi, and youth worker Rebecca Palmer.

Kwame Kwei-Armah

'Too clever for a Black kid'

I SHOULD START by saying I had a brilliant school life. I loved it. I went to primary school until I was seven and then to stage school. It was a fee-paying school called the Barbara Speakes Stage School which I attended until I was 16. I enjoyed it because of the camaraderie, the people I was at school with.

My first memory of school was of a teacher kicking me with her high heels and telling me, 'You – your brain is too big for your body.' This was at Tudor Road Primary, and I remember going home and telling my mum about the incident. That's when she decided to take me out of that school and put me into private education. My mother took from that teacher's comment that she was inferring that I was too clever for a Black kid.

So then I went to the stage school and my abiding memory of the school is the racism. My teacher would call my mother in sometimes and would say something like: 'Ian [as I was called then] is going for an audition and I know you Blacks have problems speaking good English…your lips are a bit too big and the way your mouth is constructed, blah blah blah.'

Another time she said to my mum, 'Ian has been seen holding hands with Amanda [my white girlfriend] and her father is a director and her mother works at Selfridges and they would be frightfully upset if they found out.'

When I went to the school I was the only Black kid there and over the years others appeared but were in a very small minority, by the time I left probably about five out of 150 pupils.

In the approach of the school beyond drama, how was the teaching?
The education at the school was very bad, so if you didn't make it in show business you were probably left unprepared.

One of the starkest examples was a guy called Tommy Barnet, a white boy, from Greenford. Like the rest of us he would do loads of adverts as a kid. But as you got older they became fewer and, in the case of Tommy, work dried up and within a year of leaving school he was sweeping the streets. That's a stark example but it is not untypical because the school didn't really prepare you for anything other than show business.

So what did your mother hope for you to achieve by sending you private?
She hoped that I'd end up a star – a dancing and singing star – that was her dream. And I'm glad she did, because although the education was substandard in some ways, what it did do was take me out of my immediate environment. A lot of the young boys living on my street all ended up in Borstal and got caught up in the petty crime scene. Going to the school that I did allowed me to grow up in a world of expectation – the expectation that I could be something, I could achieve something in the world. So more than anything that is why I congratulate my mum's decision. She placed me in an aspirational environment.

Did you have any education abroad? There's the argument about sending kids to school in the Caribbean?
In fact my mum did do precisely that and sent me to Grenada when I was seven. I thought I was going on a holiday. All of a sudden I'm in this school uniform and I'm getting licks. After about eight weeks my mother brought me home. I didn't think anything of it at the time but years later, when I was about 25, I asked her about it. She said I didn't get on with my cousin and she couldn't leave me in an environment where I wasn't happy.

She had ideas again about a school in Trinidad which never came to fruition, so yes, she did try that route.

What about the impact of discrimination on exclusions and other discipline in school?
In our time it was being expelled and I was threatened with it just before I

was about to sit my O Levels, and except for the brilliance of my mother who went crazy down at the school, I may well have been. Of all of my friends I was probably the only one that didn't get expelled. All the Black kids were expelled.

Funnily, I met my old headmistress the other day. And she said, 'Do you know, Ian, the most rebellious ones were the most talented.' I wouldn't say that I wasn't talkative and argumentative. I was all of those things. But without doubt there was a high level of blatant racism. This very much contributed to that feeling that when you were a boy you were cute, until you became 13 and over, and then you were public enemy number one. That made a big difference to the way in which you were perceived and the way you were communicated with.

One of the key things it seems to me, regardless of teaching method, is the question of what is taught. What do you think?
I do agree with that. I would say it is incumbent on parents to teach their children about their history – and not just the history in the West but before the Atlantic slave trade.

Bernard Coard's book – what's your take on it?
As an adult I became aware of the book and was in conversation once with Diane Abbott about it. When I think about my cousins, what I call the forgotten generation – perhaps in their 50s today – who were brutalised by the system and had no redress, we couldn't even come to our parents and say this is what they're doing to me because our parents were often so afraid they'd say it must be you. They're saying you're educationally subnormal then it must be you. So I remember all my older cousins forming sub-cultural groups when they had been excluded – expelled – from school. I'm not sure what that does to your level of self-esteem – being called educationally subnormal.

So let's look at the wider world, the 1970s, with the National Front on the streets.
I left school in 1982. The National Front was a very heavy time. By the time I was getting to 16 to 17 years old the skinhead era was coming to a close. I grew up in Southall and remember the National Front having meetings in the town hall, Blair Peach being killed. I was on the streets seeing one of my sister's lecturers being dragged away by the police and my cousins being beaten and battered by the police. I remember in the early 1980s going into

this ex-girlfriend of mine's party in Greenford and there being a bunch of skinheads in the house going 'Sieg heil, seig heil.' We ran into the toilets and were told to get the hell out because they were going to kill us. We took our exit out the window.

The politics of the period had an impact in terms of the growth of multiculturalism initiatives. Do you see a danger that this is being turned back? There's a lot of talk about children being the problem, not the system.
No, I don't. What I do sense is that there is this reinvestment going on in the idea of fearing the urban youth, in particular the fear associated with young Black youths. Although you could say it's changed now in that we won't be public enemy number one any more – we're number two after the London bombings. Our generation can play a really crucial role in healing this country because we've gone through what the young Muslims are going through now.

What about the war on terror and its impact on the Black community?
The Black community – if you talk about people of African-Caribbean and African descent – some might say is not affected, but it is. This new surveillance society that we're living in, soon we'll have ID cards, means we're the most looked upon society on earth. That affects us all.

Do you think there is or was a feeling in the African-Caribbean community that the war on terror is an issue sort of to one side, thank god it's not us, so to speak, or at least not until a Jamaican was identified as one of the suspected suicide bombers on 7 July in London.
I've heard a lot of people saying how shocked they were that one of us was involved. The authorities were as well. They've always treated Black crime as the work of boys. They call the yardies disorganised crime. We wouldn't be seen as having the political gumption or skill to organise at a high level like that. But of course the war on terror doesn't affect the African-Caribbean community in the same way as the Muslim community.

In your address to the Black child education conference last year you attacked those in the media and our own community that went along with the gangsta-rap stereotypes about Black boys. Why did you feel the need to speak out?
Because the picture painted of the African Caribbean community is not one that I recognise. We've always placed a high premium on education. I don't

know one West Indian family of our generation in which parents wouldn't say, 'Child, go fetch your book.' Now whether they could always help you with your books was a completely different subject. So I hate that stereotype. Education was absolutely key, and I refute it with my very presence.

● An interview with Gary McFarlane, conducted after the matinee performance of Kwame's play *Elmina's Kitchen*, at the Garrick Theatre, London, on 14 July 2005.

● Kwame Kwei-Armah (born 1967) is a black British actor, singer and playwright. Born Ian Roberts in Hillingdon, London, he changed his name after tracing his family history through the slave trade back to his African roots. He first achieved fame playing the paramedic Finlay in the BBC drama series *Casualty*. His play *Elmina's Kitchen*, about gun crime and young people, was shortlisted in the best new play category at the 2004 Laurence Olivier Theatre Awards. He is a supporter of Christian Aid.

Weyman Bennett

'They divide each to conquer both'

THE REPUBLISHING of Bernard Coard's path-breaking book is to be welcomed. His main point, that the West Indian child was *made* educationally subnormal, liberated thousands from the label and blame culture and the idea that there was something intellectually wrong with Black students. He identified the source of the problem in the structure of the British education system. This is heady stuff, compared to the notion that it is 'bling' culture that underlies and explains the half century of failure of young Black children.

Identifying the problem does not also indicate the solution. For example, Trevor Phillips's analysis is: 'We have to accept that our historical bleating about racist teachers, class barriers and irrelevant curricula has not moved the performance of these kids one iota. We can apply the brakes to this cycle of failure. I for one refuse to sit back and watch another generation fall by the wayside'.[1] Mr Phillips pointed to the achievements of their sisters as proof that the failings of Black boys could not be pinned on deprivation or racism. (Black girls do much better than Black boys in school.) In fact deprivation and racism are precisely the point.

Racism sharpens the class divide. The explanation for the underachievement of Black boys in school lies in the interaction between class and racism and the education system. Girls are doing better than boys in tests. The gender gap increases for all pupils between the ages of seven and 11 (key stages 1 and 2) and is wider still by the time they are 14 (key stage 3). But in the case of working class children the difference is more than twice the average by the age of 14. In one study looking at social class and GCSE attainment, Gillborn and Mirza found that, in general, pupils from non-manual backgrounds achieved more GCSEs than those from manual (ie working class) backgrounds. However, this gap in the results achieved by pupils from different class backgrounds was less pronounced for African-Caribbean pupils compared to other ethinic groups. In 1993 Black girls were attaining below Pakistani and Bangladeshi girls and managed to substantially narrow the gap by 1995. Even so, Black girls from non-manual backgrounds were still the lowest achievers compared to Indian, white and Pakistani/Bangladeshi pupils of a similar class background. So although Black girls do better than Black boys, a combination of institutional racism and class pushes down their results.

Teachers

This does not mean that all teachers are racist. Unlike the police force, teachers have a proud record of anti-racist activity over the last 25 years. Blair Peach, a teacher in east London, was killed by police on an anti-racist demonstration in Southall. Many other teachers were involved in organising against the rise of fascism in the 1970s. They also instituted and pioneered anti-racist teaching to make the curriculum more relevant to all pupils, something that has been systematically removed since the late 1980s or ridiculed as political correctness. But, of course, racist stereotyping does exist among some teachers. This is magnified by the way in which Tory and New Labour market mechanisms and competition in the schools system have encouraged discrimination. Setting and streaming are now the norm in secondary schools, and are spreading to primaries. Black pupils are more likely to be put in bottom sets. This reinforces the idea, even among the students themselves, that they are 'underachievers'.

The system still remains at fault

Coard writes:

What is needed is a system of quality education for all; and therefore, by definition, one that is not dependent on the parental income/wealth or social status and connections of schoolchildren, does not have schools providing vastly different standards of education and does not have a two-tiered, or multi-tiered system of education, providing differential education for the children of different classes, genders and ethnicities.

For any Black children to blossom they need a truly comprehensive education system.

Coard also argues for the direct involvement of pupils and parents in the education process. Personally, for me, this happened through engagement in the political struggle against the National Front, the huge Rock Against Racism events and inner city rebellions of Brixton 1981. Growing up in east London was no joke. The National Front would try and sell the fascist paper *Bulldog* at the school gates – being a Jehovah's Witness and being told the Bible demanded I turn other cheek was no help at all. One day a group of Black and white kids drove them off.

It was School Kids Against the Nazis that fired my imagination and gave me pride and confidence. It was the Punky Reggae rebellion that let me learn my place in the world. When our drama teacher put on *The Resistible Rise of Arturo Ui*, a parable play of Hitler's rise to power set in pre-war Chicago, it embraced our experience and encouraged us that we had the right to be free on the streets and in the classroom. Learning in these conditions was liberating. Personal anger at racism was turned outwards, not internalised in a corrosive way as it is today, as Black boys are blamed as the architects of their own failure. There is no space for this when you teach to test or test till you fail.

One of the best years of academic success I had as teacher was at the start of the war in Iraq when my class walked out to call for peace. Their engagement as citizens enhanced their learning experience. This is a major theme of Vygotsky's theoretical framework. He argues that social interaction plays a fundamental role in the development of cognition. Vygotsky states:

> Every function in the child's cultural development appears twice: first, on the social level, and later, on the individual level; first, between people (interpsychological) and then inside the child (intrapsychological). This applies equally to voluntary attention, to logical memory, and to the formation of concepts. All the higher functions originate as actual relationships between individuals.[2]

A second aspect of Vygotsky's theory is the idea that the potential for cognitive development depends upon the 'zone of proximal development' (ZPD): a level of development attained when children engage in social behaviour. Full development of the ZPD depends upon full social interaction. The range of skill that can be developed with adult guidance or peer collaboration exceeds what can be attained alone. This process is disrupted for many Black children because of racism and class. Students engage when they are confident but many aspects of their educational experience reinforce failure and demand conformity.

We need to change the education system, not adapt to it. We are at a critical moment. Some have argued that the segregation of Black children may be a step forward as Trevor Philips has said, or that the elitist 'Search for Black Genius' is the answer, as Tony Sewell has proposed. We should reject both these conclusions to demand resources to fund small classes, child-centred education and comprehensive learning. This is the difficult option.

Black freedom fighter Frederick Douglass said of racism, 'They divide each to conquer both.' In terms of education, the harder it is for Black boys in school, the harder it is going to be for all children. If we want Black children to succeed there has to be a root and branch change in education.

Notes

1   *Guardian*, 31 May 2005.
2   L S Vygotsky, *Mind in Society* (Cambridge, Mass, Harvard University Press, 1978), p57.

● Weyman Bennett is joint secretary of Unite Against Fascism and the national organiser of Love Music Hate Racism. He was a lecturer in Further Education for many years, teaching in inner city colleges. Weyman went to a comprehensive school in Newham, east London, during the 1970s and 1980s where he was active in the fight against racism and the National Front. All views expressed in this article are expressed in a personal capacity.

Vocalis MC (aka Wain David Williams)

The Forest Gate 1

Where did you grow up?
I grew up in east London, in Stratford. It's a great place to live if you're open to different things and different people, if you want to taste the different flavours of the world, to see different things.

What were your experiences of school?
At school I just wasn't interested. I didn't feel dumb or unable – I just wasn't interested. It's like, if you went to a science museum and look at one of those electrical balls where you touch it and all the currents meet your hands; I felt like I was trapped inside one of those balls and wanted the electric currents to escape. When I went to school and we were told, 'This is what you're going to learn today', I felt trapped; there were so many things I wanted to learn but not the things they had to teach us. I always thought there was so much more. It wasn't like I had a choice about becoming a high level academic or unemployed. I was thinking about a million things all the time.

School seemed like a dream world. It was like in a hospital when people are sat in a waiting room: they aren't interested in being in the waiting room but in what's going to happen to them; they're focused on the end. I felt like school was being in that waiting room, like I was separate from that, I had a lot of friends but felt different, like I was part of another world. My good friend Doug was on the same page as me. People were always telling us those were 'the most important years' of our lives. For some kids they need the vision of having a stable job, a big house and stuff but for others that's scary – we were under pressure from life anyway. And whose life actually works out like that? Like it's supposed to? Even the teachers' lives hadn't worked out like that probably.

I didn't know Bernard Coard's name and I suppose part of that is because my knowledge of Black history is low. Kids don't know about our history and about all the great people and great times we've had. They might know about people like Martin Luther King and Malcolm X but they don't know about the individuals who did great things on their own. Like Rosa Parks. She said, 'I am a woman. I am Black. I'm not moving because I need a seat.' What a thing to do, what a great thing to do.

When I was about 15 and MCing in class, I was told to shut up. What a teacher should really do is ask the kid, 'Is that what you're interested in?' A young woman who's singing in class, maybe someone should ask her if that's what she enjoys and let a music teacher know and give her a chance. If a kid has a passion for stories, no one should laugh at them – who knows that the kid couldn't become a writer. Black, white, Asian – whatever the colour of the kid that excitement shouldn't be stamped out just because it doesn't fit in with the curriculum. Any teacher worth their salt would be able to work out if the kid had a talent for that particular thing – they shouldn't be sent to the back of the class for showing an interest in something.

The majority of my friends are white. Growing up, my friends were of all races. I've always made friends with whoever's a good laugh and whose company I enjoy. My secondary school was primarily Black and Asian while my primary school was mainly white but I always had equal amounts of friends of all colours. I think of it in the same way I'd think of having a gay friend, like, 'This is my friend who happens to be gay.' I'm not mates with people because of their colour or whatever – I'm their mate. End of.

I did grow up in a time when some white people were standoffish though, you know, I'd go over to a mate's and his family would say, 'Better lock up the jewellery now he's here.' I didn't really understand it though at the time but as I got older and got a better vocabulary I didn't like it. When I was 16, I was at a mate's barbecue in his back garden. There were about 30 adults there and about ten kids. His dad shouts across to me, 'Were you on TV last night?' I was a bit confused and said, 'No?' His dad carried on and said, 'I was sure I saw you on *Crimewatch*.' It was the first time my blood had boiled like that. I was physically angry. I had tears welling in my eyes. When he looked at me it was like seeing someone you love stabbed. Metaphorically, he was stabbing me. So I left and they shouted me to come back but I just walked away. I was a lost soul; I didn't truly understand what it meant apart from that I was an outsider. I think it's the first time I realised there were some places I was not allowed to be – as if someone suddenly made me hypersensitive to brushes against unwelcomeness that I'd never had before.

Were you ever excluded, and if so, why?
I was almost excluded once. One day a girl at school lost her bag, books and stuff. I didn't know that and I was walking to school and saw a pencil case on the floor with pens and stuff all spread out. There were Parker pens and stuff but I didn't like them and I thought about taking the protractor but I didn't know how to use it so I left that and just took a few pens from the ground. Later in the day I was taken from class to see our Head of Year and he said, 'So what have we been up to?' I was really nervous and was like 'What? I didn't do anything.' He said a young girl had said I'd nicked her rucksack and pens. Then it dawned on me and I said, 'These pens?' He got all excited and said, 'Yes, there's the evidence.' I tried to explain what had happened and all he said was, and I'll never forget it, 'Ah ha, stealing by finding.' I said, 'So sir, if you found a £10 on the floor would you take it to the police station?' And you could see him think, 'This little idiot's right.' The Forest Gate 1 case ended there.

How have your experiences and achievements at school affected you since you left?
How has school affected me? I could say that it's harder to find a decent job because I didn't get the good grades a kid 'should'. But I genuinely believe that I didn't know what I wanted at school; I didn't have a plan about what I wanted to do afterwards. Qualifications didn't mean anything to me. You know, like I did an idiotic food technology class. If I'd have cooked rice and peas and chicken I'd have got an A* but I didn't want to. I wanted to cook handmade cheesecake because it wasn't the kind of thing we had at home, but the teacher used to say I wasn't being imaginative. But I wanted to make pizza and stuff – the things we didn't eat. You know, sometimes teachers don't look at kids in the right way; they don't consider where they're coming from.

I didn't have a passion to become an MC at school but I did always want to be entertaining. I did media studies even, but I found it very limiting. I think it's a teacher's job to look at me and tell me what they see, develop me. I wanted to make people happy and to make them laugh. You know, there's far too much to worry about in this world other than about a kid who just wants to make people happy. School can't help kids unless it taps into what they're really interested in.

What are your hopes and aspirations for your future and for young people going to school now?

I've never been one to plan for the future, or to worry about it. I don't pin my hopes and dreams on one thing; I live for the day. We have to face up to life. Sometimes we can say, 'I don't want to…' but not often. If people want to worry about getting GCSEs, A levels and a degree they should be encouraged, but I didn't. What I'd really like, the legacy I'd like, is that people say, 'He made me think about something I hadn't before', or 'I hated him' – I just want to provoke feeling, for people to feel something.

I remember three days after my fourteenth birthday deciding I wanted to do pirate radioing. I wanted to be a DJ and I started getting invites to parties and people would say, 'Come to my party and you can MC.' I make people happy with what I do. I want to be someone who gives something back. So I did a few free hall parties and then I met Jeremy Smith, my DJ Platinum, someone who saw in me what a lot of teachers didn't. We wanted to jump on that ride and do what we do and have a lot of fun doing it. Don't think kids are just disruptive. Things need to be based more than just on what someone writes on an exam paper. Being a young Black man at school and outside is different now. People club less, work longer hours, work weekends. Teachers need to concentrate on what kids are interested in and what they can do to support them. Some kids are turned off in class but they only need a football or something to come alive. They should help kids with maths and stuff but look deeper too. Don't send out matchbox kids who are all the same, who all know the same things, say the same things. I'd say this mainly about Black kids but what about all kids? We have to stop saying, 'I am', 'You are' – let's all work together to make things different for all people.

- Interviewed by Eve R Light in east London, 7 September 2005.

- Vocalis MC, Wain David Williams, grew up and continues to live in east London. He has worked in clubs around Europe for over eight years and currently has several residencies in east London and Essex, including one at Time and Envy in Romford.

Dinah Cox

A parent's choice

THE DECISION about where to send one's child to school is arguably the most important that any parent can make. Every year there is a frantic search through the newspapers when the 'league tables' are published, and estate agents habitually promote and mark up the value of properties within the 'catchment area' of prestigious schools. When my son's father and I faced this decision we both agreed that there were certain elements that were key to our choice. We wanted Max to go to a local school within walking distance of his two homes. We wanted it to be a school with a mix of children from different backgrounds that took equality and diversity seriously. We also wanted it to be secular.

The school that was nearest was about to decant to temporary accommodation and be rebuilt, so we picked Rosendale School in Lambeth as our first choice. He started in reception in January 2000.

As I write this in July 2005, Max is about to finish Year 4. He has many friends, and is achieving academically, musically and in sport. There appears to be a culture of support between the children and between the children and adults, with little or no bullying. Due to a special link with the Globe theatre his class have been learning through, and about, Shakespeare all year. He is a school council representative, and perhaps most importantly he is happy at Rosendale. They also have a voluntary organisation that runs an after-school club on the premises, Rosendale Cares for Kids. He enjoys his time here too, and it allows us as parents to continue to work, knowing he is in a safe yet exciting environment each afternoon.

No picture is perfect, and I do have some issues with Max's education. The majority of teachers are female and white, although his Year 4 teacher was an excellent Black woman. Also religion is playing a bigger part than I would like to see in a secular school. Although mixing with others of differing faiths can help Max to understand the world he lives in, I would like to see a greater understanding in the school of the majority with no religious beliefs, and a more critical approach that tackles the intolerance, exclusion, misogyny, homophobia and division religious teachings can promote. However, overall I believe Rosendale is a good place for Max to be.

So why do I feel that our original decision is the right one? As I have said, he is getting a good education and is happy, but beyond that he is gaining a broader understanding of the world we live in. Walking around the school during the school's sports day and at parents' evening we see images from many countries. The four sports teams are named after athletes including Black and Minority Ethnic women. The Ofsted report comments on the number of languages spoken at the school, and how well cultural diversity is celebrated. On parents' evening there was a concert where they played various styles of music. Of those on stage with my son, my guess is that two were of Black Asian descent, three white, four of Black African descent and two of dual heritage.

I believe that schools that have a monoculture based on class, gender, religious belief or race can make an effort to have a multicultural and inclusive ethos that teaches children about equality and diversity. However, this cannot replace the education that children get from each other by working together on a day to day basis. When I hear people complain about sending their children to local state schools I am saddened that they cannot see the benefit of having a child mixing with as many different people as possible. I also hear people saying that children are better off brought up in the countryside. I would not want my son to be an isolated Black face in a sea of white faces, the potential target of bullying and exclusion. I want him to have easy access both in and out of school to a wider and deeper pool of positive influences.

I am sure the decisions we have made would not suit everyone, and when Max grows up he may paint a very different picture of how our choices impacted on him. But I hope he continues to learn in the safe and happy environment he is currently in, and becomes an asset to our wider society with an understanding and empathy for the many people he will meet in his life.

● Dinah Cox is chief executive of Race on the Agenda (ROTA), a social policy think-tank for Black and Minority Ethnic communities: www.rota.org.uk

Opposite: Members of the Tricycle Group. Jess Hurd www.reportdigital.co.uk

Section 4
Seize the time
The way forward

I Have a Scheme by Benjamin Zephaniah

© Benjamin Zephaniah, from *Propa Propaganda* (Bloodaxe Books, 1996)

I am here today my friends to tell you there is hope
As high as that mountain may seem
I must tell you
I have a dream
And my friends
There is a tunnel at the end of the light
And beyond that tunnel I see a future
I see a time
When angry white men
Will sit down with angry black women
And talk about the weather,
Black employers will display notice-boards proclaiming,
'Me nu care wea yu come from yu know
So long as yu can do a good day's work, dat cool wid me.'

I see a time
When words like affirmative action
Will have sexual connotations
And black people all over this blessed country of ours
Will play golf,
Yes my friends that time is coming
And in that time
Afro-Caribbean and Asian youth
Will spend big money on English takeaways
And all police officers will be armed
With a dumplin,
I see a time
A time when the President of the United States of America
    will stand up and say,
'I inhaled
And it did kinda nice
So rewind and cum again.'
Immigration officers will just check that you are all right
And all black people will speak Welsh.

I may not get there my friends
But I have seen that time
I see thousands of muscular black men on Hampstead Heath
    walking their poodles
And hundreds of black female Formula 1 drivers
Racing around Birmingham in pursuit of a truly British way of life.
I have a dream
That one day from all the churches of this land we will hear
    the sound of that great old English spiritual,
Here we go, Here we go, Here we go.
One day all great songs will be made that way.

I am here today my friends to tell you
That the time is coming
When all people, regardless of colour or class, will have
    at least one Barry Manilow record
And vending-machines throughout the continent of Europe
Will flow with sour sap and sugarcane juice,
For it is written in the great book of multiculturalism
That the curry will blend with the shepherd's pie
    and the Afro hairstyle will return.

Let me hear you say
Multiculture
Amen
Let me hear you say
Roti, Roti
A women.

The time is coming
I may not get there with you
But I have seen that time,
And as an Equal Opportunities poet
It pleases me
To give you this opportunity
To share my vision of hope
And I just hope you can cope
With a future as black as this.

Bernard Coard

Thirty years on: where do we go from here?

a High quality education for all

It is my belief, backed up by recent relevant research from the US, that a successful assault on poverty, racism, gender and class discrimination, and on the income, wealth, social status and decision-making gaps which go with these in British society, requires a fundamental transformation of the British education system. It is to that wider war, a war whose slogan and rallying cry, I suggest, should be 'High quality education for ALL', that all should address their minds, and focus their organising energies to achieve. It is not that the transformation of the education system will, by itself, solve all these other problems. But it would be the decisive foundation from which all these other problems can be effectively addressed. It would empower entire future generations with the tools, the resources, the ability, to tackle these other vital societal ills. Moreover, the process of transforming the education system will itself throw up forces which will be critical in addressing these other ills.

b Education as the most important form of wealth for families and nations

Discriminatory education is a critical factor in the maintenance of *income* and *wealth* inequality in any society. Equally, the provision of quality education for the poor and the marginalised in society is critical to the closing, over time and along with other measures, of the income and wealth gaps. It is the key to ending *poverty*; persistent, generational (ie socially inherited) poverty. It is also critical to the acquisition and maintenance of – or exclusion from – such societal 'resources' as *status* and *power* within the society; and to social mobility in general.

It is also, at a national level, the decisive factor in achieving labour competitiveness in the face of globalisation. (Not a labour competitiveness born of low wages and oppressive working conditions, but one based on high skills, high productivity, and hence high wages.)

Wealth takes many forms. Perhaps its most important form is education. The academic and technical level and skills of a people constitute the most important 'wealth' of the nation. When the German and Japanese economies – their factories, ports, railways, power plants; in fact, virtually their entire infrastructure and productive capacity – were destroyed during the world war two, it took both countries less than 25 years to not only rebound but become the most powerful economies in the world after the US economy.

While all their *material* wealth had been destroyed, *their people* retained in their heads the scientific and technological knowledge, skills, and experience necessary to restore that material wealth – and more – in relatively little time.

What is true at the level of the nation-state is also true at the class, ethnic and individual family levels. For example, a well-off family which loses all its material possessions in a fire or other major disaster, and which, for the sake of argument, has no insurance cover, can, over time, rebuild or restore its relatively privileged material position, once its members are highly educated or skilled. The latter (high level of education) can be translated into the former (material wealth). But a family which starts with close to nothing and which, moreover, has little education, will simply sink even lower in the societal totem pole if faced with a disaster which wipes out the little that it has.

c **Discriminatory education as a tool of subjugation**
Discriminatory provision of education to different classes or ethnic or other groups within a society is therefore the single most powerful tool for subjugating, and marginalising those who are denied any, or inferior, education. In this context, it is no accident that, when women were most powerless in

societies worldwide, they were denied access to schools. In recent times, we have seen this with the Taliban in Afghanistan.

The discriminatory provision of education for Black people under apartheid in South Africa and in the Southern United States in the pre civil rights era, was linked inextricably to the conscious, official policy of white subjugation of Black people in those societies. Likewise, the fact that universal secondary education was only introduced in Britain halfway through the 20th century (with the 1944 Education Act), while schools for the children of the upper class had existed for centuries, tells its own story.

Moreover, the fierce battle waged by the privileged in Britain in the 1950s, 1960s and 1970s against the Labour policy of phasing out the heavily class-based system of grammar and secondary modern schools, and replacing them with one type of secondary school, the comprehensive, signals just how important a societal resource education was seen to be by Britain's traditional rulers – as also by that generation of Labour Party leaders.

d Income, wealth, power, prestige – and education

The many public debates about – and the condemnation of – those prominent white *and* Black Labour Party leaders who have gone to great financial lengths to send their children to high quality education private schools, emphasises just how important those very clever persons (and the upper and middle classes, generally) see education for their children. They perceive it as critical in terms of:

- Achieving and/or maintaining the family's access to high income, and to wealth creation opportunities.
- Access to power and high status within the society (whether in government, business, the armed forces, the churches).
- Strengthening or increasing the family's income/ wealth/ power/ status ('societal resources') with each new generation of the family.

These clever and highly successful people recognise that rises and falls in access to society's resources (income, wealth, power, prestige) by different generations of the same families are overwhelmingly a factor of education: maintaining – and increasing – each generation's access to education, in relation to that of previous generations; and in particular in relation to that of others in the same generation within the society.

I believe that it is a distraction for progressive people to condemn and vilify those individuals who opt for the best education they can access for their children. Given the centrality of education for accessing and enjoying all of the society's other resources, everyone must instead face squarely and honestly the fundamental structural problem which characterises the education system in order to seek to change it. Its discriminatory provision of educational resources to children and young people, linked to its two-tiered structure – one for those who can afford it privately, and one for the remainder of the society – constitutes the essence of the problem. The growing differentiation in the quality of education provided within the state system further complicates the situation, and widens further the disparities and inequalities which are also manifested in other areas of the society.

e **'Donkey say the world ent level'**
Children in Britain do not begin life from a level playing field, nor therefore do they enter school for the first time on an equal footing with all their fellow children-citizens of the country. As the old people in the Caribbean like to put it, 'Donkey say the world ent level.' Discriminatory access to jobs, promotion, housing, education, and other societal resources by their parents based on considerations of class, gender, race and other factors ensure that each child begins life, and school, with different degrees of 'handicap'.

They start life, and school, with different expectations, differing degrees of self-confidence and self-belief, and different language and other skills. Most critically, they begin with different amounts of financial resources and 'old boy network' resources at their parent's command. Moreover, the schools which exist demand very different degrees of these resources, in order to gain access to them.

f **Education earns money, which buys education, which earns money, which buys education...**
To summarise the above, we can say, therefore, that differential access to educational resources leads to differential access to society's other resources, particularly income, wealth, and valuable social contacts and connections. These other societal resources in turn help to perpetuate inequalities in access to educational resources, since the better off and better 'connected' tend to get the overwhelming majority of the places available at the highest-quality (and usually high fee-paying) educational establishments – thus ensuring vastly different levels of educational

achievement by the children of the succeeding generation, and hence differential access by them to income, wealth, power and prestige…and so on and so on, from one generation to the next.

Significantly, most of the limited social mobility which occurs within this self-perpetuating and fairly rigid class/race structure has come about through scholarships offered to a tiny percentage of the disadvantaged in each generation. In other words, these few children or young people were privileged to get into the quality-education tier of the education system without the normal requirement for their parents to dish out substantial sums for fees, etc – sums which, of course, they would not have had. The nexus between income/wealth and quality-education provision was broken just for these few!

g Break the link between money and connections, race and education
What is needed, instead, is a system of quality education for *all*, and therefore, by definition, one which is not dependent on the parental wealth, social status and connections; one which does not have schools providing vastly different standards of education; and one which does not have a multi-tiered system of education, providing differential education for the children of different classes, genders and ethnicities. Let us be clear about one thing: the goal is *not* 'Equality of provision of educational resources for all'. If this were the goal, it could be achieved by 'dumbing down' the excellent private schools and the better state schools to the lower standards of the many inadequately resourced state schools. Rather, the goal is 'High quality education for ALL'. This would require not a lowering of the standards of the best schools but rather a raising of the standards of other schools to that of the best ones. It would mean undertaking the necessary steps to bring all schools up to the highest standards.

h The cost and the benefits of high quality education for ALL
Some may ask whether the nation has sufficient resources to spend so as to bring *all* schools throughout the country up to high educational standards so that *all* children can enjoy exposure to these standards. The answer is an unqualified yes. Britain is a wealthy country with more than sufficient resources to do this. It is all a question of priorities. Just consider the enormous sums being spent on nuclear weapons, and on submarine delivery systems for their use; or what has *already* been spent on the Iraq war, and the answer becomes clear.

However, there is another and perhaps even more important answer to the question as to whether the nation has the necessary resources to transform all its schools into top-notch learning centres. The answer is that it has no choice, if it wishes to remain one of the leading economies in today's highly competitive, knowledge-intensive, globalised environment. The short-sighted approach to competing globally in today's cut-throat world is to restrict trade unions, dampen wage increases, slash welfare benefits, reduce workers' fringe and other benefits, lay off full-time workers and produce more with part-time, socially unprotected workers, and generally to introduce what is euphemistically called a more flexible labour force. The *real* solution is to transform Britain's working population from being a labour force, into *human capital*, through massive investment in education. It is to develop *all* of Britain's brainpower to the maximum so that Britain becomes among the most competitive in today's world.

It is important for us to understand the world we are living in today, for the kind of education system that is needed depends on our understanding this. In the pre-industrial age, the economy was *labour-intensive*. During the heyday of the industrial era, the economy was transformed from being labour-intensive to being *capital-intensive*. In today's post-industrial, globalised economy, the most successful economies are *knowledge-intensive*. Nowadays, when you buy a calculator, a mobile phone, or a watch, the plastic and other cheap materials from which these are made represent a tiny fraction of the production costs (and hence price) of these items.

It is the *'brain-labour'* of hundreds, sometimes thousands of scientists and technicians which is captured in the extraordinary range of things that these small and 'simple' devices can perform, that accounts for most of the costs of production, and which earns the companies producing them billions of dollars, and the scientists and technicians who designed their software very high salaries. It is generally not recognised that it is computer software, not computer hardware, where the highest profits – and the highest wages – are earned. Making the physical parts of a computer takes relatively old production methods. However, designing the computer software to work within the physical equipment which constitutes the computer itself takes hundreds of thousands of high-priced brain power. For this reason it is no accident that starting salaries for computer programmers are so high worldwide.

Indeed, it has been widely reported that virtually all of Microsoft's staff who have been there from the software company's start-up are millionaires, and many are multi-millionaires. *That's where high productivity, high wage, high profits, and high national income are to be found: in knowledge-intensive industries; in industries utilising highly developed brainpower in the production of goods and services. The more such industries a country has, the more wealthy and competitive the country. In turn, to have such a labour force – sorry, to have such a human capital force – requires the transformation of the education system from its present semi-feudal discriminatory system which fails to fully develop the brain power and talents of the majority of its children and students, ie tomorrow's working population; tomorrow's 'working capital', into a unified, quality education for all system.*

In today's highly competitive, globalised, knowledge-intensive production world, therefore, the way to equality is the possession of high skills, highly marketable knowledge. The present trends in the education system are geared not just to maintaining centuries-old inequalities and discriminatory treatment, but actually to worsening the class and race chasms which exist. In such an environment, a few Blacks, like a few working class whites, will rise within the system, based on a combination of fortuitous circumstances and ability. But the vast majority of Black *and* white working class children will not and cannot 'make it' within this class and race-riven system.

All people and organisations of goodwill and good intentions will need, of necessity, to focus their thoughts and energies on uniting in the great battle needed to radically transform the British education system into one of HIGH QUALITY EDUCATION FOR ALL.

i Is there a role for trade unions in this fight?

Yes, this is a task for all trade unions. Trade unions can fight in traditional ways for better wages and working conditions for their present members. True. But what is the best way to fight for *future* 'better wages and working conditions' *for the children of their current members?* Through a struggle for root and branch change in the education system so as to *genuinely* offer equality of educational opportunity for all. This is a battle, then, for parents – Black and white – for teachers, community leaders, church leaders, women and youth groups, student bodies, AND THE TRADE UNION MOVEMENT!

i Should Black people fight by themselves, or form alliances?

Black supplementary schools, and Black parents, youth, and community groups, remain vital organs in the struggle for high quality education for all black children. These many organisations in the black community must be strengthened and many more formed where there are few or none. No victory is possible without struggle, and no struggle can be won without being organised. *However,* black people, and their organisations, fighting by themselves, in isolation from other forces which have common aims, will not get far.

This is because black people are a small minority of the population. If the majority of whites (ie the white working mothers and fathers) are having difficulty getting the system to work in *their* interest, what chance is there for a small minority fighting its battles in isolation from natural allies? Yes, some individual battles may be won in relative isolation. But, to win the war of educational transformation – and hence of poverty elimination and defeat of racism and other ills – we must put sectarianism aside, and join forces with all who have the same goals of an end to discrimination and the establishment of high quality schools FOR ALL children regardless of class, race, gender, religious or economic circumstances. If all adopt this approach and organise and fight in a focused way for it, victory becomes possible – victory *will* be achieved!

© Bernard Coard 2004

Gary McFarlane

A Black school governor's view

LET'S BEGIN by considering the legacy of the education system in general and something of the social order that Black children are confronted with – the comprehensive education system and the current 'crisis' of multiculturalism. In the light of the battering comprehensive education has suffered it's worth recalling that the system was created to act as a counterweight to social inequalities in society. In the old selective set-up working class white kids were largely consigned to second-rate secondary modern schools. For African-Caribbean children, as Bernard Coard made clear in his seminal work, the deal from the state was grimmer still. The problems of struggling to get by economically were compounded by the impact of racism – both on the individual and on the community as a whole.

Multiculturalism, that other whipping boy of the media and others, arose in the 1980s precisely to undo the damage done by institutions, like the infamous schools for the Educationally Subnormal. It reflected the changes in society that today mean there is a large majority that positively supports the notion of different cultures existing together harmoniously. A BBC poll in the wake of the London bombings showed 62 percent agreeing with the statement that multiculturalism makes 'Britain a better place to live'. My daughter's school in north London has over 30 languages spoken within it. Multiculturalism is a reality in inner city schools, estates and workplaces.

But what of the multiculturalists who don't know how to defend multiculturalism? They tell us multiculturalism apparently lost its way by stressing identity over integration. It's not decades of discrimination against immigrant minorities that's to blame for Black educational under-achievement, you understand. At the same time some of these very selfsame critics say that segregating Black boys is the answer. This pro-posal is really to give up on the fight, and would create more problems than it could possibly solve.

In truth, many of the gains we started to win in the 1970s and 1980s are being undermined – primarily by the return to Victorian values and the introduction of the market mentality into education. Testing allows Black children to be readily labelled as failures. In addition, money is being diverted into the pockets of private contractors to tackle overdue infrastruc-ture improvements, but at the expense of educational resources for schools.

The problem is that the people forming and implementing education policy make assumptions that are increasingly based on a conception of the world that is totally different to the reality most of us inhabit. Previously integration into the 'mainstream' or dominant 'British' culture didn't require new Britons to change their cultural heritage, but now we're told multiculturalism has allowed all these 'unBritish' tendencies, like Islam pre-sumably, to prosper unhindered. US Senator Joe McCarthy's UnAmerican Activities Committee would have been proud.

We therefore need to reaffirm our support both for the comprehensive ideal and for the hope that the unfinished work of multiculturalism can be defended and advanced. And it is out of those two ideas – social equality and racial equality – that a solution to the problems confronted by Black kids, suffering today at the hands of an education system that's failing them, will come. Inequality in one area impacts on the other. The key point is: Black issues only got tackled because parents, educationalists, political activists and anti-racist teachers took up the cause in the 70s, against the backdrop of a comprehensive education system intended to offer equality.

Social and racial inequality must be addressed simultaneously. In recog-nising the interconnections at play we need not assign precedence to either but rather appreciate that the rundown in public services hits those at the bottom hardest – and African-Caribbeans still occupy a lower position in terms of occupation and earnings. A study of household income showed 28 percent of Black households receive below 60 percent of median income. For white households it's 17 percent.[1] There can be no social justice without the abolition of racism. Tackling the inequalities that spring from racism is a benefit to the wider community.

This is how African-Caribbean actor and playwright Kwame Kwei-Armah put it on the eve of the third 'London Schools and the Black Child' conference:

> Wherever I go in the world – and I travel a lot – I see similar trends in the working class and underclass in any society. We tend to ignore class very much in this. If you look at these boys who are underachieving we can look at their class and the overwhelming majority belong to certain social classes. Education is a way out of that: it needs to fulfil its brief of giving the best chance to everybody.
> **BBC News online, 10 September 2004**

That's why it's mistaken to conclude that, because Black working class boys perform worse academically than white working class boys, social class is not relevant. Instead we should appreciate that working class Black boys are at a double disadvantage because of social class and the colour of their skin. If class is irrelevant, why do Black and white middle class kids outperform all working class kids?

So our first task should be to defend and extend comprehensive education. In practice that means driving back the testing onslaught that makes British children the most tested in Europe. Straitjacketed testing from the age of seven introduces the notion of individual competition with your peers, as opposed to the approach of seeing education as a learning process with many different entry and exit points. Narrow concentration on the 'three Rs' in fact hampers the development of skills in those areas because it fails to provide a meaningful and relevant context for learning. As any good teacher will tell you, assessment of learners is something that is ongoing, and – at the micro level of lesson plans – checking that learning is taking place is integral.

What is required is a more progressive cross-curricular approach where maths, English, science, history, art and languages are taught in an interdisciplinary way. So when discussing the science behind the invention of the self-lubricating engine, invented by the African-American Elijah McCoy (where the phrase 'the real McCoy' is thought to come from), we could also consider the historical context in which he lived, or when learning about the history of the revolution in Haiti we might take the opportunity to learn some French. In short, the National Curriculum has to be radically transformed to accommodate this approach. Besides being of educational benefit to all, it is the only way in which a Black perspective can be adequately integrated without it being seen as something apart and ghettoised in a Black Studies GCSE – but of course there should be such a GCSE.

League tables, that force schools to compete and teachers to find shortcuts, are also detrimental to education and compound the problem. City Academies, so called specialist schools run by private companies with no particular educational expertise required, are a disaster for black kids. They represent a market mentality that ends up sucking resources from other schools and takes education out of democratic control. Children are literally seen as bags of cash. As it happens, these academies are failing even on their own terms, as recent debacles in Islington and Middlesbrough have shown. They should be abolished.

Streaming is another method used in schools that goes against the grain of the comprehensive ideal, although it's always been present in the system. It is probably not an exaggeration to say that every school in the country now uses streaming. Children are divided within years and classes into ability groups. This segmentation of the classroom is meant to provide the freedom for the more able to be pushed and the less able to be helped. But this is not actually what takes place. As David Gillborn's contribution to this collection highlights, pupils in the lower sets will be acutely aware of their lowly position, and there is no guarantee of getting that extra help given the preponderance of large class sizes. In addition the pressure to get good test results means those who are deemed likely to show the least improvement will tend to get the least attention in the name of efficiency. For the more able students, they will lose out from the lack of interplay with those at different levels. By helping others the brighter students will learn themselves. More able students are not held back by other students, but rather by the limits of the teaching experience. A good lesson plan should attempt to take account of the different learning styles of all the class members, and different abilities. Some learn through doing things themselves; others prefer a demonstration. Those who take in information visually may want to watch a video documentary while those with auditory processing difficulty might prefer the teacher's lessons to be available on an iPod to be sampled in the pupils' own time at their own pace.

Given the tools that it is now possible for teachers to deploy in the class-room – for example the fabulous interactive whiteboard, and IT resources more generally – there is no reason why a more cross-curricular approach on a well-resourced and stable platform could not be offered to our kids, except of course lack of money and political will. Streaming is an example of organising education without the learners in mind, and instead just sees things in terms of the allocation and management of limited resources. We need more teachers, a wider curriculum and the resources to realise the potential of the learning experience.

We need to spark our children's imaginations, capture their enthusiasm and build on it.

Meeting the needs of Black children

Upon leaving the primary school gates for the last time, Black boys will notice how society's view of them changes and comes into sharper relief. The cute little Black boy becomes the mugger and gangster. As a Black boy at comp you will be seen as a potential troublemaker, a low achiever with, at best, a bent for sport and music (although you'll be hard pressed to find many instruments in the average school). The negative effect of this stereotyping is reflected in the fact that at primary school Black children hold their own academically, but when they enter secondary school a gap begins to open up with their peers. Is there something wrong with Black boys, the way they live, their attitudes, or is there something wrong with society?

We're told that exclusions are so high and academic performance so low because Black boys have bought into an anti-learning culture of rap, guns and drugs. The establishment and the media are trying to say that there is indeed something wrong with Black boys rather than with the system itself. But Black boys face stereotyping and racism throughout the school system. For example, Black boys (and girls) are more likely to be excluded from primary school as well as secondary. Supposed attitudes to music, sex and gangs don't explain that.

I spoke to Dean Ryan, who works with disaffected youth in London, and this was his explanation for the low aspirations of some black youths:

> Their aspirations are lowered not by some cultural factor, but by the lack of a decent job and life chances. My job used to involve helping young people address the social problems they face. Now it is increasingly just

about getting them onto training courses. At the end of the course they come back without a job, wondering what the point was.

If Black children are going to feel that they are taken seriously and treated fairly then the fundamental issue of the lack of Black teachers has to be addressed immediately. But how? Where are we going to get hundreds of Black teachers from, fast? One answer that's been offered is to poach from those countries outside of the economically advanced regions, but don't they need teachers in Jamaica too? The only realistic and acceptable way to proceed is to make it more attractive for Black graduates to go into teaching. Part of the answer therefore means making teaching more attractive to everyone – and its least attractive part is the administration of a constantly changing, increasingly selective and marketised system. The proposals outlined earlier in this chapter, to abolish much of this baggage, would therefore be a massive help. But in addition, fast-tracking with financial incentives to Black undergraduates and new teachers is essential. The recent campaigns to attract mature graduates with financial incentives prove this is immediately possible.

That said, the commonsense assumption that Black teachers can automatically develop a more constructive relationship with Black children doesn't always follow. It can't be assumed that because you are Black you know what it takes to develop good pastoral work with African-Caribbean students. Anti-racist training should be aimed at teachers both Black and white. In relation to white teachers this isn't because Black parents and pupils necessarily see white teachers as the enemy. Training is required across the board to identify those who haven't got the message or just don't know how to relate to Black kids, in particular the boys.

An emphasis on getting more teachers from working class backgrounds into our schools will also be beneficial to our goals, given the socioeconomic profile of the African-Caribbean population.

Worryingly, anti-racism in teacher training has been progressively downgraded as the curriculum, and its delivery, has been subverted by the standards debate. This is particularly disappointing given the high level of development in the area during the 1980s and 1990s. There are outward signs that the General Teaching Council for England takes the matter seriously. In 2004 an initiative called Achieve was launched at the 'London Schools and the Black Child' conference to develop a 'network of professionals promoting race equality in schools'. But what does this mean in practice? Networking is one thing. We need funding and resources. Benchmarks also need to be established for good anti-racist practice in teaching by creating centres of excellence to run accredited training as part of continuing professional development.

The chance to talk to a sympathetic, credible adult in school, who is not a teacher, and is going to start by listening and helping through example, is enormously important. Mentoring programmes seek to do this and should be widely instituted, and not just as fleeting pilot schemes. Trained youth workers make excellent mentors but there should also be funding provided for Black practitioners in various professions to go into schools and for students to visit workplaces as mini-interneeships. Mentors should also be paid – in other words it shouldn't be left to volunteers, but seen as a professional practice and a student's right.

To facilitate parental involvement in their child's education and school life in general, paid leave from work should be encompassed within parental rights. And there is the wider issue of an overworked population with less and less time for the kids. The government's move to extend the school day to take account of working parents is in fact a way of offering childcare on the cheap and is likely to lead to people working even longer hours, not less. Black families, like everyone's, want and need more time to spend with their children in both recreation and education. Indeed the two often go together.

Supplementary or Saturday Schools, many of which have their roots in the struggles of the 1970s, should be financially assisted by the state and their work more closely correlated with local schools. The example of self-help the schools represent is in itself a testimony to the thirst for educational attainment that exists in the community. It's about time the government guaranteed funding for these initiatives, to end their hand to mouth existence.

Permanent exclusions must be drastically curtailed. Instead only internal exclusions should be allowed – where pupils are taught in the school but in a special fully resourced department. Schools exclude pupils far too quickly – often lacking the resources to deal with disruption. The easy answer is, get them out of the school environment. For the kid who's been excluded it makes them feel precisely that: excluded. When the system washes its hands of you, it becomes even harder to acquire aspirations beyond the limits of your immediate environment.

Northumberland Park School, Tottenham, almost written off as a failing school a few years ago, has been trying to address some of these problems. The most likely candidates for exclusion are usually the Black and Turkish boys and a minority of girls. One of the main reasons teachers gave for disruptive behaviour from pupils was the fact that they didn't understand what was going on in lessons. Every year might have half a dozen such students. To tackle the predominance of African-Caribbean kids among the disruptive element, the Aiming High programme was introduced. It's targeted at five schools nationally, including Northumberland Park, with a focus on Years 9 through to 11. Youth workers are assigned to the programme to work with students on issues such as anger management. Parents are also encouraged to come into school to help with out of school activities, such as trips to museums and theatres. Emphasis is placed on avoiding exclusions by using internal exclusions, which essentially amounts to one day off the timetable, and is often seen by pupils as the more arduous of the two options. The programme has had some impact in reducing the number of exclusions but the scheme is far too small and piecemeal.

Finola Brennan, a senior teacher and one-time mentor at the school, praised the programme and other attempts to curtail disruption and exclusions, but also pointed to the fragility of its funding:

> Much of my time was taken up in preventative work and with the local primary schools. We started with six mentors but now we only have two, each with a caseload of maybe ten to 15 students.

But the downside is best summed up in the catchphrase of the new head at the school: 'Everyone has the right to an education but no one has the right to disrupt.' There is still the danger, then, that the disruptive ones are seen as the problem instead of tackling what it is that makes them disruptive. Nevertheless, the school does have an internal pupil support unit although it only takes ten pupils, and with two to three members of staff allocated to the unit, its operation is considered 'expensive'.

We need to introduce structures in schools to allow pupils to challenge racist attitudes. A sort of school council cum watchdog should be created in schools to allow aggrieved pupils to find an outlet and redress for actual or perceived wrongs.

Urgent change is needed, but we aren't going to get it from this government without a fight, fixated as it is with 'choice' for the middle classes. And neither is private education a solution. In fact private schools are part of the problem because they help to uphold the idea of elitism in education and, besides, their fees are out of reach for most of us.

Schooling does not take place inside a vacuum and our fight to get a decent education for our children should link up with social movements that are trying to turn back the tide of privatisation and market economics that is plaguing Britain and the world. The recent European Social Forum in London was a prime example, but it was wasted. Our campaign should be seen as part of the movement for progressive change in this country. And it needs to be a real movement, not a conference once a year, as good as it is. That means taking up the issues raised in this book and demanding change at national and local level. Another world is possible and so indeed is another education system.

In conclusion then, contrary to the stereotypes, Black families have always placed a high emphasis on education. The disproportionate levels of GCSE 'failure' and exclusions among Black boys are because of racism. Blaming individual teachers won't do. The teachers are working in a framework of league tables and testing where the 'weak' fall by the way-side and teachers are overworked. Also, the national curriculum is a disgrace. Black history doesn't get a look in. Science and literature are taught with no regard to placing the subjects in a context that shows the contribution of Black people. And above all else Black children demand respect as individuals who also have dreams, but need help overcoming society's obstacle-course of institutional racism and prejudice.

Note

1   Office of National Statistics, 'People in Households Below 60 Percent Median Income: by Economic Status and Ethnic Group, 1996-1998', *Social Trends* 30 http://www.statistics.gov

●   Gary McFarlane is 45 and works as a journalist in London. He is currently the production editor at *Moneywise* magazine. He is a governor of Coleraine Park Primary School in Tottenham and was a lecturer in web design and project management at City and Islington College. He is a member of North London Respect and stood as a candidate in the 2004 European elections.

●   For more information on measures to overcome Black underachievement see the recommendations set out in Part 7 of the London Development Agency's research report, 'The Educational Experiences and Achievements of Black Boys in London Schools 2000-2003 – A report by the education commission at http://www.lda.gov.uk/upload/pdf/Main_Research_sect7.pdf

Sharon Geer

The ACE Project: working successfully to ensure the attainment of African- Caribbean boys

Introduction

When I was appointed Ethnic Minority Achievement coordinator with a specific brief to address the attainment of African-Caribbean boys at Forest Hill Boys School in 2002, I had an open brief. It was set against a national and local picture of underachievement among Black boys that is still familiar despite the numerous interventions to support raising attainment in schools.

The head and senior leadership in the school had a clear vision. They wanted an offer that was led by senior staff, and it was to be part of the school's development plan on raising attainment. After many years of trying different interventions run by outside agencies, they were clear about who they wanted to lead the project. It must be a teacher, an expert practitioner who understands the issues and dynamics of classroom, the complexities of the curriculum, and the nature of classroom interaction. The outcomes were never going to be evaluated by a single measure, and it was not budget sensitive. Nor did they want a closed offer – they wanted an entitlement offer to as many students as they could. They wanted it to become firmly embedded in the school over the next few years.

Basic principles

Some basic principles guided my thinking and influenced the way I set up the project. Far too frequently in the past, targeted interventions had been made, but the focus was on behaviour management, setting up a pre-exclusion project or working with the disaffected and disengaged in a way that treated the students as a problem. I fundamentally rejected these notions for the following reasons.

- I did not ever perceive Black boys to be a *problem*.
- I rejected the view that Black boys were intrinsically less able to access the British educational system.
- I was determined that the intervention must always be positive.
- I recognised that if I wanted to raise attainment I must focus on learning, not behaviour.

Once I had identified the issues, the challenge was to develop solutions that were possible, achievable and likely to be effective – out of this ACE was born.

Focus group

I invited a group of representatives from across the school to discuss the issues in the specific context of Forest Hill. We analysed data, identified a target group, and considered different models aimed at establishing and organising an entitlement offer of additional support. Among the issues we discussed were the time commitment required, the resources needed to run the programme effectively and the curriculum offer to participants.

As a result of this process the following decisions were made:

- There would be an entitlement offer to all African/African-Caribbean and mixed heritage students. This would dispel any notion of deficit.
- The programme would be based on group sessions. Six weekly courses per year – therefore a group would be seen five times in Key Stage 3/4.
- The students would be withdrawn from Personal Social Health and Citizenship Education (one taught period) for six weeks per year. It was vital that the sessions were conducted in school time/curriculum time and that the programme was seen as relevant and part of the curriculum, not an add-on.
- At Key Stage 4 there is another offer – 15 students identified as not

meeting 5 A-C targets were targeted for one on one academic tutoring (weekly sessions).

- The ACE Project is part of an integral whole-school drive to raise attainment of all pupils. It is complementary to other attainment-raising initiatives in the school, and to the support offered to other targeted groups.

The curriculum

Clearly the students had to be offered a curriculum which was specific to their age and stage. The focus of the work is building success in the curriculum and equipping pupils with key skills to enable them to become more effective learners.

There are separate programmes designed for each year group to ensure appropriate development and progression. The main topics include:

- Organising yourself for learning.
- Effective learning strategies – learning styles.
- Study skills – independent learning.
- Managing the dynamics of the classroom.
- Peer pressure/stereotyping.
- Culture identifying/self.
- Aspirations – planning for the future.
- Thinking skills.
- Communication – talking and thinking about their learning.

All sessions are 'talk sessions' – they are discussion based, and use solution-focused approaches. Students are encouraged to talk, debate, outline, rehearse, discuss, question and express their ideas. These are fundamental to the process of learning. It is a time out – a reflective space to consider the activity in which they are engaged for the rest of the time. They develop skills and strategies which they can take back to the classroom to support their learning.

Does it work? Has it been successful?

The results and outcomes of the work are quantifiable if one were to examine the 'raw' data. By the end of 2005 the gap between white students and African-Caribbean students had narrowed to just 2 points.

Forest Hill	Black A/C	White	Difference
2002	26.5	44.4	17.9
2003	26.7	35.9	9.2
2004	44.4	46.4	2.0

The project has had a powerful impact on the students. In December 2004 we ran a questionnaire/focus group session which revealed that students felt attached, empowered and confident as learners. The response of one student is simple but telling. He commented that ACE is important because 'I am being listened to.' Another suggested that 'it helps you see how to put things right'.

The power of the positive group dynamic is key. The groups are mixed – all pupils are different. Some are able, some disaffected. There are students with learning needs and others with behavioural needs. Their togetherness in a group is a key to the success in the project. Again, this is borne out by the students' own remarks. One respondent indicated that 'it gives me confidence I can speak out in this group. It helps me in other lessons,' and another admitted, 'We share some feelings about confidence problems – [we] talk together about how to express yourself in class.'

One student readily admitted that if it had not been for ACE he would have spent his time socialising rather than revising for exams. He attributed the improvement in his SATs results to his participation in the scheme. Another critically important aspect of ACE is the strength it gives students to avoid some of the more negative aspects of peer pressure. One of our students said, 'It gives you confidence, helps you to decide that you don't have to take part in something... You can walk away. The pressure is still there, but not as strong.'

Peer mentoring

We encourage our students to establish positive relationships with one another by building peer mentoring into the initiative. Successful older students on the project from years 11/12/13 talk to the younger students about how to be successful in school. These are extremely powerful sessions and have an enormous impact on the younger students. They remember the session, the talk, and they see the older boys as role models. When asked to comment, one of the mentors declared, 'Education sets you free... I want to tell the young ones...student to student is powerful!'

Impact outside of school

The success of the project has been acknowledged by the Department for Education and Skills which included the ACE Project in the 2003/4 London Challenge KS3 strategy. At a conference for London secondary schools entitled 'Ensuring the Attainment of Black Caribbean Boys', the work of the project was presented to a London-wide audience. As a lead practitioner I have written part of the accompanying handbook which has been circulated to all schools in London, and which is the most requested publication on its website (www.standards.dfes.gov.uk/keystage3/respub/ws_inc_bcb). A DVD on raising attainment which features the project has been produced and distributed nationwide.

Conclusion

The most evident and important thing about ACE is the impact the project is having on the students. They really enjoy it – they are usually extremely disappointed when the six sessions end, and are eager for the next year. There is increased attachment to the institution – the students feel they have a vested interest, a stake in the school's success.

Mediating the institution to the students and vice versa is an integral part of ACE. The students learn how to make it work for them. In order to be successful learners pupils need to understand the institution: its processes, relationships, classroom dynamics. They also need to be understood within it. 'ACE teaches us about ourselves and our future, and what we need to do to be successful,' commented one project participant.

It is possible to have a highly successful mainstream comprehensive school where Black boys are valued, not stereotyped; cared for, not controlled; empowered, not powerless; attached, not disaffected; perceived as norm, not other: and, most importantly, are successful learners. The ACE Project has proved this, and young Black men at Forest Hill School are thriving and learning in mainstream comprehensive education.

I leave the last word to Aaron Lee (Year 8) 'The Ace Project is important for me as a Black person because it makes me feel special... Like I have been chosen... Even though the media is representing us as young Black boys who are not achieving, we know we can achieve – we are successful and ambitious.'

● Sharon Geer is an advanced skills teacher in raising attainment and Ethnic Minority Achievement (EMA) coordinator at Forest Hill Boys School in south east London.

Julie Hall

What can teachers do?
What can parents do?

THIS CHAPTER aims to provide a resource for teachers, teacher trainers, and parents for, if we are enthused and angry by what we have read, we have to respond with action. The first session is aimed at teachers and teacher trainers and the second at family members and carers involved in bringing up young people.

What can teachers do?
As David Gillborn (1999) says:

> The responsibility for changing this situation lies primarily with teachers, head teachers, LEAs, education policy makers, their numerous advisers, and ultimately with government. It is time we stopped looking to Black students, their families and communities for the causes of, and answers to, problems rooted in systematic racism.

We have two choices before us. One is to aim to raise awareness of cultures and equal opportunities. As this book explains, this approach has been part of mainstream education policy for some years, it is what most teachers are taught through their training and many schools are very committed to this.

However, the fact remains that Black boys are being failed by an education system embedded with this approach.

The second choice is to aim to provide real equity within the classroom and across the school. Central to this is freedom from bias and a recognition of the multiple, complex interconnections between race, poverty, class and power in today's society. This goes beyond the diversity celebrations of the first choice to an attempt to get to the root of racism through exposing and exploring power structures and the role of race and class in society.

As Coard argues here in his article 'Thirty Years On', what we need is 'High quality education for ALL'. For whatever the teacher does in response to the issues raised in this book will result in improved education for all the students in the class and an improved experience of teaching for the teacher.

As teachers we are of course constrained by the environment in which we operate, for example the constraints of the National Curriculum, the culture of testing and the marketisation of education – targets, league tables and inspection regimes.

However, there are still many things we are doing or we can do in terms of:

- What we teach.
- How we teach.
- Building an anti-racist school.

1 What we teach
Ask yourself these questions as you deliver your curriculum:

- Can I adapt this to challenge commonly held assumptions, eg that migration is a recent phenomenon, or to link with events which will have touched the lives of the young people.
- Am I delivering an Anglocentric view of, eg, history or literature or geography? Can I find other perspectives?
- Can I use the topic to explore how race and class and gender are mixed up with, eg, economics and history?
- Can I use this as an opportunity to challenge stereotypes, eg to show that the origins of the alphabet lie in the Middle East, or that the Black presence in the UK goes back many, many thousands of years or that many African cities are vibrant and modern?
- Can I use this topic to generate new knowledge from my class, eg on the numbers of languages people speak, the number of countries people

have experienced, or to engage young people in sharing some of their life experiences?

- Am I rejecting tokenistic examples of multiculturalism and doing more than presenting other cultures as exotic, or focused around the usual examples of music or food?
- Where can I attempt a cross-curricular approach, which, for example, looks at the history behind mathematics?
- Can I include activities that allow young people to explore real facts and figures relating to, eg, migration or discrimination and notions of social justice and democracy?
- Can I build on the lived experiences of my students and their families? Can the class bring in items from home or can I invite parents, carers or members of the community to contribute?
- Can I help to show that cultures are all dynamic, evolving and connected?
- Can I use this topic to encourage young people to aim high, plan their future and consider their role in shaping it?
- Can I show Standard English as one form among a repertoire of many other valued styles of English and help students make decisions about when it should be used?

2 How we teach
a Classroom activities

- Have your learners at the centre of your mind when planning – ask yourself how can you spark their imaginations, capture their enthusiasms, relate to their lives, communicate passion about the subject?
- Ensure that students are learning actively, bringing much more of themselves to their learning through group discussions based on experiences, sharing ideas and activities to explore the issues facing them.
- Commonly create activities where young people are made to feel proud of their backgrounds, where they build on their lives and interests, enhanced perhaps by visiting community speakers or extended family members. Appreciate their unique talents and help students consider their futures.
- Avoid directing discussions around particular groups – allow discussions and debates to grow from students' contributions. Don't shy away from issues which students show a need to discuss – where possible show sensitivity to the issues in your young people's lives.

- Plan activities which encourage collaborative learning in peer groups and consider the use of peer assessment where appropriate.
- When providing resources or examples ask yourself whether they are appropriate for your group. Do they reflect their lives? Do they challenge stereotypes?

b Classroom relationships

- Provide safe space in your class to allow young people to challenge racist attitudes, to share realisations of how they might be viewed by others and to come to understand what might be happening to them.
- Ask yourself whether you are teaching with emotional intelligence, ie that you are responding to each student as a distinct, unique individual, that you are showing that you care about them and that you have some understanding of them. How they are feeling will have an impact on the level of their learning.
- Celebrate the skills and knowledge of those students who can speak more than one language or who have lived in other countries and present this as a really positive contribution to the class.
- Don't try and de-emphasise your teacher power. As Friere (1999) asserts, 'Dare to teach ' – really engage and push your students to engage with and critique commonly held assumptions.
- Don't aim to dominate or scare your class. Once you have firmly spoken to someone ensure you don't hold a grudge. Follow up at the end of the class or at the end of the day with any young people who seem upset or uncomfortable during class.
- Express high levels of warmth and low levels of criticism while setting and enforcing clear boundaries.
- Provide clear leadership in terms of encouraging supportive, positive behaviour, modelling, reflecting and developing positive attitudes, creating a safe, open climate and challenging assumptions and stereotypes. It can be difficult at first to strike the right balance between fixing clear boundaries and showing you are responsive and caring. Talk to colleagues about this and arrange to observe others if you can.
- Before you challenge someone's behaviour or attempt to summarise their approach to learning, perhaps in a report or at a parents' meeting, check yourself. Are you misunderstanding them or stereotyping them? Do you need more information before you make a judgement? Contact the

parents/carers from the beginning to ensure there are no misunderstandings.

- If you feel that you don't understand the lives of your students, ask for training and consider observing other learning environments such as local youth clubs or after-school activities.
- Be wary of interpreting noise levels, 'looks', body language or passionate exchanges of opinions as inappropriate. Be culturally sensitive to ways of communicating.

c Achievement

- Be aware that testing results in racialised patterns of achievement.
- Remember that 'ability' is subjective and dependent on a number of factors including the young person's self-esteem, their relationship with the teacher and motivation.
- When asked to band or set children attempt to measure potential rather than narrow definitions of ability and be highly conscious of stereotyping.
- When agreeing levels for GCSE, be as transparent as possible, discuss and explain decisions to parents and fight against putting 'the safe bets' into the higher tiers. This can have life-changing results.
- Express high realistic expectations of success, especially for Black boys and young men, and encourage them to contribute to and monitor their goals.
- Where extra support is required for a young person, create this as a real opportunity to do even better rather than a stigmatised or ghettoised place for underachievers. Monitor its effectiveness and keep parents informed.

3 Building an anti-racist school

- Build networks within and outside school.
- Encourage your school to fully comply with the Race Relations (Amendment) Act 2000.
- Ensure that patterns of achievement are monitored and discussed regularly.
- Work with your colleagues to build up resources which are accurate, relevant and challenging.
- Encourage others to see the school through the eyes of families who might not fit people's 'norms' and explore ways of reaching out to all and involving them in the school.
- Ensure invitations to families and carers are multilingual where required.

- Encourage teams to observe each other's classes in a supportive and constructive way and call for training in areas where people have identified further development.
- Develop strong links with local clubs and community groups.
- Work with others such as parents to provide after-school activities that really reflect the lives of the young people.
- Support new staff and trainees, encourage them to engage with these issues and be particularly aware that new Black staff may also be affected by any institutionalised racism at the school or college.
- Include the whole school community and learn from each other, particularly teaching assistants and young people who will provide valuable insights.

What can families and carers do?

Coard's orginal book ends with a number of suggestions for parents. Unfortunately these are still very relevant today. In addition people may want to also consider the following:

a   Choosing a school for your child
Research indicates (Blair, 1998) that a number of elements are necessary for a successful multi-ethnic school. Therefore where possible arrange to meet the head before choosing a school or attend an open day to ensure that:

- Staffing is stable and attempts to reflect the ethnic makeup of the school.
- There is a highly visible, committed school leadership team.
- There is a highly visible attempt to reflect the ethnic makeup of the school in its displays, resources and activities which aim to challenge stereotypes and commonly held assumptions.
- There are strong community links.
- Active involvement of parents is encouraged.
- There is compliance with the Race Relations (Amendment) Act, ie ethnic monitoring data is available and action plans are in place.
- Staff receive training in this area.
- There are clear policies on bullying and harassment.
- There are high expectations of success.
- Supportive, collaborative learning is encouraged.
- Be on guard for what Gillborn calls 'naive multiculturalism'.
- There is a range of interesting and relevant after-school activities.

However, it is fair to say that this cannot guarantee a racism-free experience for your child. As this book highlights, institutional racism is pernicious and we still have a long way to go.

b Monitoring your child's progress

- Each year find out as much as you can about your child's curriculum and the expectations of the teacher in terms of homework, approaches to learning and classroom culture.
- Don't wait till parents' evening if something is of concern. Contact the teacher either by letter or via the school office and arrange a short meeting or telephone conversation.
- Always end the meeting by agreeing some kind of action and fixing a date to review how things are going, and take a friend or colleague with you where possible.
- Don't be afraid to ask for information on school policy such as Special Educational Needs, exclusions, banding and behaviour, including racial bullying.
- If you feel your child isn't reaching their potential, speak to the teacher. The school has a responsibility to show individual learning needs are being met.
- If you are asked to attend school over a behaviour issue, ask to see the behaviour policy first and ensure the correct procedure has been followed. Where possible ask for proof and witness statements and talk to your child.
- If you feel your views are not respected or that you are being stereotyped raise this with the teacher and if you are still not satisfied speak to the head. Your final recourse is to the governing body.
- In a year where your child will have a SATs test, ask for past papers to practise with your child and talk to the teacher about their expectations for your child. Ask to see some examples of good answers.
- In Year 9 young people will begin to be banded in preparation for GSCEs. Find out which exam board is being used for each exam and buy specific revision guides for every subject. This is a very important time to be in communication with your child's teachers as they will be assessing your child's chances of success. The teacher's assessment of your child's ability will result in a decision on which level they will be entered for. Many Black children are denied access to the higher tiers.
- Build up your networks – other parents, people interested in this area of education, community support groups.

- Provide consistent support – especially through secondary school.
- Never think you're being over-protective, 'over the top' or over-sensitive. All the research points to the crucial part played by parents.

What can we do together?

As Coard argues in his updating, we must join forces to end discrimination for all children regardless of class, race, gender, economic circumstances or disability. We need to be organised and focused. The trade unions can help us, as can community groups and our own networks. We need meetings in schools, colleges and churches to raise the matters addressed here more widely and we need to call our education authorities and local and national politicians to account. Through the meetings our networks will grow and our voices will become louder. It's not difficult: book a room, find a speaker, advertise it locally and begin. Together we can make a difference!

Resources

Find out about customising the curriculum at www.qca.org.uk/8529.html
A toolkit for auditing practice and setting targets: Commission for Racial Equality, *Learning for All* (2004).
Resources for anti-racist teacher training www.multiverse.ac.uk

References

G L Brandt, *The Realization of Anti-Racist Teaching* (Falmer, Lewes, 1986).
M Blair and J Bourne, *Making the Difference: Teaching and Learning in Successful Multiethnic Schools* (Sudbury, DfES and Open University, 1998).
S Dadzie, *Toolkit for Tackling Racism* (Trentham Books, 2002).
P Friere and D P Macedo, 'Pedagogy, Culture, Language and Race: a Dialogue', in Leach and Moon (eds), *Learners and Pedagogy* (Sage, London 1999).
A M Ingram, *Good Practice in Raising the Achievement of Black Caribbean Heritage Pupils in Islington Primary Schools* (London CEA@Islington Ethnic Minority Achievement Service, 2003).
V Laville, *How Can Teachers Raise the Educational Achievement of Black Male Pupils in the Classroom?* (Goldsmiths University, 2005).
A Rampton, *West Indian Children in our Schools* (Cmnd 8273, HMSO, 1981).
T Sewell, *Black Masculinities and Schooling: How Black Boys Survive Modern Schooling* (Trentham Books, 2000).
Lord Swann, *Education for All: Final report of the Committee of Inquiry into the Education of Children from Ethnic Minority Groups* (Cmnd 9453, HMSO, 1985).
D Walker Tileston, *What Every Teacher Should Know About Diverse Learners* (Sage, London, 2004).

- Julie Hall is a parent of three children and has worked for many years as a teacher in inner London. She now works as an educational developer and researcher at Roehampton University. Julie is very active in her local community in Brixton.

Steve Sinnott

Bringing down the barriers: raising the attainment of Black Caribbean pupils – an NUT perspective

THERE IS no disputing the fact that Bernard Coard's publication in 1971 of *How the West Indian Child Is Made Educationally Subnormal in the British School System* was seminal. It had an enormous impact on the educational establishment and in particular made Black parents acutely aware of what was happening to the education of their children across the country.

The Coard book also had a tremendous impact on the conceptualisation of Special Educational Needs, contributing to the 1978 Warnock report's shift from the medical model of 'mental deficiency' to an educational needs based model.

Over the past 34 years since the publication of the pamphlet, much has improved in the education system. Equally, some things have not improved as much as we might have hoped. While the attainment gap between Black Caribbean children, particularly boys, and others has reduced in recent years, it still remains the case that their attainment at GCSE remains unacceptably low and well below the national average.

The National Union of Teachers (NUT) was not immune from the impact of the Coard pamphlet. Activists who were involved in the NUT at the time recall that the pamphlet galvanised the NUT to focus on race equality issues in education in a much more sustained manner than before. The NUT has always been at the forefront on equality issues in education and its archives are a testimony to this commitment. The Coard pamphlet, however, gave the NUT a very particular focus on issues related to the attainment of minority ethnic pupils, in addition to its already well established policies on equality in general.

Writing in February 2005 in the *Guardian*, Bernard Coard said, 'It is my belief that the turnaround in the establishment's response also owed a great deal to the support which the contents of the book, its main thrust and objectives, received from thousands of teachers – white teachers, including several headteachers – up and down the country.'

Coard is making an important statement about the vital role of teachers in eradicating the attainment gap between Black Caribbean pupils and the national average. Teachers have a key role in tackling discrimination and promoting equal opportunities in schools and creating a positive school environment for all pupils. Research evidence is very clear on the impact of teacher expectations on pupil achievement.

Research evidence also shows that during the primary phase Black Caribbean pupils do not fall behind, but that something happens during their adolescence which negatively impacts on attainment. Precisely what happens is both a complex and familiar debate involving analysis by Tony Sewell of the impact of street culture to continuing criticisms of teacher-pupil relationships and expectations. This is a continuing and important debate.

Due to its role in enhancing the life chances of pupils, the education system has a clear and particular responsibility to ensure that teachers are equipped with the knowledge, skills and understanding as necessary tools to challenge their own and their pupils' stereotypical views about particular Black and minority ethnic groups.

In 1980, in its evidence to the Rampton Committee of Inquiry into the Education of Children from Ethnic Minority Groups, the NUT stated:

Within the education system neither teachers nor pupils are blind to colour, and it would be insufficient for teachers to claim that they give all their pupils equality of treatment within the classroom. They have to cope with social pressures from the outside world – for the classroom does not exist in a vacuum – and attitudes of racial intolerance, prejudice and a stereotyped view of ethnic minority groups will often percolate through into schools. If teachers are to play their full part in changing this climate by educating their pupils to respect and welcome ethnic and cultural diversity then they need help in their training to foster positive attitudes among those they teach.

In order to achieve this aim, the NUT argued that it was important that teacher education played its part in preparing teachers for teaching in a culturally diverse society. How successful was this call from the NUT and others? The response from teacher training institutions was varied across the country. Furthermore, any work in this area was often dependent on the dedication of individuals rather than the institutions themselves. Many such people were appointed during the 1980s with a 'multicultural' brief. When funding ran out, they were seldom replaced and the institutions reverted to their former practices. Any changes were not grounded in policies, practices and procedures.

It is true to say, however, that many teacher training institutions responded enthusiastically to this challenge. There are many positive examples of teacher education institutions which attempted to ensure that the curriculum they offered to trainee teachers was capable of delivering teachers fit to teach in our increasingly ethnically diverse schools.

The establishment of the Teacher Training Agency (now the Training and Development Agency – TDA) standards for initial teacher training may have been a setback for anti-racist teacher education. Teacher training institutions which had pioneered anti-racist teacher education felt that they had to scale back their activities in this area due to the overloaded and tightly defined standards for trainee teachers. Anecdotal evidence suggests that this is particularly true for one-year courses, such as the Postgraduate Certificate in Education.

Evidence from the TDA annual newly qualified teacher survey seems to confirm the NUT's concerns about the preparation of teachers to teach in a culturally diverse society. Over the last three years the TDA survey has shown that large proportions of NQTs (Newly Qualified Teachers) feel that their training does not adequately prepare them to teach pupils from minority ethnic backgrounds. In 2005, for example, the survey showed that NQTs' perceptions of how well their training had prepared them to teach minority ethnic pupils (35 percent rated this good or very good) was only a marginal increase on the 2004 survey, which showed that 32 percent rated this aspect as good or very good in their initial teacher training. Clearly teacher training needs to do better.

In the years following the Coard pamphlet, large numbers of teachers rose to the challenge of tackling racism and discrimination in education. Teachers took their lead, particularly in London, from the now dismantled Inner London Education Authority (ILEA), which made available resources for schools and teachers, including professional development courses and advice and guidance for schools. The ILEA's influence spread to many other parts of the country. Yet the coherence of the practice that it generated has waned over the years. While there are now many examples of good practice across the country, they are not consistent and lack a coherent national direction.

Teachers during this period were highly active in the anti-racist movement. The Coard book triggered the establishment of many national anti-racist groups, the Association of London Teachers Against Racism and Fascism (ALTARF) and the National Anti-Racist Movement in Education (NAME) to name just two. A large proportion of the teachers involved in the activities of such organisations were NUT members.

At the same time, along with Black parents, Black teachers were also politicised by the Coard report. Black teachers developed their own self-organised groups and in time this led to the establishment of Black members' courses and an annual Black Teachers' Conference within the NUT. To this day the conference is a highlight of the NUT's calendar and annually attracts large numbers of Black teachers who have increasingly become more active within the NUT.

The NUT's Black Teachers' Conference is complemented by a highly successful professional development programme for teachers. Anti-racist teacher training and continuous professional development are the key to unlocking any closed minds which exist within the teaching profession. The NUT's professional development programme has a strong focus on race equality issues which aims to provide teachers with the knowledge, skills and experience necessary to promote race equality in schools.

The greatest sea change has occurred as a result of the Stephen Lawrence report. The debate around the impact of institutional racism, particularly in the public services, has galvanised awareness – a debate which rightly still continues.

This article argues that the dismantling of the ILEA had a negative impact on the capacity of teachers to deliver anti-racism at the chalkface. The abolition of the ILEA occurred as part of the Education Reform Act 1988 and its associated National Curriculum, Local Management of Schools and the policy of parental choice. Many of us remember the painful vilification of schools and teachers in the media and by politicians of teachers' efforts to promote anti-racism in schools. Despite the odds, many schools and teachers have continued to make valiant efforts in this area and the NUT has been behind them all the way.

The causes of Black Caribbean under-attainment are complex. Those who over-emphasise the negative role of teachers in the context of a blame culture create the conditions in which a positive and proactive dialogue is dogged by organisations and individuals taking entrenched positions. A reasoned and mature debate on the causes of Black Caribbean under-attainment in schools would bear more fruit. It is the case that the academic debates on this issue swing between the impact of peer pressure, the socio-economic nature of the Black Caribbean community, the relations between parents and schools, the low expectations of teachers and institutional racism. So the solution needs to be multi-faceted and concerted. There are no magic solutions.

In his updated essay in this collection, 'Thirty Years On', Bernard Coard issues the rallying call 'High quality education for ALL' and argues:

> ...that a successful assault on poverty, racism, gender and class discrimination, and on the income, wealth, social status and decision-making gaps which go with these in British society, requires a fundamental transformation of the British education system.

The NUT couldn't agree more. We believe that it is the development of a truly comprehensive education system which will deliver the aim of closing the gap between the attainment of Black Caribbean pupils and other pupils. In its education statement, 'Bringing Down the Barriers', published in 2004, the NUT says:

> Comprehensive education is about tackling barriers to high quality education. No government committed to raising the living standards of its people and to playing a progressive role internationally can afford to have an education service which is shaped by barriers arising from, for example, the influence of social class and economic and health issues, race, gender, disability or sexuality.

The terms 'comprehensive education' and 'equality of opportunity' are synonymous. As the OECD's Programme of International Student Assessment (2000) report demonstrates, the best education service is one where there is a single non-diverse system of well resourced provision within which the needs of all children and young people are targeted and met.

Within such a system there should be a sustained attack on the root causes of social and economic deprivation. There needs to be proper joined up thinking on how initiatives in communities to tackle social and economic deprivation can link up to education and anti-racist strategies locally.

The greatest potential for such joined up thinking lies in the widely welcomed 'Every Child Matters' agenda which recognises and sustains the idea that every school is at the centre of its community.

If schools are essential to their communities, then all parents should be entitled to send their children to good local schools and live up to the responsibilities that go alongside such entitlements. All the evidence points to the fact that this is the wish of the vast majority of parents. Indeed, local schools are enhanced by their communities and communities are enhanced by their local schools. The journalist Fiona Millar, at a recent NUT conference, called for good local schools for all. This is the idea behind which all stakeholders should put their energies.

It would be profoundly pessimistic to assume that the idea of good local schools for every community is a less powerful idea than the concept of the 'right to choose' schools. Indeed, the idea of 'choice' can exacerbate social division. The right to choose a school can only be used by those who have the capacity to make such choices. Discrimination, and economic and social disadvantage make the idea of school choice being equally available to all an illusion.

Schools' intakes reflect their communities and there is still much work to be carried out on targeting funding which tackles social disadvantage, preventing admissions arrangements disadvantaging both socially deprived communities and minority ethnic communities. Disproportionate numbers of Black pupils are still found in schools in areas of greatest social and economic deprivation. That is why the vision of high quality local schools for all supported by highly trained teachers (including in anti-racist practice) is so powerful.

The vision and the only viable solution for tackling the unacceptably low attainment of Black Caribbean children described above will not be achieved by providing 'diversity' in the structure of education that the government so favours. 'Diversity' of provision is a powerful background factor against securing equality of opportunity, particularly in redressing the impact of social and economic disadvantage.

The realisation of NUT policies contained in 'Bringing Down the Barriers' provides the best chance for Black Caribbean children. The NUT, therefore, invites parents – Black and white, teachers, community leaders, faith leaders, student bodies and the trade union movement more widely – to join hands with us to ensure that in a decade's time we do not still regret the relative under-attainment of Black Caribbean pupils.

- Born in Liverpool, Steve Sinnott became general secretary of the NUT on 29 June 2004, having been deputy general secretary since 1994 when he was elected in the middle of his year as national president of the NUT. Steve was the first president of the union to have attended a comprehensive school. He took a four-year BA in Social Sciences at Middlesex Polytechnic, graduating in 1974, and a PGCE at Edge Hill College in Ormskirk in 1975. His first teaching post in 1975 was at Shorefields Comprehensive in Toxteth, Liverpool, where he taught humanities. In 1979 he moved to Broughton High School near Preston, where he became head of economics and business studies until his election as deputy general secretary in November 1994.

Paul Mackney

The relevance of Coard's pamphlet today

EVERY NOW and then you read something that opens up your eyes and makes you think in a different way. Bernard Coard's pamphlet *How the West Indian Child is Made Educationally Subnormal in the British School System* did just that for many people including me.

When it was published in 1971 Hans Eysenck and other 'experts' were telling us all that Black people were less intelligent than white people and that this could be measured by tests. Despite the high aspirations of West Indian parents for their children, they were bound to fail, do the worst paid and most repetitive jobs, because experts had shown they were intrinsically less intelligent. Rae Davis, now the Principal of the Jamaica University of Technology, recalled to me the impact that this had upon people from the Caribbean at the time: '[We] were somewhat on the back foot and losing our confidence. But Coard's pamphlet changed all that.'

For those of us with even a sketchy knowledge of imperialism and its brutal and demeaning enslavement and wastage of millions of people, it was easy to acknowledge at a theoretical level the continuation of racist views. Furthermore, white 1960s radicals such as me had often read the definitions of institutional racism by Stokely Carmichael, Hamilton and others. The very political ones among us had read C L R James's triumphant assertions of Black intelligence in *The Black Jacobins*. But these were discussed in small political millieux.

Coard came out of the same traditions but he also gave us something that we could do, which related the theory to practical activity. With his concrete examination of the interstices of the process by which society divides people on racial lines, he gave us elements of a contemporary theory of learning (and the failure to learn) that had immediate practical application.

Coard wrote at the start of his conclusions chapter, 'This booklet has been written for the West Indian Community in Britain.' But it also presents lessons for us all. It challenges white teachers to examine their own practice, to listen to what the Black parents are saying and to work for institutional changes as well. To the Black community it gives the imperative of self-organisation, Saturday Schools and so on.

For unions, though it may seem very different, Coard's message on race is not dissimilar to some of the early precepts of working class self-organisation that were central to the development of trade unions. After all, the establishment had originally held the view that workers were too stupid to be educated, with the sub-set that, if they were wrong on that, it was nevertheless dangerous to do so. In this context, it is interesting to note that Coard now presents his argument in the context of campaigning for 'High Quality Education for ALL'.

It is possible to argue that just as schools have failed Black children, so unions have failed Black people in society.

But the message from Coard's pamphlet that suggested that the thinking and practice of many teachers might be racist and (unintentionally) discriminatory or inadequately attuned to the problem was not popular with many teacher unions in the 1970s.

There have been enormous advances in both thinking and practice since then, but the impulse to defend teachers at any price is still strong. Thus the leader of one large schoolteacher union said the definition of institutional racism presented in the Stephen Lawrence inquiry report was 'gobbledygook' and irrelevant to education. Other institutions have also found the lessons hard to digest. Some have understandably invoked Bernstein's crie de coeur that 'education cannot compensate for society'.[1] But this has never stopped unions trying to argue for practices that prefigure a better set-up in any other area of activity.

There are major implications in Coard's analysis for unions. Teacher unions, in particular, have an obligation not merely to pursue better terms and conditions for their members, but also to critique and work to improve the education system within which they work.

In the further education colleges and the new universities where Natfhe members work, the proportion of Black students is double that in the populations as a whole. This is largely because of the GCSE achievement rates and the difficulty in finding work. But the number of Black students is not reflected in the workforce where there are only six Black principals (four of whom have been appointed since the time of the Stephen Lawrence inquiry report when there were only two), while 25 would be proportionate to the population as a whole

The TUC estimated that unemployment stood at 11 percent for Black workers and 5 percent for whites in June 2005.[2] Whatever their level of qualification, an ethnic minority person is more likely to be unemployed – 'for example a white person who only has GCSEs is more likely to have a job than a Black job hunter with 'A' levels'. More hopefully, however, the TUC noted, 'There are now more Black and Asian people in work than there were seven years ago, but progress is slow. If the employment rate for Black workers continues to rise at its current modest pace, it could take 46 years before employment is as high among the Black working age population as among the white.'

Unions have a duty to be at the cutting edge of equality practices. In view of this, Natfhe, the employers' organisations and the funding bodies established the Commission for Black Staff in Further Education. Its aim has been to get to the roots of the problem of under-representation of Black staff in colleges.

The commission established witness days around the country where Black staff described their experiences, often in harrowing detail. There were painful echoes of Coard's pamphlet and, in response to requests, Natfhe has distributed over 100 'pirate' photocopy editions of the pamphlet in the last five years!

The principal recommendations of the Commission for Black Staff in FE, to improve the number and conditions of Black staff at all levels, echo Coard's final sentence calling for 'more Black teachers'. The report, recommendations and handbooks of the commission go a long way to providing a strategy to achieve that.[3]

But the commission's proposals, good as they are, are all set in the framework of current employment legislation that does not permit more than positive action to remedy historic discrimination. Even if every college implemented every proposal there would still be a major problem 20 years down the track.

All these issues also have major implications for the structures of unions (well summarised in the Labour Research Department's pamphlet *Black and Minority Ethnic Workers* – June 2005). Natfhe and its partner in a potential merger – the Association of University Teachers – have been giving much thought to enhancing the best of the traditions from both unions in the proposals for the new union of 120,000 members.

It is our intention to build a union which transmits a clear anti-racist message from the top, that is seen as a champion of race equality, that listens to its Black members and provides many routes to their participation in the leadership. The new union will connect the struggle against racism and for the rights of Black members with the battles of other equality groups and movements for social equality and justice.

For us this will mean special measures to recruit and involve Black staff, including a strong Black members network, annual equality conferences of Black members, a national Black members committee, an NEC equality committee and reserved equality seats on the National Executive Committee including two seats for Black members.

It is also clear that the new union's staff must reflect the populations it serves, with a Black Official as part of an Equality Unit and with an appointments procedure that is not only 'equality proofed' but also focuses on equality outcomes. Training representatives and officials will be emphasised so that Black members have confidence – and can become involved – in the way race discrimination cases are handled.

These commitments, however, cannot be made in a vacuum. Employers and the government must also move beyond equality proofing to creating a positive action employment environment with colleges and universities implementing and acting upon existing national equality agreements.

This approach will only work if it is united. All teaching unions must commit to ensuring a racism-free environment for all students and education workers, with a zero tolerance policy for fascist activity on campuses. It is clear that we have to prevent the development of a political culture that threatens minorities, parading as academic debate by those who wish to achieve an all-white UK by any means. Many unions now have a policy of expelling organised fascists and the new union will have rules to enable expulsion of those engaged in fascist behaviour from the union.

And unions must keep a critical eye on the government's immigration and asylum policies and challenge the new racism, fuelled by globalisation, which focuses particularly, but not exclusively, on Muslim people. International tensions and the rise of fascism have also led to a substantial increase in anti-Semitism. The promotion of tolerance and a strong stand against all manifestations of fascism are of crucial importance – not only in this country but also in fortress Europe. This can be achieved by creating active alliances with other unions, student organisations and broad based campaigns such as Unite Against Fascism.

In his pamphlet Coard cited the warning from the director of the 1970 Survey of Race Relations in Britain that 'by 2002 Britain will have a Black helot class (modern-day hewers of wood and drawers of water) unless the educational system is radically altered'. This is a message we would all do well to heed. Just as we have an obligation to ensure that this generation learns about the Holocaust and genocide we also need to explain the legacy of the old racism – that slavery leaves its mark on many generations (both white and Black).

This stain will not easily be removed or be glossed away by harmony committees that provide the window-dressing behind which the institutional discrimination and injustice continue. Because those who are not part of finding a radical solution will be part of the problem, there will inevitably be conflict with entrenched interests. For, as the Black freedom fighter Frederick Douglass said, 'Without struggle there is no progress. Those who profess to favour progress, yet deprecate agitation, want crops without digging up the ground. They want the ocean without the awful roar of its waters.'

Notes

1 B Bernstein, 'Education Cannot Compensate for Society', in *New Society*, no 387 (1970), pp344-347.
2 TUC, *Black Workers, Jobs and Poverty* (June 2005).
3 See *Challenging Racism: Further Education Leading the Way*, full report of the Commission for Black Staff in FE (2002).

● Paul Mackney is 55 and has been general secretary of the university and college lecturers' union Natfhe since 1997. He is on the TUC General Council and serves on their Race Relations Committee and Stephen Lawrence Task Group. He was instrumental in estblishing the Commission for Black Staff in Further Education and was a founder member of Unite Against Fascism. Paul was Natfhe West Midlands regional official for five years (1992-97). In the 1980s he was president of Birmingham TUC and head of Birmingham Trade Union Studies Centre. He discovered Bernard Coard's pamphlet during his first teaching job establishing ESOL courses in Hall Green Technical College, Birmingham, in the 1970s.

Hugh Muir

We need allies to win these battles: we should heed this prison-cell warning of the perils of trying to beat inequality alone

A GENERATION OF Britons, black and white, has never heard of Bernard Coard. There is some excuse for this. Since 1983, when Ronald Reagan 'liberated' Grenada from the intolerably lefty government of Maurice Bishop, Coard, who was one of Bishop's lieutenants and then his foe, has languished in jail in the Caribbean.

But before he became a veteran political prisoner, he was a revered figure in Britain's Black community as the man who deconstructed for a first disappointed generation of West Indian immigrants the ways in which their children were being ill-served by the education system. He became a respected voice.

Now, from prison 4,300 miles away, he has spoken again to protest that the plight of many Black schoolchildren has barely improved in 40 years. But perhaps the most pertinent point Coard makes from his cell is to warn about the perils of a minority community believing that it can tackle social inequality alone.

Communities looking to self-sufficiency is surely a good thing. I admire the work being done by Black Saturday schools and voluntary organisations providing services for our community. But we must beware an activism that renders us blind to the opportunities for cooperation with others. The future belongs to strong lobbies that know how to make a case, to empathise and to strike a deal with others.

The Commission for Racial Equality has been a concert master for many years, bringing together the disparate players. But with so many groups emerging, including those who prioritise religion above race, it cannot hope to micro-manage minority affairs in the way it has.

The most obvious example of how to do better has been provided by Muslim communities post-9/11. Much divides the many Muslim groups, but when faced by an onslaught from the police and the Home Office on one side and ignorant sections of the public on the other, they have been able to find common ground. Prominent figures have been able to present a reasonably united front and to agree priorities. They have then been able to pitch coherent messages to the external forces who might further their cause, whether they be white MPs keen to woo the Muslim vote or anti-war activists.

It pays to make friends. Witness the speed with which pressure from Muslim communities and their allies brought forth the law against religious discrimination.

By contrast, after 50 years of mass immigration, Black communities still lack internal cohesion, viable leaders and clout. The Black church, for all its potential, remains insular. There is still no Martin Luther King, no priorities, no route to achieving them.

What is more, we rarely reach out to others. Consider that not long ago sections of our community seemed to be defending the right of dancehall artists to threaten violence against the gay and lesbian community.

Our silence over the war on terror also speaks volumes. We understand more than most what it means to be detained in dubious circumstances. The stop and search tactic, which currently plagues young Muslim men, has been our cross to bear for 40 years. These are things we know about. It is absurd that we appear to have nothing to contribute, nothing to say.

Bernard Coard is right to warn against the perils of sectarianism. The battle for better schools, as well as for human rights, decent jobs and housing, is being fought in many communities. In the years to come, minorities who make common cause with others will prosper; the isolationists will fail.

● Hugh Muir writes news and comment for the *Guardian*, having also worked for the *Evening Standard*, the BBC, the *Daily Telegraph* and the *Mail on Sunday*. He was the first winner of the Commission for Racial Equality's Race In The Media Award. He also serves as a school governor. The article reprinted here was first published in the *Guardian* (hugh.muir@guardian.co.uk).

Hassan Mahamdallie

Is this as good as it gets?

IF ONLY we could treat Bernard Coard's book solely as a historical document, a comforting reminder of how far we have come since 'the bad old days' of the 1970s. But it is not possible to read it without drawing comparisons between the situation he described and the present crisis. Hard questions confront us – how far have we progressed, if at all, and are we still advancing, or is this as good as it gets?

That is not to say that Coard's pioneering tract has no historical weight. Far from it. Its author belongs to a tradition stretching back to pamphleteers like Robert Wedderburn, the early 19th century Black firebrand whose writings called for a simultaneous uprising of the plantation slaves and the British working class. Wedderburn was also incarcerated for his political convictions.

Like Wedderburn, Coard's writing has an agitational purpose. He directly addresses those he sees as the agents of change – the Black working class and its allies. Coard seeks to place the victims of oppression in a position where they can begin to shape their own destiny.

How the West Indian Child is Made Educationally Subnormal in the British School System is also one of those rare polemics that not only argued for struggle, but actually inspired it – becoming the analytical touchstone for the Black Parents Movement of the 1970s. This movement was spearheaded by the radical North London West Indian Association (NLWIA) and by individuals such as the Trinidadian socialist John La Rose, who founded New Beacon, which published Coard's book.[1]

But after we have contextualised the book, the disturbing thought lingers that not only is the 'scandal' that Coard exposed still around, but that the establishment appear increasingly reconciled to its continuing destructive nature. The injustices that Black pupils suffer are one of those glaring inequalities that persist in the early 21st century – the pay gap between women and men is another – that we are supposed to somehow regard as an inevitable fact of life.

Meanwhile another generation of kids is being de-educated in Britain's schools, or as one expert recently put it, 'Black boys are in serious trouble.' All the negative factors Coard identified are still at play, albeit in modern forms. Cognitive ability tests, SATs, league tables, streaming, two-tier GCSEs, low school and teacher expectation, racist stereotyping, an arid and rigid curriculum and the stigmatisation of 'failing' urban schools interact to push down a significant proportion of Black children.

These factors have been intensified by the New Labour government's attempts to remove the egalitarian heart of the comprehensive ideal, and its replacement by free market forces. So we now have the prospect of City Academies handed over to corporations and billionaire hedge fund gamblers.

In 1971 Coard identified the link between the needs of capitalism for a pool of manual labour and the systematic lowering of horizons inflicted on the Black child. Coard wrote that 'ESN schools are designed to assist each child…to realise his assumed low capabilities so that he will on leaving school be able to hold down a simple job' – a process in Coard's words of 'social adjustment'.

How much has changed? Some things have clearly progressed. At a social level the present generation of Black Caribbeans is arguably more integrated than the generation Coard was writing about. In a graphic way the inner city uprisings of the 1980s in Brixton, Toxteth and elsewhere were a measure of this – the riots saw Black and white unemployed youth joining together against the brutality of 'Thatcher's Britain'. Today there is a general level of social mixing and cross-cultural respect that the parents and grandparents of today's young Black population would perhaps envy. London is now known as 'the multicultural capital of the world'. But it is not at all clear that these social advances have been matched on the wider institutional and economic fronts.

Take just one example – the labour market. In the late 1970s Black Caribbeans were twice as likely as their white peers to be jobless. Twenty years later government figures showed their sons were now over twice as likely to be unemployed as white British men of the same age. Even after class factors are taken into account, there still remains a dogged 'ethnic penalty' weighing down Black youngsters and hampering their chances of a decent job.[2]

The situation in Britain's educational institutions is proving to be just as intractable. Over a decade ago it was reckoned that Black pupils were around three or four times more likely to be excluded than their white counterparts.[3] Figures released in 2005 show that permanent exclusions in schools in England had risen 6 percent in the previous year, and that Black children were around three times more likely to be punished in this way than their white counterparts. Schools minister Jacqui Smith celebrated the figures, saying that 'we want a zero tolerance approach to disruptive behaviour'. But there was no mention of 'zero tolerance' to the racist stereotyping of Black children.[4]

Statistics show that the gap in educational achievement between working class pupils of Black Caribbean, Pakistani and Bangladeshi origin and their higher achieving counterparts is not narrowing at all.[5] As one statistician recently put it, the educational progress of these children is 'stagnant'.

However, we do have some knowledge that was not available in 1971. Research shows that at least one local education authority manages to buck the national trend of poor educational performance for each of the minority ethnic groups. Some authorities are managing to make a difference, for example Tower Hamlets' relative success with Bangladeshi children.[6] So we know that not only is the present crisis not inevitable – it can be reversed.

However, it remains astonishing, especially after reading Coard, to reflect that government ministers and policy makers still appear mystified as to why Black children crash out of the schools system. In 1999 a report by schools inspectorate Ofsted stated that Black Caribbean pupils tended to start off in primary schools doing 'reasonably well'. It then observed that, 'at secondary level, the data indicate that Black Caribbean pupils underachieve. In some cases they are the lowest performing group at GCSE level. *It is therefore urgent that secondary schools establish what is happening to Black Caribbean pupils to cause a good start in primary schools to turn into such a marked decline and take action to reverse it*' (my emphasis).[7]

Can we possibly still be on the starting blocks, facing educationalists who have yet to 'establish what is happening'?

Crucial issues about the schooling of Black children remain neglected, now casualties of a rightwards lurch of the state discourse on race. In a peculiar sense New Labour seems to have done the most extraordinary thing – it has banished racism.

Not literally of course. Quite the reverse – the government, through its attacks on asylum seekers and Muslims post-9/11, has fuelled racism to an extent not experienced for decades.[8] At the start of August 2005 the Metropolitan Police released figures showing a 600 percent rise in hate crimes in London directed at Muslims, as the blowback from the war in Iraq shook London. In the same week a racist gang in Liverpool, perhaps buoyed by the general racist atmosphere, murdered Black teenager Anthony Walker with an axe.

In much the same way as Tony Blair's initial refusal to link his war on terror with the London bombs diverted hostility onto Britain's Muslims, the government has sought to deny that the most debilitating aspects of racism 'originate in the operation of established and respected forces in society', as the 1960s Black Power activists Stokely Carmichael and Charles V Hamilton argued.[9] A government minister or adviser would have to break ranks and go against current orthodoxy to even come close to the analysis that the continuing 'abysmal failure' of Black children in British schools can best be explained by 'the racist policies and practices' of the school system.[10]

Once the institutions have been cleared of blame, logic demands that the problem has to lie with the individual child or family, or with negative traits assigned to their ethnic group. For example, the 'underachievement' of African-Caribbean boys is to be traced back to a host of supposed factors, from instability in their family lives, lack of role models, fixation with guns, ghetto life and gangsta rap, all the way through to bigoted notions of innate laziness, propensity to violence and biological inferiority. These 'explanations' don't fit Pakistani and Bangladeshi boys, so a whole new set of problems are constructed, including their bilingualism, the 'back home' mentality of their parents, self-segregation, and a culture clash generated by the backward nature of their religion and cultural practices.

This 'race revisionism' is also happening on the other side of the Atlantic in relation, it should be noted, to a Black population with a very different history to our own. Yet the same arguments arise. A recent exchange in the *New York Review of Books* (NYRB) centred around a publication that reportedly argues that 'Blacks' average academic achievement...is now not equal to whites' mostly because Black community culture doesn't value education the way the culture of middle class whites does. As a result, Black students don't try hard in school, and schools in turn, don't expect much of black students'. The authors go on to advocate that Black pupils should concentrate on acquiring 'basic skills'. Racism is no longer a factor – at best it is an excuse. As the *NYRB* reviewer wrote, 'The premise that racial discrimination has been erased and that the remaining reason for differences in the relative earnings of Blacks and whites is a difference of skills has become an article of faith among conservatives'.[11]

Sadly, the establishment's refusal to contemplate the obvious is not confined to the US. There is also a history of this in Britain. In 1981 the Rampton Committee into the education of West Indian children reported to the Thatcher government. The report was promptly disowned by ministers when they found Rampton had identified racism as the problem and anti-racist policies as the solution.

So the government ditched Rampton and set up another inquiry under Michael Swann in the hope that he would water down his predecessor's findings. A red herring was waved around to skew the debate early on. The government wondered how racism could be the problem when other minority groups, for example 'Asians' who also suffered racism, seemed to do better at school than Caribbeans. At best, all this really proves is that some members of some ethnic groups can, through various alleviating factors such as class and wider society's perception of them, somewhat mitigate against racism in the education system, but it certainly does not prove an absence of racism.

Unfortunately for the Tories, Swann, like Rampton, could not ignore that which stared him in the face. His report 'Education for All' confirmed not only that structural racism was indeed the problem, but that its negative effects were being compounded by class inequality. The Tories again disowned their own report and made it clear that money for new initiatives would not be forthcoming.[12] We now live under a New Labour government whose public commitments to education and a 'fairer society', let alone their historic reliance on the Black vote, should make for a more progressive stance. Yet we find the same red herrings and refusal to acknowledge basic realities.

The Home Office's 2005 document 'Improving Opportunity, Strengthening Society: The Government's Strategy to Increase Race Equality and Community Cohesion' states that 'in education... some groups, such as Chinese pupils, are now generally thriving but others, such as African-Caribbean, Pakistani and Bangladeshi boys, are performing much worse'.

The 'underachievers' are variously described as having 'low attainment', suffering 'disadvantage', being in 'great need' and 'falling behind'.[13]

There is no suggestion (or acknowledgement) in the document, which lays out New Labour's third term policies towards minority ethnic Britain, that racism in the education system is wrecking the life chances of the present generation of Black school students. In fact the word 'racism' is not mentioned in relation to any of the institutions that dominate society. Instead it is carefully and narrowly bracketed under 'extremists who promote hatred',[14] a phrase designed as much to catch political Islamists as well as members of the British National Party.

This disappearing trick extends to other areas of policy. Despite the mountain of evidence and the collective experience of many Black men, the Home Office refuses to make a firm link between institutional police racism and the disproportionate stop and searches Black people suffer. According to Home Office officials the causes of this disproportionality remain 'complex' and not fully understood.

The British Transport Police, capitalising on the nervous mood in the wake of the 7 July London bombings, dispensed totally with this debate by stating that discriminatory racial profiling of groups for stop and search purposes didn't need justifying – in other words racist harassment by officers was now the price every 'Muslim looking' person was expected to pay.

It was in 2001 that the rightward moving nature of government thinking on race became apparent in ministerial reaction to the riots that took place in Oldham, Bradford and Burnley. The then home secretary, David Blunkett, damned the victims as authors of their own misfortune. Instead of pointing to the provocation of fascist gangs, Blunkett attacked those who had fought to protect their communities. He recast people who lived and worked in Britain for generations as foreigners endangering the social fabric of this country. He prescribed the now familiar demand that Muslims accept British 'norms of acceptability' and demonstrate their 'Englishness'.[15]

In the 2003 new year's honours list Doreen and Neville Lawrence were awarded OBEs. A fortnight later Blunkett effectively trashed the Macpherson report into Stephen's murder when he remarked that 'the slogan created a year or two ago about institutional racism missed the point'. Rumours began to emanate that Blunkett had banished the phrase 'institutional racism' from the mouths of Home Office ministers, officials and policy makers.[16]

Shortly after this Doreen Lawrence observed publicly that progress had indeed stalled in the aftermath of the 2001 riots. Mrs Lawrence revealed that

Blunkett was usually absent from the Home Office steering group she attended, even though he was officially chair. She said that Blunkett had lost interest in the whole area, and that he was now downgrading racism issues.[17]

Since then the government has developed a vocabulary consciously employed to obscure the processes of racism. As we have seen, racism (except in relation to 'extremists') is no longer to be acknowledged as a powerfully distorting feature of British society. It can only be alluded to via its specific and isolated manifestations – 'disadvantage', 'discrimination', 'disproportionality', and so on. The multicultural notion of integration based on mutual respect has been replaced by 'community cohesion' and aggressive demands for assimilation.

Today Blunkett is wheeled out by Gordon Brown to periodically obsess over the nature of 'Britishness'. Missing from all of these debates is the voice of Black communities themselves. Their historical experience does not 'fit' and so is not acknowledged. In their place have rushed policy wonks now emboldened to give their 'take' on race – in the summer of 2005 one such figure informed a conference, 'Just to talk about racism and discrimination misses much of the point. We're now in a world of variable geometry where there are many kinds of exclusions and many kinds of discrimination, many kinds of disrespect, and where class is every bit as important as race'.[18]

This 'deracialisation' of the official discourse on race is not a new feature, but it has clearly developed a particularly insidious strain under New Labour, one with policy consequences – for if racism doesn't exist, then why dedicate resources to tackle it? So at the start of 2005 there was no new money on the table from the Home Office to help Black pupils– just a pledge to better target the £162 million Ethnic Minority Achievement grant.[19] £162 million spread across the whole of England to dig a whole generation of working class Black boys 'out of trouble'– is this as good as it gets? There is also an increasing tendency for politicians and commentators to counterpose the needs of Black and white working class pupils. They argue that there are only finite resources, and that if we allocate more to Black children then we are somehow guilty of oppressing poor white children.

How strange it must be for white working class children, usually looked down on by the entire British political elite, to find well-heeled Oxbridge educated right wing/New Labour pundits suddenly jostling to champion their cause over that of their Black Caribbean and Pakistani schoolmates. Coard has a powerful retort to this divisive argument: 'High quality education for ALL.'

Parents of all ethnic groupings have an interest, in the first instance, to fight for more resources. Britain at 4.7 percent still spends less as a percentage of its GDP on education than 13 other European states, including Poland (5.6 percent), Hungary (5.1 percent) and Italy (5 percent). Even Mexico at 5.1 percent spends proportionately more on education than New Labour.[20]

If the pot is so small that the government says it has to take from poor Peter to pay his Black classmate Paul, why don't we make the pot bigger? One wonders how many of those pundits 'defending' white working class children would agree to a modest proposal to increase the top rate of income tax to allow Britain to reach the European average education spending.

The domestic political and social arena is inextricably linked to what is happening at a global level. I have already talked about how the blowback from Iraq is fuelling racism here. The war is also draining the Exchequer. The Iraq Analysis Group (IAG) estimated that by April 2005 the government had so far spent somewhere in the region of £5.5 billion on the invasion and occupation of Iraq. The IAG estimated that this sum, if diverted to education, would 'fund the recruitment and retention of over 12,000 new teachers for ten years'.[21]

The unifying nature of Coard's slogan encourages cooperation and common cause across racial boundaries. The struggle cannot merely be about raising Black children to the level of their white working class counterparts – replacing third best with second best – it has to be a strategy that places wider transformative demands on the system.

Over 9,000 pupils, the majority teenage boys, were permanently excluded in 2003-2004. Although Black boys are disproportionately represented, the majority are still boys from white working class backgrounds.[22] Surely it is in the interests of parents (and boys) of both groups to work together. The general argument that these boys have a right to be educated with their peers is a shared one, even if specific solutions may differ.

An aggressive approach to tackling racial inequality has the potential to generalise across the system. Take Coard's original recommendations: extra 'opportunity' classes to bring pupils back into the mainstream (not 'ghetto' streams); moving away from testing as a method of measuring potential; hiring teachers young people can relate to; making children feel proud of their backgrounds and raising their self-esteem; the active involvement of parents; and a richer, more relevant and flexible curriculum – all of these are methods to raise the heads of all working class children.

Coard's plans would also be attractive to teachers angry at the way their 'right to teach' has been eroded. They therefore also contain the seeds of a challenge to the whole way in which the education system is organised.

How positive it would be if the republication of *How the West Indian Child is Made Educationally Subnormal in the British School System* acted to encourage the founding of a new radical movement. After all, how many working class families, Black or white, can afford to face the grim prospect that this may be as good as it gets?

Notes

1   See T Carter, *Shattering Illusions: West Indians in British Politics* (Lawrence & Wishart, 1986), ch 4.
2   See H Mahamdallie, 'Racism: Myths and Realities', *International Socialism* 95 (Summer 2002), p13.
3   J Bourne, L Bridges and C Searle, *Outcast England: How Schools Exclude Black Children* (Institute of Race Relations, 1994), p41.
4   See R Smithers, 'Permanent Exclusions Rise', *Guardian*, 20 June 2005.
5   For the best recent survey of all evidence see D Gillborn and H S Mirza, *Educational Inequality, Mapping Race, Class and Gender: A Synthesis of Research Evidence* (Ofsted, 2000).
6   As above, p11.
7   *Raising The Attainment of Minority Ethnic Pupils: School and LEA Experiences* (Ofsted, 1999), p11.
8   For background to this see H Mahamdallie, 'Racism'; in *Anti-Imperialism: A Guide for the Movement* (Bookmarks, 2003).
9   S Carmichael and C V Hamilton, *Black Power: The Politics of Liberation in America* (Pelican Books, 1969), p20.
10 B Coard, 'New Introduction'.
11 R Rothstein, 'Must Schools Fail?', *New York Review of Books*, vol 51, no 19, 2 December 2004.
12 See T Carter, as above.
13 'Improving Opportunity, Strengthening Society: The Government's Strategy to Increase Race Equality and Community Cohesion' (Home Office, 2005), p8.
14 As above, p13.
15 See H Mahamdallie, 'Black and White Lies', *Socialist Review*, January 2002.
16 See H Mahamdallie, 'Blunkett Trashes Anti-Racist Fight', *Socialist Worker*, 25 January 2003.
17 Doreen Lawrence, speech to National Assembly Against Racism, 22 February 2003, quoted in IRR news bulletin.
18 Geoff Mulgan, director of the Young Foundation, to CRE conference, 12 July 2005.
19 'Improving Opportunity', as above, p26.
20 In N Grant, 'Hands off our Schools: A Critique of the Department of Education and Skills 5 Year Strategy for Children and Learners' (Ealing Teachers Association [NUT], 2005), p27, www.ealing.teachers.org.uk
21 IAG, April 2005, http://costofwar.com
22 R Smithers, *Guardian*, 20 June 2005.

● Hassan Mahamdallie has written and lectured widely on race in contemporary Britain and on Black history. He is a founder member of Unite Against Fascism. He presently works at Arts Council England. This article is written in a personal capacity.

Appendix: Committee for Human Rights In Grenada (UK)

The Committee for Human Rights in Grenada (UK) was set up in 1983, shortly after the US invasion. It developed links with the trade union movement on the island, and aimed to publicise and campaign against the violations of human rights in Grenada following the invasion. The committee is best known for its campaign in support of Coard and his 16 co-accused, who have always maintained their innocence, and it was instrumental in organising the worldwide campaign that led to the commutation of the death sentences of the prisoners.

A number of legal experts, including the former US Attorney-General Ramsey Clark, have raised very serious concerns about the trial of the Grenada 17. Among these concerns:

- That the US government gave the government of Grenada 'financial aid' for their legal system coincident with the period during which the trial was held and ending immediately thereafter (which raises the possibility of undue influence).
- That the jury panel was selected by a newly appointed registrar who had formerly been a member of the prosecution team.
- That the jury panel was also selected in a manner which grossly violated prescribed legal procedures. Had those procedures been followed, only one of the 12 jurors who rendered the verdict would have been on the jury!
- That the jury panel from which the actual jurors were selected were openly hostile and threatening towards the defendants and their lawyers, some of them even making blatant 'cut-throat' signs with their fingers.
- That the judges, at both the trial and appeal level, were under specific contract for this case alone and had no security of tenure, which raises questions about the degree of their freedom to act independently of the government.
- That documents seized by the US which the defendants maintained could have established their innocence and the falsity of key evidence given against them were withheld from the defendants, who were legally and morally entitled to their return. Recent documents obtained under the US Freedom of Information legislation show that the documents had been returned to Grenada, but were never made available to the 17 defendants.
- That during long portions of the trial the prosecution presented its evidence without defendants or defence counsel present.
- That the jurors were forced to sign their names on verdict sheets. In view of the 18-month US military occupation of Grenada and the millions of dollars spent by the US in Grenada before the trial on propaganda asserting the guilt of the prisoners, this was clearly designed to pressure jurors and thus ensure the convictions.

Beyond these irregularities, the defendants repeatedly alleged that they were tortured, and that the statements extracted under torture were used as evidence against them. The trial judge refused to have admitted into evidence their medical files which recorded two prison doctors' findings following their interrogations by foreign policemen. Both the trial and the appeal took place in a largely secret court on the grounds of Richmond Hill Prison, and in an unconstitutional court, dubbed a 'Court of Necessity'. This necessity disappeared the moment the Grenada 17 appeal was over, for Grenada then immediately rejoined the Eastern Caribbean Court System. And even now, 14 years after the Grenada Appeal Court's oral verdict, the 17 are still waiting for the written judgment, this unconscionable delay allegedly stemming from a dispute between the government of Grenada and the judges over payment of the judges' salaries.

Following what turned out to be the most expensive trial in the history of the Caribbean, the 17 were denied the right to appeal to HM Privy Council – a right enjoyed by all Grenadian citizens from the day Grenada restored its Constitutional Court system, within two weeks of the end of the Grenada 17 appeal. Even now, after a protracted and costly legal battle spanning 14 years, the 17 are not permitted to appeal their convictions to the Privy Council. In a desperate effort to obtain justice, however, they have filed a Constitutional Motion – and although many of the illegalities of their trial cannot be argued under this motion, they have finally obtained permission to argue this motion before the Privy Council. Their appeal to HM Privy Council was due to be filed in the autumn of 2005.

● For further information about the Committee for Human Rights In Grenada (UK) email chrguk@tiscali.co.uk

● Amnesty International's report can be accessed at http://web.amnesty.org/library/index/ENGAMR320012003?open&of=ENG-GRD